EXPERIENTIAL LEARNING IN SPORT MANAGEMENT

TITLES IN THE SPORT MANAGEMENT LIBRARY

For a current list of Sport Management Library titles visit
www.fitpublishing.com

EXPERIENTIAL LEARNING IN SPORT MANAGEMENT

Internships and Beyond

Second Edition

Susan Brown Foster

Saint Leo University – Saint Leo, Florida

John E. Dollar

Northwestern State University of Louisiana – Natchitoches, Louisiana

FiT Publishing
A DIVISION OF THE INTERNATIONAL CENTER FOR PERFORMANCE EXCELLENCE
375 Birch Street, WVU-CPASS ▪ PO Box 6116
Morgantown, WV 26506-6116
www.fitpublishing.com

Library of Congress Card Catalog Number: 2017939674

ISBN: 9781940067247

Cover Design: Wendy Lazzell, FiT Publishing
Cover Photo: Wrigley Field (Photo © JPaulB | iStockphoto)
Stock photo ID: 458122541
Production Editor: Kassandra Roberts
Typesetter: Scott Lohr, 40 West Studios
Proofreader/Indexer: Deni Remsberg
Printed by Sheridan Books, Inc.

10 9 8 7 6 5 4 3 2 1

FiT Publishing
A Division of the International Center for Performance Excellence
West Virginia University
375 Birch Street, WVU-CPASS
PO Box 6116
Morgantown, WV 26506-6116
800.477.4348 (toll free)
304.293.6888 (phone)
304.293.6658 (fax)
Email: fitcustomerservice@mail.wvu.edu
Website: www.fitpublishing.com

Table of Contents

Dedication

To Dr. Susan Foster, my distinguished colleague in this endeavor, for her unwavering dedication and commitment to making this project a first-class experience in every detail, and for being most understanding when my daytime duties as a department head would have me perform otherwise.

To Dr. Jerry Elledge and Dr. Paul Batista, mentors extraordinaire, for their encouragement and support to pursue my work with integrity and ethical diligence to all tasks.

—*John E. Dollar, PhD*

To "Dr." Dollar, a long-time colleague with experiential learning background, whose after-hours work on this project assisted in making this book significantly better than I could have ever done alone! Your sense of humor has always made our collaboration fun!

To all of my former teachers and college professors—while in school, a student often does not fully appreciate the dedication and commitment it takes to include experiential learning projects and content until long after they have graduated and entered the work force. Each one of you played a role in molding my career!

Thank you is simply not enough because learning is truly life-long!

—*Susan Brown Foster, PhD*

Foreword

Everyone has a story to tell. This one statement has resonated with me for the last 10 years of my 20 year career working in baseball. As you read through *Experiential Learning in Sport Management: Internships and Beyond,* you will observe in the sports industry the fact that sports professionals come from all types of backgrounds before making their way into the game. For many of you, your interest in sports was sparked at a young age, driven by your youth teams then culminating with the opportunity to play high school sports and possibly at the collegiate and/or professional level (if you are one of the fortunate few!). No matter how far you were able to play, you were hooked! I can still remember growing up as a kid in the Baltimore, Maryland area, making the trek to Memorial Stadium with my father to see the talented Orioles teams of the 1980s (yes, 1983 World Champions!) that included individuals like Hall of Famers Eddie Murray (my all-time favorite) and Cal Ripken along with a great supporting cast that included solid players (and loveable characters) like Ken Singleton, Al Bumbry, John Lowenstein, Rick Dempsey, and Gary Roenicke and pitchers such as Hall of Famer Jim Palmer, Mike Flanagan, Scott McGregor, Dennis Martinez, and Tippy Martinez. I can say to this day it was significant for me that I was able to see fellow African-Americans like Murray, Bumbry, and Singleton, who I could personally identify with, providing a backdrop that I could dream and one day put on a major league uniform like them. Unfortunately, the dream to play in the major leagues did not happen for me, but now after 20 plus years of working within Major League Baseball, I know my passion to be around this great game was fueled by those early childhood memories.

The pathway to a career working in sports is truly a journey. Be sure to enjoy the ride! First and foremost, you have to start somewhere. As you will find from reading through this book, there is no exact recipe for starting your career in sports, but you will see by following your passion and showing perseverance, you can have a long and productive career doing something you love to do. In my role with Major League Baseball as the senior director of the Front Office and Field Staff Diversity Pipeline Program, I talk to prospective industry candidates (students, job seekers, former players, etc.) a good chunk of the time and I always want to genuinely understand their motivation for pursuing a career in sports (specifically why the game of baseball). In some ways, it's like being a guidance counselor as I try to dig to the depths of their heart to fully grasp their want and need to pursue a career in the sports industry. I completely understand that many of you could excel in a career outside of the sports industry thanks to your skills and experiences, but the lure of being in the arena, stadium, or ballpark is something that powerfully draws us all in!

I speak to current students all the time about the value of internships as they are huge staples (and labor) of our sports marketplace. Internships give you the opportunity to get first-hand experience of the work environment on a daily basis and demonstrate your value to your employer. Secondly, the organization offering the internship is getting a chance to see how you enhance their culture by not only reviewing your work product, but seeing where your personality fits among fellow employees and their surroundings. I've been on the hiring end of searching for interns numerous times, and one of the biggest questions an employer is trying to answer is if this potential candidate is the right fit. In a fast-paced and ever-changing working environment like the sports industry, we all become "teammates" upon whom we have to be able to trust and rely. Are you dependable? Can I trust you to complete your assignments? Are you willing to get out of your comfort zone by asking for additional challenges? From my own personal experience starting in this business as a baseball operations trainee (intern) in 1996, I do not know where I would be today without my first opportunity to break into baseball with the Atlanta Braves. My internship experience was a true life changer! Making copies, driving minor league players to doctor visits, and entering data into spreadsheets might not seem glamorous, but I immersed myself in every task and was always asking for more to not only build my knowledge base but to also build trust and confidence among my co-workers and superiors.

With any internship experience, you need to survey the surroundings and consider ways to make yourself valuable to the organization. Self-evaluation is the key. What do I do well? Based on my skill set, how can I immediately make an impact within the organization? What areas do I need to address that would make me more competitive for future opportunities? Talk to any employee, no matter the industry, and in every job there are tasks that he or she would rather avoid or push off to someone else. Gain an understanding from your superiors about tasks they would prefer not do. By possibly getting out of your own comfort zone, you are making the job of someone else easier and adding value to your inclusion in the work environment. Don't forget, you only have one opportunity to make a first impression!

Ask any successful person, regardless of the industry in which they work, and they will tell you that someone (a supervisor, co-worker, mentor, etc.) helped them along the way. You can't do it alone! I had the great pleasure of starting my career under the tutelage of John Schuerholz, one of the greatest baseball GMs in the history of the game, who took his well-deserved place in the Baseball Hall of Fame in Cooperstown during the summer of 2017. If you follow John closely in his interviews, he will readily admit, in order for him to win World Championships in both Kansas City and Atlanta (the first GM to win in both leagues), it took a dedicated staff of men and women by his side to lead those organizations so successfully. I am still in awe and amazed how Schuerholz was able to guide the Atlanta Braves to a record 14 straight division titles (1991–2005), an achievement that will probably never be matched again. Schuerholz is quick to credit Hall of Fame manager Bobby Cox, executives like Paul Snyder (longtime Braves Scouting Director), Dayton Moore (former Braves Assistant GM and now GM of the Kansas

City Royals), Dean Taylor (former Royals and Braves Assistant GM) and Frank Wren (former Braves Assistant GM) along with many dedicated and loyal scouts and coaches for their success. As someone who came in and worked under all these talented individuals, I'm appreciative they each made me better by challenging me and providing opportunities to learn and grow. During this process, I had to first earn their trust and support to move up successfully within the organization.

As you can see from the example above and throughout the book, the network you build around yourself has substantial value in assisting you along this journey. I've never forgotten the individuals who have made a major impact on my career, as their willingness to share their own stories and answer my probing questions provided insight into the journey ahead of me. In 2009, after much thought and personal reflection, I created the Baseball Industry Network on LinkedIn, a baseball networking resource group that has now grown to over 32,000 members throughout the world. Through the Baseball Industry Network, I have attempted to foster an environment where current and former baseball professionals are willing to reach back to help the next generation of future industry professionals. Your turn is coming in the near future, so be prepared to tell your story! Please enjoy *Experiential Learning in Sport Management: Internships and Beyond* as it is my hope the stories you read here will truly be life changing!

—*Tyrone Brooks*
Senior Director, Front Office and Field Staff Diversity Pipeline Program
Major League Baseball
Founder, Baseball Industry Network

Preface

FOR THE STUDENT

Students, this book is written for you! Many skip reading the preface of many books. While we address this preface to both student and professor, in this introductory page, we speak directly to you in this section. We provide a rationale for how we developed this book and why we structured it as a text that can be used at the beginning of any educational degree, throughout that degree program, and as a reference for climbing a sport business career ladder. Please read on!

Experiential learning is a seriously important factor in the landscape in American education. As you will read, some research has indicated those who have participated in internships have a better chance of being hired into a full-time position. Collectively, we have more than 50 years of experience in supervising students in field experiences. We bring that experience to you. We have seen what might be characterized as the good, the bad, and the ugly. Trial and error has taught us the more organized the entire experience is from the managerial side and the more serious the student is about searching for and selecting the right field experiences, the better the resulting experience/internship is for the student.

We hope this book will become a great reference for you and one that will be kept throughout your educational experience and beyond. It is intended to be a program-required text and a useful resource to be used over and over. Chapter 1 introduces you to the sport business industry from a very easily read theoretical base focusing on how important it is to get experience early on in order to build the résumé prior to graduation or applying for any position, full- or part-time. It also includes an experiential learning model that stresses the importance of continuing to gain experience. This chapter also exhibits how large the sport business industry really is and emphasizes there are plenty of jobs for everyone who seriously pursues a career. This is important because many outwardly state there are not enough jobs. This is because some only focus on the popular industry segments such as college athletics and professional sport. But, oh, there is so much more! Many positions in these two industry segments, due to their popularity, pay less to entry level individuals than other industry segments. We challenge you to look far and wide! Do not give up your pursuit of a career in this exciting industry without being persistent and leaving no stones unturned!

Chapter 2 is written for those looking for a sport management program at any level. We realize most individuals reading this book have already selected a sport management program. However, some may still have questions about program accreditation and how to find a graduate school with a specialized sport-related emphasis or faculty members. This chapter assists parents and students with hard-to-find information.

Chapters 3–5 build on this introduction by providing over 30 Time Out Interviews. In these interviews, we have invited current sport business practitioners in all different types of sport organizations to provide you with very clear explanations of their academic preparation, how they entered the sport business industry, and how their career has progressed by exhibiting different job titles and sport organizations for which they have worked. Basically, these interviews are snapshots of how they climbed the ladder getting to where they are now in their careers. We do not believe any other textbook about sport business internships or field experiences has included this type of information in the detail we have.

Chapter 6 introduces teaching sport management as a full-time career. Many individuals do not think about this type of career or may not be considering graduate school. However, as one progresses through their career or pursues graduate school, the reality that this type of career is rewarding personally, professionally, and financially becomes a consideration for some. Our Time Out Interviews from faculty members provide insight into graduate assistantships and the life of a professor. Graduate assistantships are a form of experiential learning and a way to pay for graduate school. This chapter, as well as Chapter 2, discuss graduate assistantships and many of the associated benefits.

Chapters 7–9 include tips and examples we have garnered over the years from sport industry professionals on writing résumés and cover letters. This is not our opinion: It is what is expected by the industry. We have updated this information to include more information on how to prepare your materials for online applications. Also included are strategies for you to save and budget your money during a required full-time internship and how to market and network yourself to organizations. In fact, we feel networking is so important, we have devoted an entire chapter to this topic (Chapter 9). Even if you are not required to complete a full-time internship, we challenge you take a full semester to do this before you graduate. Many organizations do not like the student coming in and, in essence, dictating a work schedule to the employer. While many state they will work around a student schedule, if full-time interns are working for the organization, often it will be the full-time intern who gets the full-time job offer. Additionally, if you are able to perform this full-time experience after you have finished all your courses, you will then be available to accept the full-time job offer. You will not have to turn it down to complete coursework and your degree! A full-time experience gives you the opportunity to experience a 40-hour a week schedule and what it is like working in the real world with a sport organization! We are constantly being told by some of our students they have never held any job, and it seems this scenario has increased in recent years. By working in several experiential learning opportunities prior to applying for full-time positions, you will learn from mistakes and how to behave in the professional environment by the end of your academic experience. Thus, you will not make the mistakes some first year professionals make and prevent yourself from being let go by an organization. Chapter 10 helps you in this process and offers how you can transition from student to professional.

We also encourage you to read the foreword written by Tyrone Brooks, a senior director in the office of Major League Baseball and founder of the Baseball Industry Network. Tyrone is a very down-to-earth approachable colleague who began his career in sport as an intern with the Atlanta Braves. He is always willing to work and consult with students regarding careers in sport and baseball.

Thank you for reading this preface! Do not skip any chapters! We believe each chapter has great information and strategics to ponder as you prepare for an exciting career in the sport business industry!

FOR THE FACULTY MEMBER

In searching for a publisher of our first edition, Fitness Information Technology embraced our topic and vision following their very successful 1990's book titled *Field Experiences in Sport Management.* After the success of this text and our first edition, our belief that this was a very necessary and important resource was confirmed. Faculty members who adopted the textbook provided helpful comments for this revision. We believe our book is the most organized experiential learning text on the market with the most useful information provided to students. Thus, the book can be purchased for use in an introductory class, as a text for experiential learning courses where students also attend class, and finally, as a book in a pre-internship class to prepare students to enter an internship and the industry as a polished professional. Different chapters can be used in the different classes. In the age of expensive textbooks, the book can be purchased once, kept, and used for several classes, thus reducing the overall textbook costs to the student. As an added bonus, this edition of the book is available as an e-book. We believe you will find this book very useful.

We are passionate about quality experiential learning. The book provides information from industry professionals employed in a variety of positions within the sport industry with perspectives on their own career paths, their insights, and their comments on particular topics. We have tried not to date the book. In other words, it has been written in a manner by which the information will remain relevant for several years to come.

Many textbooks of this type include chapters in which the student may not have much interest. Sample internship affiliation agreements, information about developing the working relationship between the educational institution and the internship site, and institutional oversight bare very little interest for the student. Our book is different! There are faculty contributions at the end of each chapter from our sport management colleagues that you could adopt as projects for students in your classroom or foster your own creative juices to design projects fitting your teaching style. Additionally, useful faculty information is available in an online supplement for professors who adopt the textbook for classroom use and who are tasked with the development of an experiential learning program.

The Foster Five-Step Experiential Learning Model in Chapter 1 was not developed just for this textbook. It was conceived after years of experimentation with experiential learning concepts regarding what worked the best in helping students explore various career paths. We believe the more opportunities an individual has to learn about an industry segment, the earlier they will discover a comfortable career choice—one for which they can become passionate in its pursuit. Thus, we introduce a progression of opportunities and include your projects in the classroom as one of the steps of experiential learning.

We realize many professors approach experiential learning differently. However, three common threads were discovered after collecting internship syllabi from numerous sport management colleagues, by pouring over entire sport management curricula, and when discussing the internship process.

First, and foremost, is an early introduction—the earlier, the better—to the sport industry through volunteering, activities sponsored by a sport management majors club, class assignments, or an early formal experiential learning encounter. Most sport management programs provide one or more of these experiential learning activities. A second thread was the appearance of a culminating internship where a student worked full-time for an extended period of time without interruption. The third commonality discovered was the existence of a full semester pre-internship class. All of these seemed to be the most direct path for full and complete preparation of a student intern, especially at the undergraduate level. But experiential learning is important at any educational level, so the concepts of the book are applicable from high school through graduate school (Chapter 6).

This book can be used for many purposes. It can be the book for introductory or foundations sport management class because of its breadth on the discussion of the sport business industry. We have never taught an introductory course teaching management and marketing. These concepts are often taught in the more advanced core or business school courses. We exposed students to guest speakers following in-course discussions of each industry segment. This would have been a very valuable book in that process had it existed early in our careers.

This book can be just as valuable when preparing students for a practicum or internship at any educational level with certain chapters being used in different courses. Students who are exposed to it immediately upon arrival on campus or at the beginning of an online educational program, including graduate students, should have a head start on their decision to pursue a career in the sport business industry. We believe it will provide information and tips for an extended period of time as the search for a dream career position is pursued.

Another main purpose for writing this book was because many colleagues have indicated their administrators do not approve of internship courses deserving of a grade versus a pass/fail evaluation. Some of our experiences have been opposite of that perception. Experiential supervision courses can and are treated as respected academic courses when substantial evaluation and course assignments are required. Preparation for these assignments required during the internship can be accomplished during a pre-internship class. Thus academic rigor can be accomplished by requiring a total analysis of the sport organization sponsoring the internship from management and evaluation practices, strategic planning and goal setting within the organization, an investigation of marketing and ethical processes, and more. Sometimes, administrators must be convinced any experiential course should reward the professor in promotion, tenure, service, and pay, but more importantly, should be worthy of an A-F grading system. When these courses only evaluate the student on a pass/fail basis, students are not challenged to do their best work; rather, some do just enough to pass the course. Rarely, do students fail an experiential learning course, but when administrators allow these courses to be graded with rigorous assignments, students must do excellent work to get a good grade that will appear on their transcript. We feel this textbook supports you, the faculty member, in your efforts to design a strong experiential learning program and provides a practical text for the professional preparation of your students for the sport business industry.

Most individuals may believe an internship book is only valuable for the undergraduate student. Since many institutions will accept graduate students for master's and doctoral students, some of these students have little to no background in sport management as well as no undergraduate degree in sport business. This text is a great way to introduce these students to the very broad scope of the sport business industry. We have even included a chapter with Time Out interviews from different types of sport management faculty members to introduce master's and doctoral students to this career path. Many doctoral programs focus on preparing students to be researchers. In reality, the majority of institutions need professors who embrace teaching. Thus, this textbook will introduce and educate them to the industry and how to educate the students they will encounter in their first years of their college teaching careers. We are confident no other experiential learning book has included this type of discussion!

Finally, to the high school educator, we realize many high schools are now including courses involving event management, sport marketing, or an introduction to our industry. This book is useful for you and your students. High school juniors and seniors can learn about this exciting career field and ease their transition into a collegiate degree program.

To all educators who have passion for teaching in the sport management field, enjoy!

Acknowledgments

We would like to acknowledge the assistance of several individuals who supported our passion for this project.

To all of the individuals and colleagues who graciously gave of their time in the development of the chapter introductory and practitioner comments, Time Out Interviews, and end-of-chapter teaching and program experiential learning ideas—without your assistance, this book and the quality thereof would not have been possible.

To my husband Joseph L. Foster, III who always supports my career, projects, and after hours work load.

To the following Saint Leo University sport business majors/student workers:

Zachary Smith for his internet research, appendices work, and formatting many of the Time Out Interviews; Andrew Thriffiley and Savannah Mitchell for their internet research efforts and timely work in finalizing many items throughout that needed attention to detail and online ancillaries available to professors.

To Doris Van Kampen-Breit and other Saint Leo University Library faculty and staff and Christopher Wiginton from University Technology Services who helped make my library research much easier.

To my co-author's family Janet and Justin who cooked and hosted me during a long weekend to finalize this book and for Justin's graduate student perspective and assistance with PowerPoints and updating appendices.

—*Susan B. Foster, PhD*

To the following Northwestern State University of Louisiana Graduate Assistants:

Justin Kern-Dollar, Steven Tjaden, N. Garrison Burton, and Nathan Dunams, for assistance with references, e-mail correspondence, and internet research, pursuant to the completion of this project.

To the more than 2,300 apprentices, practicum students, and interns we have had the pleasure of supervising, past and present, whereby their dedication to performing quality work, played a role in building the sport business/management programs at the institutions where we have taught. For believing that a quality placement is as much about their hard work and personal sacrifices as it is about their willingness to accept a mentor's guidance. Your work was a significant building block in the writing of this textbook.

For the administrators and colleagues who believed in our background knowledge about the sport business industry and our confidence in building quality programs; who understood an experiential learning program is a key ingredient to becoming a top sport business/management program—your support when we made positive curriculum, policy, and program changes will never be forgotten.

To the many internship site supervisors who have provided experiential and career opportunities for our students.

—*John E. Dollar, PhD*

CHAPTER

1

Introduction to Experiential Learning and the Sport Management Industry

"Open yourself up for new experiences and ideas. It expands the possibilities. Don't limit yourself by becoming a specialist."
—Buck Rogers, Vice President, Fort Wayne Mad Ants, Fort Wayne, IN

THE WARM UP

Sport as an industry dominates the economy. Leagues, teams, and sporting events on both the professional and amateur stages will always be a primary staple of North American society. Internationally, sport is growing as evidenced when new countries participate at each Special Olympics, Paralympic, and Olympic Games. Many countries are realizing the importance of grassroots sport programs to improve the quality of life and foster a strong interest and desire in youth to become athletes who will then represent their countries well in international competitions. Many foreign students desire an education in the United States, but prefer to intern or work in another country, perhaps their home country. Whatever the venue, there will always be a need for qualified sport managers and sport organizations willing to design quality internship positions thus allowing the hard-working individual to gain experience through a variety of experiential learning opportunities.

UNDERSTANDING THE SPORT BUSINESS INDUSTRY

The sport business industry is large and complex. In 1995, from a financial perspective, it was reported to be a $152 billion industry (Lambrecht & Kraft, 2009) in the United States, and in 2008, it was reported to be "more than $225 billion—far more than twice the size of the U.S. auto industry and seven times the size of the movie industry" ("Academic Degrees," 2008, p.

29). PricewaterhouseCoopers reported the British sports industry grew by 23% between 2006 and 2007, and the global sports market (non-US) was expected to increase to more than $140 billion by 2012 (Associated Press, 2008). In 2015, Heitner indicated the sports market in North America was expected to reach $73.5 billion by 2019; Plunkett Research indicated the United States and world markets in 2015 to be $472 billion and $1.5 trillion respectively (2016). So, whom do we believe?

Two economic professors, Humphreys & Ruseski (2010), justify it is nearly impossible to calculate the size of the sport industry. First, they explore the many definitions of sport appearing in the literature and state the economic activity of sport includes "watching, listening, and following sport competitions on various media" (p. 60), something many ignore when reporting their dollar estimations. Chelladurai (2014) explored the potential size and economic significance of the industry and somewhat confirmed the difficulties. In evaluating the work of Broughton (2002), who reported $194 billion in spending in 40 categories, Chelldurai explained Broughton left out expenditures such as recreational, tourism, and family activities involving sport and also questioned how one should truly count expenditures within the field of sport media and broadcasting. He states,

> Assume that a broadcaster pays $10 million to broadcast a football game. The broadcaster then sells 30-second and 60-second spots to several corporations for a total of $12 million. Should we include both amounts (i.e. $22 million) in estimating the size of the industry? (p. 9)

So, we will leave the proposed size of our industry to the continuing efforts of the number crunchers. Our main point is this: the industry you are studying to enter ranks among the top industries and could possibly be the largest industry worldwide. If you want to work in sport and are passionate enough to do well in classes, get volunteer and paid experience early on in your journey to a professional career, do not limit your internship possibilities, and learn the art of networking, you will reach your goal. The ensuing pages will challenge you to not cut corners and put into practice our years of experience in assisting students entering the sport business industry.

THE SPORT EMPLOYMENT MODEL

Sport crosses other industries in a manner that is often difficult to describe. Figure 1.1 portrays a Sport Employment Model that encompasses the athlete or consumer, the two drivers of the sport industry. Included in the model are 11 components that encompass the breadth of possible employment opportunities in sport. While many will not take you to the ballpark every day, an entry-level position in any of them could lead to contract deals with top athletes, a position where services provided touch each athlete, or to an eventual transfer to an organization where sport is the main product. Subsequent chapters in this book will investigate many of the core components. Thus, this chapter will serve to explain the model and provide initial insight into the scope of the industry.

In the Sport Employment Model, the athlete and consumer are at the center and are the very heart of sport. The athlete or participant, whether professional, collegiate, recreational, young, or old, is the core ingredient for an event to happen. The consumer may be the spectator or the individual purchasing merchandise or tickets. Regardless, the entire sport industry would collapse without the athlete and the consumer. Later in this chapter, we expand your concept of the breadth of the industry. This model attempts to categorize everything you can find in sport into 11 components. The model focuses on the United States sporting landscape even though we do discuss opportunities in various international locations within the book. We realize there may be some overlap between segments. Due to the vast nature of our industry and the multiple ways each segment can impact another, this cannot be avoided.

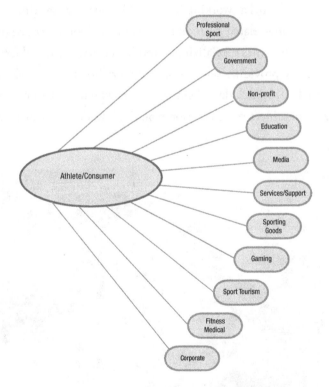

Figure 1.1. Sport Employment Model

Professional sport, at the top of the model, is a prime employment destination for many individuals. Defined as "any sport activity or skill for which the athlete is compensated" (Gladden & Sutton, 2011, p. 122), this component is constantly expanding. We realize the individual participating can be involved in the gaming industry described below as a separate category. We are using *government* to explain all non-educational programs or departments sponsored by a branch of a city, county, state, or national government. Examples include city recreation departments and sports commissions or authorities. *Nonprofit* is being used to capture any non profit sport-related foundation or private organization. YMCAs, Boys and Girls Clubs, Little League Baseball, a private foundation that sponsors golf tournaments for the purpose of fund-raising, or an organization such as Special Olympics would fall into this category.

Education, of course, would encompass college athletic and recreational sport management departments and any kindergarten through 12th grade sponsored sport program. This model would put all of the college bowl games, the National Collegiate Athletic Association, all high school athletic association offices, and collegiate sport athletic conferences under this umbrella. Arguably, some of these organizations can very appropriately fall under the label of nonprofit, but we chose to place them in this category because the central component of all of these events is the athlete participating within an educational setting or because of their enrollment.

Media—Newspapers, magazines, television or radio, and websites tied to sport create numerous positions we would label as working in sport. One may be covering a live event or working in a paid communication-related position tied to fantasy sports. *Services or support businesses* are large components. Companies specializing in food, security, event and facility management/design, and marketing are providing services or a support function to operate a sporting event or facility, large or small. This includes all entrepreneurs who own their own sport-related firm. Law firms specializing in athlete representation would fall under this category.

Students can learn important skills used by the media through internships at on-site locations. (Courtesy of Big Stock)

Sporting goods needs little explanation and includes apparel, equipment, and merchandise, as well as shoes, fitness clothing, and sporting equipment needed for participation. This is a very broad category as it can include anything a team, sport participant, or fan may need or wish to purchase tied in any way to a physical sport. We are not including gaming products in this category.

Gaming includes the popular games tied to sport and played on systems such as Xbox. Electronic sport (eSport) enthusiasts participating in live real-time events would also fall into this category as would live poker and horse racing. Purists who subscribe to the most basic definition of sport and believe a sport must have a fitness or activity component may not see this segment, or certain entries in this segment, as part of the sport industry, especially when gambling or games involve an element of luck. Take also into account professional sport teams are buying into the eSport phenomenon, and German Sports University researcher and professor Ingo Froböse, an expert in prevention and rehabilitation, found professional eSport athletes having been exposed to a level of strain never observed in other sports that require a high degree of hand-eye coordination (Schütz, 2016). Considering, too, ESPN chooses to cover events within this segment, we felt it important to include all of them in this category.

Sport tourism is a new component to the model. Sport tourism, in its simplest form, is travel for the purpose of sport. Gibson & Fairley (2014) break this down into active sport tourism (travel to play a sport) and passive sport tourism (travel to watch a sport). This segment can have a model all its own because it is directly tied to sport economics. Any city, town, or state will measure the money brought in when hosting any sporting event, but the public generally only hears about the monetary impact when there are major sporting events or the government wants to justify to their tax-paying customers the need for a sport facility infrastructure. As an example, when Tampa hosted the Outback Bowl and 2016 NCAA Football championship game just seven days apart in the same facility, local news broadcasters interviewed sport managers about the importance of the number of individuals coming into Tampa for those events. Money was spent on food, gas, lodging, and trips to local attractions such as Busch Gardens, the Florida Aquarium, Florida beaches, and more. However, sport tourism does not just involve major events; adult and youth sport tournaments account for a great deal of sport tourism where immediate and extended families travel to see a family member participate. ESPN's Wide World of Sports at Disney World in Kissimmee, FL, was built for this primary reason. We discuss this topic more fully in Chapter 5.

Fitness and medical must be included in this model. Certainly, the fitness of an athlete is of utmost importance at any level, especially to prevent the athlete from having to seek out medical services. Athletic and fitness trainers and team doctors play extremely important roles in sport from preventative and rehabilitative perspectives. However, this text will not delve heavily into careers falling into this category. Students wishing to pursue a career in this segment can also work within, manage, and/or establish a fitness center. A business background is beneficial, but knowledge of anatomy, physiology, and kinesiology is paramount. Certainly, there are existing curricula including this content as a concentration or minor. However, since they are not part of the mainstream sport management/business curricula of today, we have not placed a great deal of emphasis on this segment within the book.

To complete the model, *corporate* is defined as any organization using sport to market their non-sport product. Companies such as Coca-Cola and Bank of America have long been corporate sponsors of sport and have several individuals within their companies whose positions are very closely tied to large and small sporting events and facilities. Time Out Interview 5.3 (in Chapter 5) is with the director of marketing for Pepin Distributing, a beer distributor and Tampa, FL, based company that sponsors many of the sporting events in that geographical market.

COMMON SAYINGS: MYTH OR REALITY?

There are several sayings you may hear relating to getting your foot in the door of the sport business industry. Some are part myth, but all are based in reality. The first saying that needs discussion is "it's not what you know, but who you know." This may be true in some pockets of the industry, and some influential individuals might be able to help you land your first position or a new position once you are firmly entrenched within the industry's walls. However, two alternate sayings portray a better reality and an introductory strategy for everyone.

First, "it's not who you know, but who knows you." Inviting guest speakers to a college campus is a great way to start, but getting beyond the walls of a specific class or outside the college by meeting people—networking— is equally important. Attending conferences, volunteering to work sporting events, meeting influential individuals, and starting a personal network of professional contacts are all paramount to career success. There are positive steps a student can take that will draw the sport business professional into the student's personal network where that individual will know and, hopefully, remember the student. Examples include thank-you notes, a student business card, and an offer to volunteer at the next event. All initiatives, when properly planned and executed by the student, can reap future benefits in ways that may not immediately be revealed. Associate Sports Information Director Lindy Brown began his career by working for five years as a student in the sports information office at Western Carolina University. During that time, he met the sports information director (SID) from Duke and stayed in touch with him; four years after his graduation, a position opened at Duke, and Lindy was hired. It was all about networking and experience. Of course, Lindy had over eight years of experience by the age of 26, and he had also attended his first sport management conference as a college freshman.

The second saying, "it's not who you know, but what you know that keeps you in the industry," provides important food for thought. While a friend or relative might be able to get you in the door, without the prerequisite knowledge to handle the responsibilities, your stay may be short-lived. A great example of this is the appointment of Michael Brown by President George W. Bush to lead the Federal Emergency Management Agency (FEMA) and Brown's subsequent resignation two weeks after Hurricane Katrina hit New Orleans in 2005. He certainly had connections to get appointed, but keeping the position proved difficult. According to a *Time* news article, Brown's only experience in emergency management was three years serving as an assistant to the city manager of Edmond, OK, who oversaw the emergency services division. Brown had no responsibility for anyone and did not personally oversee any aspect of the division (Fonda & Healy, 2005).

IMPORTANCE AND DEFINITIONS OF EXPERIENTIAL LEARNING

Experiential learning can typically take several forms such as part-time/full-time work experiences or a classroom assignment. Volunteering is even a form of experiential learning, although often in a very informal format. Thus, it is important to define the terms that will be used in this textbook. Internships can be defined in many ways. Individuals can volunteer and someone will call it an internship. However, gaining experience is the focus of this book, and having a general understanding of how the industry is organized can be important. Experiential learning can be categorized in many ways and often has one of many labels. Volunteering, an apprenticeship, a practicum, an internship, cooperative education, service learning, and a graduate assistantship are the more common ones. Service learning has gained a great deal of publishing ink and the federal government also has official definitions that include student learner and learner (Employment, 2005). Regardless of the label, the individual is generally working or volunteering for an organization in order to gain on-the-job experience in their preferred field of work before graduation from an academic program. However, some organizations will hire individuals and label them an intern even if they are not formally part of an academic program or curriculum. This may soon end, because current case law in certain Federal Circuit courts are mandating unpaid internships be part of an academic semester (*Glatt v. Fox Searchlight Pictures, Inc.,* 2015; *Schumann v. Collier Anesthesia,* 2015). Throughout this book, when referring to specific types of field placements, each will be identified by the appropriate name as defined below. When referring to all types of experiences, the terms field experience or experiential learning will apply.

Volunteerism probably does not need any formal introductions, but for the purpose of this book, we will define it as any unstructured experience where one willingly provides hours of their time without academic credit or financial reward in order to gain experience in some area of the sport management field. This is often where many individuals find their passion for working in sport or get their start. From a legal standpoint, the federal government defines a volunteer as "an individual who performs hours of service for a public agency for civic, charitable, or humanitarian reasons, without promise, expectation, or receipt of compensation for services rendered," and their services must be "offered freely and without pressure or coercion, direct or implied, from an employer" (Application, 2007, 1). While the government's definition does not fit most learning experiences in sport, it does provide a framework for understanding the legal aspects of any acceptance of a paid or unpaid learning experience.

An apprenticeship will be used to define a part-time position that can last anywhere from 5–15 hours per week for a semester or be used to explain a cumulative hourly requirement (e.g., 100 hours) established by some institutions. While it may seem odd to leave out those working 16–19 hours, it would be difficult to find an institution that defined their requirements using this type of workload. Practicum is the more recognized term derived from the word practice, which certainly defines the experience. One is practicing on the job and learning a skill or becoming more proficient in industry practices.

Some institutions use the term apprenticeship and, when operationally defined, apprenticeship fits within an experiential learning model. Formal definitions of an apprentice in Webster's online dictionary ("Apprentice," 2010) include "one who is learning by practical experience under skilled workers" and "an inexperienced person." Certainly, these definitions describe a sport management student that is just beginning to build their skill set. Oddly enough, the federal government uses apprenticeship extensively and offers grants to organizations who establish an apprenticeship program to give individuals an opportunity to gain experience. These apprenticeships do not have to involve individuals registered within an academic program.

Cooperative education is typically defined as an experience that combines skills and components learned on the job while integrated with a classroom experience. While many sport management programs do not directly utilize this definition, a university office may classify all experiential learning as cooperative education on their individual campus. Some students will take time away from campus and classes and work full-time for an organization; this is often labeled as a cooperative learning program by the organization.

Service learning is defined by many educational institutions. In general, service learning is an experiential learning strategy that integrates instruction, community service, and often a measurable project and/or research. Reflection and learning outcomes may also constitute evaluative measures. In the educational environment, sport management classes can become involved in sport-related activities and events that fulfill this definition. This form of experiential learning has been gaining momentum at universities and in the media even though its conceptual theory in education has been around for quite a while (Bennett, Henson, & Drane, 2003). Bush, Edwards, Jones, Hook, and Armstrong (2016) completed an impressive study involving a short-term service learning project as part of a psychological and cultural dimensions of sport. Their research exposed sport management students to the "potential value of service" (p. 133), and the students reported a "heightened sense of social consciousness" (p. 133). Thus, service learning, as a form of experiential learning, enhances the student's awareness that there is more to the sport industry than financial statements, ticket sales, and economic impact.

Graduate assistantships are part-time work related positions for graduate students pursuing either a master's or doctoral degree. We hesitate to use the word employed to define the experience because some courts and some states choose not to classify a graduate student as an employee. Regardless of how an individual entity may define an assistantship, this type of position is typically offered to qualified individuals by colleges to provide experience for 20 hours per week in a position that assists the institution in completing necessary projects or fills employment vacancies. In exchange, the student usually provides a service for anywhere from one to four years depending upon the time it will take to complete their graduate degree. These positions are an excellent way to obtain an advanced degree while gaining experience in the college environment as an assistant coach or athletic department assistant. One can also serve as a teaching or research assistant to a college professor. These latter positions are usually reserved for students pursuing a doctoral degree with hopes of entering the college teaching profession. Often a graduate assistantship takes the place of a culminating internship or other required work experience while attending graduate school. More information on graduate assistantships appears in Chapter 6.

The term internship is not well-defined in the literature. We are defining the internship as a 400-hour minimum, high-impact capstone experience lasting at least 10 weeks. These parameters allow for a strong work relationship to be developed by the student with the sponsoring organization. Some organizations prefer an even longer period where interns may work an entire sport season or academic year. This sets the internship apart from shorter work experiences and should not be given the same label where students are simply getting their feet wet in earlier experiential opportunities within the curriculum. Labeling all volunteers and students as interns is troublesome. Research by DeLuca and Braunstein-Mikove (2016) reported site supervisors felt interns were lacking in coachability, communication, organization, and accountability. The study only labeled the students as undergraduates but never clarified their academic classification (i.e., sophomore, senior). If the interns were underclassmen, one would not expect their performance to equal that of a capstone student. Sport management academia has not collectively defined this term. Thus, all internship studies have this preset limitation. College instructors, by official label, do not possess the same qualifications as a full professor. Neither should a freshman possess the same intern label as a capstone student. Once academics have agreed on this definition, practitioners could then begin to understand and differentiate between apprentices, practicum students, and interns, and research results on experiential learning categories will have stronger implications.

THE FOSTER FIVE-STEP EXPERIENTIAL LEARNING MODEL

Dewey, Kolb, and Fry are names well-known in the history of experiential learning, and many educators and researchers constantly quote these individuals for good reason. Dewey (1938), a philosopher and educator, wrote about a "new" and "progressive" education completely founded in promoting the idea that experience should be integrated into education and one role of an educator is to constantly monitor the quality of the experiential learning. In essence, the professor has experiential maturity versus the student who cannot know what a future experiential opportunity will bring. In fact, Dewey ends his book stating a "need for a sound philosophy of experience" (p. 91). Kolb and Fry (1975) developed a four-part cycle explaining that experiential learning was an integrated process utilizing observation, reflection, and analysis to create new learning experiences.

The key to developing the Foster Experiential Learning Model presented in this chapter (Figure 1.2) is an integrated process, as described by Kolb and Fry (1975). Learning is optimized when reflection and growth take place as the student and professor observe and evaluate to obtain a more mature process for designing future experiences. If one is to simply get the same experience over and over without introducing new parameters and/or new environments, learning will take place, but at what expense if the student is not aware of other possibilities? This was the basis for Dewey's book that dissected the meaning of experience in great depth, calling the experiences of the professor the maturity that enhances the learning cycle.

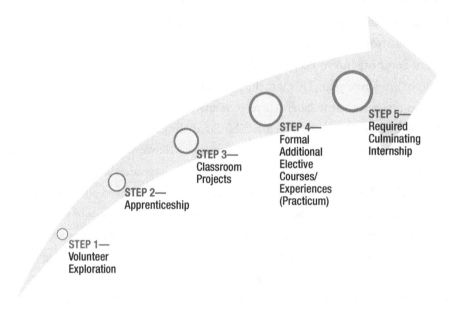

Figure 1.2. Foster Five-Step Experiential Learning Model

Support for the development of formal experiential learning practices can be found throughout the domestic and international literature (see Suggested Readings for this chapter). In fact, Parkhouse (1987) reported research results over 25 years ago that undeniably claimed field experiences to be extremely important. Kelley, DeSensi, Beitel, and Blanton (1989) presented a research-based undergraduate curricular model describing practica and internships as a "series of professionally related work experiences that should move from general to very specific" (p. 24). Furthermore, they indicated the internship should be a "one semester full-time applied work experience directly focused toward each student's professional sport management outcome objective and should be the culminating experience" (p. 24). The Foster Model supports this research but takes practical experiences much further—spreading experiential learning across the entire formal academic curriculum. It encompasses informal and formal, student- and professor-initiated experiences from matriculation to graduation. Kang & Hedstrom (2016) presented a similar idea through a stepwise advising development guide where students progressively move through a four-year curriculum by creating clear action steps each year. Progressively, these years are labeled explore, engage, expand, and experience.

The Foster Model is supported by the work of the theorists, researchers, and authors mentioned above and within the suggested readings for this chapter. The learning process behind the Foster Five-Step Experiential Learning Model has been followed for over 25 years. It was designed by Susan Brown Foster as a way of getting students involved very early in their education and to then build upon those experiences in hopes of developing a more mature learner as the student progresses to graduation and into their sport management career. The model has proven to be extremely successful throughout the years of its use based on internship site supervisor final evaluations and continuous offers of employment to interns from the institutions where the model was practiced.

Two recent studies also lend credibility to the model. Sattler (2016) surveyed sport management faculty and found all components of the model being used, but found classroom and internships to be the most popular. Respondents to this study stated in open-ended responses that more than one of the techniques in the model were effective. Sauder (2014) suggested there is value when engaging students in "early experiential learning endeavors" (p. 136) following her research involving 139 students completing a capstone experience in sport management. Furthermore, the Council on Sport Management Accreditation (COSMA) lists practical and experiential learning as "characteristics of excellence" in sport management education (2016, p. 1, 3).

It is easy for sport management professors to facilitate the experiential learning process as the sport business industry presents many learning opportunities. However, the educator does not have to be in a large metropolitan area to facilitate that learning. Classroom projects are experiential learning. Student major clubs facilitate opportunities for individuals to learn leadership and to participate in team projects. Most small towns will have opportunities to learn event management through local road races and festivals. The following sections explain the Foster Experiential Learning Model in detail.

Step 1: Volunteer Exploration

This step can begin as soon as the student steps foot into a high school that introduces formalized industry learning, on a college campus, or begins graduate school. The purpose of step one is to introduce the student to the industry as soon as possible. For college freshman and graduate students, this can involve membership in an on-campus sport management association and volunteering to work an on-campus sporting, recreation event, or concert. The faculty advisor should be able to assist the student in finding industry-related volunteer positions with a local organization. Some opportunities may exist in an athletic or intramural/recreational sport department or public relations office and can provide a quality learning environment. Many sport organizations will accept all types of volunteers, and first-year students can certainly become involved in this manner during the first semester/year. Examples of experiences may include volunteering as a parking attendant at a college football game, serving as an usher, or working in the concession stand as part of a fundraiser. Large metropolitan areas obviously offer a variety of opportunities, but if someone is isolated in a smaller geographical location, opportunities to volunteer and obtain that first experience can always be found. Nonprofit organizations or foundations often look to sport to raise money. This often happens through golf tournaments, sport memorabilia auctions, or road races. Regardless of the role an individual may accept in any one of these initiatives, just getting started is important. While beginning to build the résumé is a main objective for step one, learning basic skills and observing sport managers on the job rounds out the overall learning objective for this step. The curriculum may require all students to take a first-year foundations course, but without this requirement, students can still begin step one of the Foster Model.

Many students can start by finding a mentor or shadowing an employee during any event. If these types of opportunities are presented to you, jump on it. Even better, ask for them. Why? The number one reason is your foot is now in the door, and professors with industry experience often tell students they must learn to sweep the floor. While you may not literally undertake a maintenance position, we want student learners to focus on learning the basics. If you learn the very rudimentary operations of an organization, you will be a better intern, entry-level employee, and manager because you will have first-hand experience with and knowledge of the foundations of an organization. If you have learned what it is like to be an usher, to work in a concession

Volunteering to work local events can assist in building one's background knowledge and skills. (Courtesy of Susan Foster)

stand, or to understand the questions consumers pose when they call the organization, you will have a clearer understanding, and perhaps more empathy, for lower wage earners and their tasks. As a future employee climbing the ladder within an organization, you will learn the organization inside and out. This will be beneficial when you reach the management level and is especially helpful within smaller organizations where climbing the corporate ladder may be swift. Thus, step one can be a very important and fruitful step for you, the student. You are learning from the ground up through the simple act of volunteering. Your sport management curriculum may require you to volunteer or present opportunities for volunteering. Your professor is the mature component of the learning theory presented early by Mr. Dewey. Take advantage of any and all opportunities even if it means getting up early on a Saturday morning to setup for a 5k run.

Step 2: Apprenticeship

The second step of the experiential learning model is the apprenticeship or other early formalized entry-level work experience. We recommend this be a required element of the sport management curriculum taking place as soon as possible after a required introductory sport management class is satisfactorily passed. Having a classroom component tied to the apprenticeship applies Dewey's mature leader component of his theory. Discussing each student's apprenticeship experiences in the classroom as it takes place is crucial for full implementation of the model. The professor, as the mature experiential leader, learns more about each student and each organization. Additionally, each student expands their knowledge of the experiences other students are having. Perhaps a student will seek out an experience another student presented. It may not be necessary for the class to meet every week, but periodic classroom sessions enhance the experiential learning process for all involved. Perhaps one session will present the first opportunity to begin the development of a professional résumé while others will require the opportunity to practice presentation and listening skills through a formalized and graded short presentation summarizing the sponsoring organization, skills learned, and unique experiences. The main purpose of this step is for a student to get some formal learning experience early in the academic process thus allowing them to learn where the opportunity can take them toward a career. If graduate students are entering a sport business master's level program and do not have an undergraduate degree in a field related to sport, this can be a formalized starting point as well.

Institutions may assign anywhere from one to 15 credits for an experiential learning class. Many institutions today may limit the number of credits required for a major. A one-credit class is usually easy to fit into a class load and just as easy for the sport management faculty to fit into a total credit hour count. Some institutions may allow you to repeat an experiential learning class more than once. Consider this opportunity if afforded to you. This is explained more thoroughly in step four.

When starting early in gaining experience, one of two things will happen for you, the student learner. First, you discover the experience is not what you believed it would be. It is very good to learn this early on when it is not too late to change your industry segment focus. If your institution is fully implementing the Foster Model, you still have time to gain formal experience. Of course, you can always volunteer on your own to learn about other segments of the industry. Second, you discover you absolutely love your apprenticeship and believe it is the area of sport you wish to pursue. Finding what you like early will assist you in focusing future experiences and perhaps class assignments/projects on a preferred industry segment. Move forward without hesitation; you are well on your way! Find as many opportunities as you can to build your résumé in the chosen area. Summer jobs, community events, certifications, and leadership positions will all boost your employability in the future. In summary, these early experiences can teach you which areas you may or may not wish to pursue.

When choosing an apprenticeship, seek out a great opportunity. Your college may allow you to select an apprenticeship during any academic semester, but many students will select this opportunity during the summer. This is especially true for college athletes due to practice schedules during the regular academic year. Your main goal is to select an organization that offers you a great chance to learn and grow. If you believe you want to work in professional sport, finding a professional sport organization that will accept you is your best route. The old saying that practice makes perfect only when it is perfect practice is very applicable. If you wish to work for a professional sport team and select an apprenticeship in a YMCA because it is conveniently located close to your residence, will prevent a long commute, and you know somebody who can get you hired—well, ask yourself if you are going to learn or get a feel for what it is like to work for a professional baseball team by working at your YMCA. Absolutely not! Professors have had students who wait until a senior internship to obtain their first experience in what they believed to be their dream job only to find out, they did not like it. Selecting what is easy or convenient may not assist you in making an early decision and actually can prevent you from practicing networking skills discussed in Chapter 9. Work with your academic advisor or program chair in finding a position that best fits you. Maybe you volunteered for an organization under step one, and you really liked it. Perhaps contacting the organization again to formalize an entry-level work experience for you will be a starting point.

The overall guidelines for this level are to identify a sport organization that will allow you to volunteer/work at least one day a week for them. This should be a minimum of five hours a week during an entire semester. Remember, the key here is that the organization is accommodating you. Show up on time, maintain a regular schedule each week, and be reliable. This is extremely important. You want to come out of this experience with an understanding of how an organization operates or projects it completes. Additionally, you want a strong positive recommendation from the individual who supervised you. This will add to your professional network of individuals that know you. Some organizations will find it difficult to fill four to five hours in one day. It also may be difficult to obtain a class schedule that gives you a block of time on one day unless hours are available at night or on weekends. Thus, the minimum work schedule you may want to establish is two and a half hours per day, two days a week, at the same time each week for the academic semester. Most class schedules and organizations can accommodate this format, especially if their normal work hours are 8 a.m. to 5 p.m. Many employees love mentoring an individual eager to learn the business and can expose you to many opportunities.

Typical assignments one may encounter in an apprenticeship certainly can vary. You may encounter a different project each week. Other organizations will use an apprentice to prepare for upcoming events. Be prepared to assume the role of a data entry clerk in positions where you may assist a college athletics compliance coordinator or an organization's finance office. Be flexible in accepting assignments. While an organization appreciates your ability to show up on time for work on a regular established schedule, they may ask if you can work an event on a weekend. Whenever possible, work the events in addition to your weekly schedule. This will exhibit to a supervisor that you will do whatever it takes to get your foot in the door. Yes, volunteering often means without pay, and this can be difficult to do with bills to pay. However, a formal first experience can launch your career.

Some institutions require a student to work a number of hours, let's say 60, to get their first experience. A student takes this to heart and obtains an assignment that allows the student to work three weeks in a college athletic department at night and on weekends. This is certainly possible at a large university with major college football and men's and women's basketball programs. You think, "60 hours. Great, I'm done," but have you established a strong relationship with one person who would vouch for your work ethic? Was your working relationship strong enough where one person supervised you for the entire 60 hours and will remember you next year when you need a recommendation? Regardless of the institution's requirement, take it upon yourself to view the requirement not as an academic credit to fulfill, but your first position in the industry. Make the most of it and come away with a strong recommendation from at least one person that can attest to your reliability and work ethic.

Apprenticeships can also be easy to find if your institution is simply concerned with you getting that first experience regardless of the responsibilities. During spring break, find out in advance if you can interview for an usher or a concessionaire position at a sport facility or team somewhere close to where you will be living for the summer. Get a jump on the summer part-time job application process and use your spring break to find an opportunity. It exhibits passion and an eagerness to learn. Summer apprenticeships away from campus can fulfill a classroom component using today's technology. Weekly assignments can be submitted and weekly discussions conducted using the variety of available online educational platforms. In today's e-learning environment, most academic curricula are supported by electronic submission, and email is an easy alternative. We believe the online opportunity does not create the best learning environment for the classroom portion of an experiential learning class as the benefits of face-to-face discussions have their time-tested advantages. However, in a well-structured online component with mandatory discussion postings, even the very shy student may contribute more than in the traditional face-to-face classroom environment.

Step 3: Classroom Projects

Aw, the classroom! Homework! This step asks you, the student, to be passionate about your classroom learning—particularly those that will be very applicable to your future career. This step really starts as soon as you take your first college course, whether it is sport-related or not, but certainly in your first sport management class. This step was strategically placed in the middle of the model because it can happen anywhere during the college experience. However, many universities do not allow students to engage in major coursework until their sophomore or junior year or after formal acceptance into a rigorous program requiring application to the major. Hopefully, your curriculum permits you to start early with one or two classes.

Step three allows faculty to be extremely creative and develop meaningful assignments to enhance learning about the industry. Service learning projects can also be incorporated in this step. Field trips (Pate & Shonk, 2015), guest speakers, role-playing, and even term papers can open doors. Exposure to all types of elements that exist in the industry can be the end result of an in-class team assignment. You can come away with a great personal project; in a job interview, you can provide an outline of the completed project to the interviewer or submit it as part of a professional portfolio. A project well done can set you apart from other candidates where you become the only contender for hire. Get fired up about one of the possible assignments your professor may require in a list of sample classes provided below. Yes, even if it is a term paper. Approach it with passion and get started long before the due date. You may be surprised what you can learn by researching the literature for a term paper especially if you approach the assignment with the attitude of trying to learn anything that will help in your future career. Here are some examples of experiential learning projects your professor may require in a formalized class.

- **Introduction to Sport Management.** An internet assignment asks you to find ten actual job announcements in ten different industry segments. One purpose is to help you understand the breadth of the industry. Do you know the differences or similarities between college sports information, professional sport public relations, and community relations segments of the industry? This assignment can help you focus on choices you may wish to pursue in an apprenticeship or in step four. See the end of chapter classroom assignment in Chapter 3.

- **Event Management.** Develop a small, individual sport event from start to finish by applying formulas for tournament scheduling.[1] Consider that you are required to develop a double elimination tournament for your classmates using any sport-related computer game or by developing something as simple as a horseshoe tournament on one of the recreation fields. You must create the tournament schedule in two different processes. One requires you to use an online scheduling program. The second requires you to apply tournament scheduling formulas. Your classmates are divided into groups and you must run the tournament all within one 80-minute class period for one group. Each group has ten members. Develop the rules and draw the tournament chart. Conduct the tournament and award prizes. This was done in an actual class and one student went so far as to obtain a sponsor, and the sponsor provided the prize and drinks for all contestants. This is homework? C'mon!

- **Risk Management in Sport.** Write a risk management plan for an on-campus facility incorporating guidelines provided. While this assignment may not sound as much fun as the previous class—well, after all, this is school—one can learn a great deal and apply this in a future internship or job. Picture a job announcement that describes assisting an organization's risk manager in developing a safety conscious work environment and a risk management plan. You are the only applicant that has had this experience, and you have the completed project to prove it! Provided you approached the assignment with the same awesome attitude you have brought to every homework assignment, you may be a slam dunk for the position. In a tight economy when positions for event managers and market researchers are scarce, you want to do everything possible to increase your positioning. It may not be your dream job, but you are now in the door!

- **Sport Marketing.** Your class is visiting a local professional sport team and the vice president (VP) of sales will teach you how to work their ticketing software. The VP offers each one of the class members the opportunity to sell a certain number of tickets, and if the entire group sells at least 500 tickets, the class receives a one-on-one half day meeting and luncheon with the team owner. The top seller within the class receives eight prime seat tickets for another upcoming game. Of course, you are going to be the top seller with your awesome attitude toward homework!

Imagine this favorite story that started with a class assignment requiring a face-to-face interview with a sport industry professional the student did not already know. Kerryann Cook (Time Out Interview 3.6 in Chapter 3), a sophomore seeking a career in college athletics, approached her advisor and asked if she believed Pat Head Summitt, the very successful former head women's basketball coach at the University of Tennessee, would grant Kerryann an interview for a class assignment. The advisor suggested she make the phone call, and Coach Summitt not only granted the interview, but spent approximately 90 minutes with her. Kerryann ended up driving two

---

[1] *Note.* Yes, very simple algebraic formulas exist for constructing tournament brackets. Why is this important to know? You can set up a nice computerized schedule, but you get to the field and one or more teams had to cancel. Experienced recreation participants know how double elimination tournaments are supposed to work. Do you? In fairness to the teams, especially when your tournament has seeded participants, knowing how to reconstruct the tournament brackets and properly re-seed the participants can be crucial depending upon the level of play and participant expectations. Not all outdoor facilities have Wi-Fi available where you could set up your computer and take the time to reconstruct a bracket. Both of your authors have taught tournament organization, scheduling, bracket development! If you watch the March Madness shows for men's and women's basketball on television, all you see are the results of the bracketing. There are actually basic rules for setting up any tournament bracket. We are sure the selection committees use computerized programs. However, if one has the background knowledge and rules for setting up a large tournament, the process for seeding teams and placement of those seeds is more easily understood.

hours one way on a weekly basis to perform an apprenticeship with the Tennessee Women's Athletic Department the following semester, after which, she was offered a full-time internship in her senior year followed by a graduate assistantship. Kerryann has been practicing law in New York City and owns her own sport agency representing female professional basketball players and other professional athletes. Her career truly began with this one interview and her own motivation.

The above examples display just a few assignments that can actually give a student additional insight into the corporate sport business world. Of course, as much as we would like it, not every student approaches every assignment with their best work ethic. This is what sets apart those who get the job and those who do not. Perhaps this is the exact work ethic that got Theo Epstein the Boston Red Sox's general manager position at the youthful age of 28. He began as a summer media relations intern for the Baltimore Orioles at the age of 18. He had not been a star athlete and had no relative in baseball making calls for him as he was promoted through the ranks (Riordan, 2002). The Red Sox won the World Series under his tutelage. During the writing of the this edition of the textbook, he was also the general manager for the Cubs during their 103 regular season winning record and World Series championship in 2016. Jon Daniels was 28-years old when he was appointed general manager for the Texas Rangers. He also started as an intern with the Colorado Rockies (Fisher, 2005). Tyrone Brooks (Time Out Interview 3.1 in Chapter 3) is a top executive with Major League Baseball. He started as an intern with the Atlanta Braves, and he graciously wrote the foreword for this text.

Step 4: Formalized Additional Elective Courses or Experience (practicum)

The purpose of this step is to gain additional experience through another formalized opportunity, by taking an additional class not required in your curriculum, or even staying an extra semester to complete a minor. Your choice. It is a résumé builder. It is offering you the opportunity to become a more mature experiential learner by evaluating more opportunities and to see what else is out there. Some institutions will offer formal junior-level or graduate student for-credit opportunities, and some may require them. Some universities require a student to take a certain number of electives. This is where you can possibly repeat a one-hour apprenticeship and select a different sport organization. Perhaps your university has a longer formalized three-credit hour requirement similar to the apprenticeship. Many institutions call it the practicum where you may have to work between 10 and 20 hours a week. It might end up being a formal independent study supervised by one of your professors with specific industry experience with a project you propose. You can never stop learning about opportunities within the sport business industry. Regardless, the purpose of this step is to simply get more experience with different responsibilities or possibly with another organization in a different industry segment. As mentioned earlier, maybe you were not thrilled with the experience you had during your apprenticeship because you observed employees working nights and weekends for 10 days straight.

Perhaps professional golf has always been a passion of yours and you can get involved in the planning of a major professional men's or women's golf tournament that is hosted near your university. Find the right contact. Call them and offer to send your polished résumé via email or propose to drop it off when their schedule permits. Again, yes, emailing it is easier, but the latter suggestion is better because it creates an actual face-to-face networking opportunity—just make sure you dress appropriately. Your goal is to learn about another industry segment because you are not quite sure where you want to intern during your senior year or in meeting a graduate level internship requirement. The moral to the story is never put off investigating career interests. There are plenty of opportunities to volunteer and learn how professional golf tournaments are run without waiting to gain academic credit for the experience. Going back to step one on a regular basis gives you more opportunities to examine career interests. The Professional Golf Association (PGA) and the Ladies Professional Golf Association (LPGA) Tours have internship opportunities that are extremely competitive. Having already worked in the planning of a professional golf event as a volunteer or apprentice may make you a top candidate for the internship as described below in step five.

Step 5: The Required Culminating Internship

Bell and Countiss (1993) described the internship as the cornerstone of a student's academic preparation and Sutton (1989) called it a core component. In our model, the internship is designed as a full-time capstone experience after all course work is completed. Two primary reasons exist for this. First, when a student does a great job, the possibilities are increased for being offered a full-time position. If the internship is performed prior to this time, students have to make a choice. Do you accept, thus not completing your academic degree, or is the position turned down and you return to campus? An organization may state they will hold a position, but often another intern comes in and does as good a job, if not better, and is immediately available to begin work on a full-time basis. The organization might also realize they need a full-time position filled immediately and cannot delay another year.

The second primary reason for requiring a culminating internship is because coursework is completed, and students have been exposed to the entire curriculum. Most institutions have several courses with critical sport business concept knowledge toward the end of the degree program. Performing an internship before these important courses are completed may diminish the optimum performance level of the student. For example, if a sport marketing or sport sales course is one of these courses, a student in a sales or marketing internship may not have learned information beyond the four or five P's of marketing. The staff may determine the student was inadequately prepared to accept the position. Not only has the supervisor formed a less than optimum opinion of the intern's work knowledge, other interns from the same institution may not be offered future positions. This is especially true if interns from other organizations are performing a culminating internship and have been exposed to the requisite information in their course work. Research supporting the importance of a culminating internship was found by Batty (2011) when 25% of 92 undergraduate students at two public universities reported fears of not being prepared for the internship. The study did not report if any preparatory class was provided prior to the internship, work hours required, or if the internships were capstone experiences. However, responses by the students when asked their purpose for selecting an internship implied some, but not all, needed the internship for graduation.

The culminating internship is the time to shine! Don't be a clock watcher! The clock watcher arrives just before starting time with only seconds to spare and is first out the door as the clock strikes 5:00. Projects are left uncompleted; sometimes employees or even your site supervisor are held up in their work because the clock watcher was more interested in leaving than in the overall goals or needs of the work place.

Yes, we all know some sport organizations do not operate on an 8:00 to 5:00 work schedule, though some do. Private sport marketing firms may be one that does unless an important meeting is coming with a potential sponsorship client and final work must be done on a proposal or additional research needs to be conducted. The intern who is truly interested in making it in the sport business arrives early, is ready to start or has already started work on assigned projects, and puts in enough quality time to complete a project needed very early the next day by another individual in the organization. Even if a deadline is not looming, completing work ahead of schedule is recognized as a good time management skill. However, caution must be taken. One should not rush into finishing a project without proofreading one's work, reviewing the project to see if any holes exist, and perhaps without conducting additional research or gathering more information that may make the work even better. An example of this in one's coursework is when a student asks how many pages it has to be. While some professors may provide a page requirement, one's goal should be to make it the best possible paper with quality work and research done in advance. Waiting until a week or two before a paper is due is not the prime way to approach an assignment nor is it a good way to approach work assigned by your internship supervisor. If unexpected things come up at the last minute such as illness, your work is not done and either someone else has to pick up the slack or has to wait for you to return. If sufficient time was provided to complete the project, weak time management skills have been exposed to the organization.

If your position happens to be in professional sport, let's say baseball, during the season, full-time employees may be working a 10-day home stand, which could mean a 70- to 80-hour work week. Long hours are also to be expected in college athletics. If you truly want this, you may be sleep deprived, but take the extra effort to do the little things that complete your job before you leave. For example, if you are assigned to your team's merchandising efforts, rearranging products on the store shelves exhibits pride in your position and advances work for the next day. Of course, some assigned tasks can be left when you come in earlier than other interns the next day to prepare for the incoming spectators.

Another way to shine in one's internship is offering to help someone else who might be falling behind. Perhaps your site supervisor has had to leave the office to take a child to the doctor's office or has been asked by their supervisor to take on additional responsibilities. By finishing your tasks ahead of time, you may have some free time or can stay a little later to assist if possible.

Some individuals have the misconception that doing things in advance, offering to help others, or staying late to help the boss is brown nosing or kissing up to the supervisor or organization. Your goal is to be the best possible intern. What you do not want to do is become boisterous or arrogant about being recognized by the organization if complimented or given additional responsibilities. Just go about the work in the best possible way using great time management skills. If one is concerned about the perceptions of others, in some positions, you can take work home. Nobody has to know how you spend your evenings or what time you awake to get a head start in the morning before leaving for the office. Just stay ahead of the game and do not be one that is constantly running behind. Meet all deadlines!

The culminating internship may be one's first full-time opportunity to work with a sport organization, and you want to be there to see the entire operations from sunrise to sunset. Some internships may be seasonal such as those existing in collegiate athletics. The organization may want you to begin in mid to late summer to prepare for football season and stay until the last pitch in the baseball College World Series in late June (if your internship institution's team should make it). This could mean an intended nine-month internship is stretched to 11 months. You can do this because you have completed your course work; you have done an outstanding job in this collegiate internship and have made yourself indispensable. You now are offered a full-time position! You have skipped the entire process of having to send out résumés, submitting job applications, waiting for organizations to respond, and participating in those nerve-wracking interviews. How much better can it get?

Summarizing the Model

Williams (2002) reported that institutions recommend students perform multiple internships. The Foster Model has many advantages, as described, to facilitate these opportunities formally or informally (steps two, four, and five). Implementing the entire model on one's own, or within a sport business program, provides a very manageable road map through the maze of preparation, planning, and networking that can lead to full-time employment. A major advantage the model implies is that varying levels of academic credit should be available because sport organizations, or the FLSA will require an intern to be enrolled for credit even if the institution does not require it or only requires one internship. This is where a one- or three-credit experience such as the apprenticeship and practicum (steps two and four) assists the students from a financial perspective. Paying tuition for a one-credit opportunity on an elective basis is much better than requiring the student to pay for a full six or 12 credit internship for an additional elective opportunity. Many outside organizations do not care what the course is titled as long as the student is enrolled at the institution for academic credit while participating in any experiential learning opportunity with the organization. This fact is not presented in this matter to trivialize academic credit. Written work should be a part of any experiential learning opportunity for credit even if it is an elective, especially in today's outcome-based, measured requirements for academic work. Managerial participation on the part of the internship site and the host institution ensures an increase in the level of learning, thus justifying academic credibility. Jowdy, McDonald, and Spence (2004) very clearly presented an in-depth approach to internships by applying the Wilber's All Quadrant, All Level Theory of Everything (TOE) that included the faculty member's role in assisting a student in making sense of all elements of their self-development. Therefore, one should expect a faculty advisor to monitor/require assignments that assist the student in applying theory to their experiential learning opportunities.

STUDENT MOTIVATION TO BECOMING SUCCESSFUL

The Foster Five-Step process described in this chapter can be formally and informally applied. Most institutions likely apply at least three of the steps (e.g., classroom assignments, events identified as volunteering, and work experiences). You, the student, can be self-motivated to find events in the area or in your hometown for which to volunteer. Finding summer positions that very closely align with one's intended career path is recommended.

This first chapter has utilized an experiential model that is time-tested. Students at six institutions where we have worked have been exposed to all or parts of the model to advance their careers, and it works! However, self-motivation is part of the process. One can minimally meet requirements or go above and beyond to be at the top of the game. Alumni of the process are team and business owners, vice presidents, sports information directors, facility and event managers, athletic directors, coaches, and consultants in all types of sport organizations.

Does everyone make it? Of course not, but our experience working with students has elicited patterns of employment. Motivated individuals who are not concerned initially with salary, location, or work hours will succeed in the sport business industry. Others may as well; it might just take them longer to get their foot in the door and climb the ladder. Patience and persistence are crucial in our industry. An academic program can provide background knowledge, the sport business network can get you started, and tips and tools can enhance your employability, but a student's desire to be the best at every stage completes the proven formula for success.

FROM INTERNSHIPS TO FULL-TIME POSITIONS

Due to the glamour of the sport business industry, many may believe it is difficult, if not impossible, to get their foot in the door. Dismal pictures have been painted in key newspaper articles. In the first edition of this book, we shared comments from two leading publications. The *Wall Street Journal* (questioned if sport management programs were "the tickets to great sport jobs" (Helyar, 2006, p. R5) and the *New York Times* stated individuals would stay in "low-paying, unglamorous jobs like selling ads, tickets, and concessions" (Belson, 2009, para. 1). However, it seems as if the tide has turned with perceptions of the breadth of the sport industry and position availability. The *New Haven Register* did report career opportunities in private event management, talent booking, marketing, public relations, and more without even mentioning the typical professional sport or college athletic industry ("SCSU offers new degrees," 2014). Social media is exploding with personal and professional opinions about the breadth of the industry. While the authors of many of these posts may or may not be qualified, one bares mentioning. The Ninth Inning Blog reported 30 legitimate and unique career options, once again, without specifically mentioning professional sport or college athletic administration (2011). SportsCareerFinder.com lists 23 specific industry categories. Nobody can dispute the rise of career positions within social media itself. According to Keen (2012), digital technology has quickly transformed social media into a central part of life instead of a secondary tool. All sport organizations necessarily have had to increase their staff size to incorporate the fan or customer involvement with the various forms of social media.

Even though we have provided you with the Sport Employment Model in Figure 1.1, it is hard to get a full picture of the employment opportunities in sport. The 2015 Plunkett analytics report indicated 447,900 individuals were employed in performing arts, spectator sports, and other components of the live entertainment industry within the US. Clearly, this is good information but only presents a limited view of the employment landscape of the sport industry. Humphreys & Ruseski (2009) imply it is nearly impossible to get an accurate accounting of the number of positions attributed to the sport industry. There is no way to precisely count the number of jobs related to our industry just inside the United States. The two authors above stated in 2005 there were "49,169 firms in the industry employing over one million workers… about 118 million participated regularly in sports…and 227 million attended spectator sporting events" (p. 94). That is quite a while ago! With new leagues, new sports, and growing international opportunities, we agree with these authors and offer additional support for this belief in the following paragraphs.

There are 11 components within our Sport Employment Model described in Figure 1.1. Working in one of the five major professional leagues or within college athletics in the United States may be an ultimate employment goal for many. The number of minor leagues, teams in professional sport, and college athletic departments is mind boggling, but let us offer the following opportunities within the sport industry:

- over 100 amateur and professional national governing bodies in the United States alone such as USA Basketball, the United States Table Tennis Association, the United States Association of Blind Athletes, the Ladies Professional Golf Association, and the Florida Facility Manager's Association;
- local organizing committees for major sporting events (e.g., professional golf tournaments or the Paralympic Games);

- major sporting facilities such as the Amalie Arena and Raymond James Stadium in Tampa, FL;
- large sport management facility firms such as Comcast-Spectacor with operations in venues around the world and all but four states in the US;
- nonprofit foundations such as the Women's Sport Foundation and foundations established by professional athletes to raise money for charitable causes;
- sports commissions or authorities that have the job of attracting major and minor events to their cities to foster economic growth;
- private sport marketing and event management firms;
- sporting goods stores and manufacturers of sporting equipment and apparel;
- YMCAs and Boys and Girls clubs;
- local organizing bodies that plan and manage professional golf or tennis tournaments
- large and small campus recreation departments;
- high schools where a sport management degree may be acceptable to fill physical education teaching, coaching, and athletic director positions;
- city and county public recreational programs and facilities;
- collegiate and high school conference offices such as the Atlantic Coast Conference (ACC) or the Florida High School Activities Association (FHSAA);
- Bowl games;
- state games and senior games such as the Alabama State Games and the Florida Senior Games;
- publications and websites reporting and supporting sport and sport media;
- television and radio stations that broadcast sports or stream live video;
- youth league organizations, both local and national, such as Little League Baseball;
- ESPN Wide World of Sports;
- lifestyle, non-traditional, extreme, and alternative sports;
- private sport agencies such as athlete representation firms and concierge services; and
- all of the sport leagues, events, and organizations that exist outside of the United States, which we expound on in the next pages.

Thinking outside the box, online gaming in the form of fantasy sports and eSport is included in our Sport Employment Model. Many individuals question whether eSport is truly a sport. However, in 2013, the U.S. government officially declared "professional video gamers as individual athletes" (Pedersen & Thibault, 2014, p 8), which gave foreign gamers the opportunity to travel to the United States on visas granted to other professional athletes. Major sport team owners are purchasing or announcing partnerships with eSport teams. The year 2016 seemed to be a banner year for eSport as FIFA announced it was entering the eSport market, the French

Professional Football League announced a partnership with EA Sports, and mobile eSports company Skillz announced it eclipsed $50 million in prize money with over 10 million players involved and 70 million tournaments projected to take place that year (Cynopsis, 2016). We are quite positive no other professional league experienced such growth in the history of sport. Consider, too, that colleges are now offering full scholarships to gamers (Jenny, Manning, & Keiper, 2016; Ross & Nelson, 2016) and a new association, the National Association of Collegiate eSports (NAC eSports) offered its first invitational event during the spring of 2017 ("Why Sports," 2016).

Yes, jobs and, more importantly, career positions abound. The explosion of career opportunities is not confined to the borders of the United States. Several articles published since 2012 praise the increase in career opportunities in India (Dabhade, 2016; Gupta, P., 2012; Gupta, S. D. & Rane, G., 2016; Kashmir Times, 2015; Pandya, 2013). Subramanian (2012) reported that sport has had a significant impact on the economy of India including positions with lucrative salaries. Lu (2012) reported many new small to mid-size sport-related businesses have formed in Taiwan; their government is dedicated to building sport facilities, and the country produces 90% of all bicycles worldwide. More expansion is also seen in the Asian cities of Shanghai, Singapore, and Kuala Lumpur as all have been building their sport infrastructure (Yuen, 2007).

In October, 2016 the Fédération Internationale de Football Association (FIFA), the international governing body for soccer, announced a 10-year vision that included spending $4 billion on expanding the game whereby they hope 60% of their population will be participating in some form by 2026. Australia unveiled a 20-year plan for the expansion of football (soccer) in 2015 whereby they recognized a future need for 100,000 coaches, a new organizational infrastructure, and new facilities (Football Federation Australia, 2015). Add to all of this possible National Football League (NFL) and National Basketball Association (NBA) expansions into Europe (Chiari, 2015; Edelman & Doyle, 2009; Kerr-Dineen, 2016) and initiatives established by other countries for expansion of sport at grass roots and professional levels. Well, obviously, these initiatives all create jobs under the sport industry segment.

What about the sport of Quidditch? If you are a Harry Potter fan, you are familiar with this. But is it a real sport? According to Cohen (2013), students in Vermont, bored with recreational sport offering at their school, began forming teams to play Quidditch, which is made up of seven player teams ("Rules," n.d.). Volleyballs, dodge balls, goals or hoops, and a tail similar to a flag football belt, are used to play on a pitch or court. As it caught on at universities, the International Quidditch Association was formed. As of 2013, over 350 teams were reported to be participating throughout the world (Cohen, 2013). This was all formed by volunteers, but as a sport grows, so does the need for full- and part-time event managers. Leagues are created, office space established, and paid employees must become part of the formula if any sport is to continue to grow.

There are probably many more possibilities we have missed. In summary, the number of positions to be counted would take a great deal of time to mention. In fact, a full-time position could possibly be created just to count and keep track of the number of positions available in sport. We want to go on record stating, unequivocally, if all sport and the supporting infrastructure is considered, career positions are increasing in the sport business industry. The possibilities are only limited if one is simply considering popular organizations or professional teams. We do not recommend you put limitations on yourself organizationally or geographically as you embark on your career. Michael Mondello (Time Out Interview 1.1), the Associate Director of the Sport and Entertainment Program at the University of South Florida, recommends you be receptive to nontraditional jobs to get your foot in the door.

Time Out Interview 1.1 with Michael Mondello
LEARNING ABOUT THE INDUSTRY

Position	Professor, Department of Marketing Associate Director, Sport & Entertainment Program
Employer	University of South Florida
B.S. Degree	University of South Florida—Secondary Education
M. Ed. Degree	University of Florida—Sport Management
Ph. D. Degree	University of Florida—Administration/Finance
Career Path	• Assistant Men's Basketball Coach – Santa Fe Community College – 4 years • Director of Sport & Fitness Program – University of Florida – 4 years • Assistant, Associate, and Full Professor of Sport Management – Florida State University – 14 years • Associate & Full Professor of Sport Business; Associate Program Director – University of South Florida – 5 Years • Faculty Extern – Tampa Bay Rays – 1 year

Employment Recommendation

"Be open to broadening your lens—it is fine to have a focus, but try to have an open mind and be receptive to thinking about other non traditional jobs or organizations. Furthermore, it is more important to go work for someone who can mentor you and develop your talent than a particular organization."

Yes, as with other industries, the recession hit the sport business industry hard in 2008 and jobs were lost. Even storied sport management programs with a strong track record for graduate job placement experienced problems (King, 2009). As the economy has rebuilt, so, too, has the sport industry traditionally known to do better than others in difficult times. Many believe social media has led the increase in the number of positions available in the industry (Popp &

Woratschek, 2016; Sanderson, 2011; Vann, 2014), and it certainly helps sell tickets (Moore, 2011), which can lead to a team needing to hire more sales staff. Internet broadcasting has also led to the need for more broadcasters and serves as a training ground for aspiring professionals in this area of employment (Kozma & András, 2016).

However, the competition can be fierce for many positions. Individuals with a variety of backgrounds and college degrees apply for career opportunities in our industry. As one example, an accounting background can create your entry into the sport industry. Athletes, teams, YMCAs, leagues, conference offices, and other sport businesses need accountants. Brandpoint (2015) broke accounting into segments including entertainment accounting, sports accounting, international accounting, and nonprofit accounting. Andreff wrote a chapter on sports accounting in a 2006 book titled *Economics of Sport.* Perhaps getting a second major or a minor in accounting with your sport business degree will make you unique. Yes, some organizations may want a certified public accountant (CPA) or a degree in accounting. However, many sport organizations want individuals with a strong background in the management of sport and events. Later in this chapter, we discuss the positive attributes of having a degree in sport management, sport business, or sport administration. With more and more sport management programs moving into or being founded within schools of business, sport management students are qualified to work in the business of sport since many are required to take several business courses. We both have had students enter accounting/finance positions in sport without a minor in either domain. It is most likely one of your professors has experienced this as well.

In summary, thousands of jobs exist in many hidden corners of the sporting world. One just has to seek them out. Chapters 3–6 will expand on many opportunities. The aspiring sport career professional should be aware, regardless of the economy, there will always be excellent opportunities for those who are motivated and patient to work their way up a career ladder just as in any other industry. Patience and persistence are key attributes. Very few start in the sport business industry, or any industry, in a top position, which is the level to which many sport management majors aspire. Sport seems glamorous to many, but beyond the glitter and glitz, very good careers exist with good salaries. And, as one works in sport, the glitter and glitz one perceives decreases. However, sport managers typically love their careers and experience a variety of daily scenarios far different than the everyday doldrums of many jobs. Even the seasoned veteran rallies with excitement when their team, event, or business hits a home run! Thus, any negative publicity sport management programs receive fuels the already passionate desire of the authors to drive sport management students across geographical regions toward a clear understanding that a career in sport business is more than possible. Indeed, careers in this field are extremely desirable, fun, exciting, rewarding, and many are very financially rewarding. Six figure salaries exist in numerous segments of the industry. Seven figure salaries are atypical but do exist.

Is the path to obtaining a full-time career easy? Absolutely not, but neither were the on-field practices or days in the weight room that some athletes, perhaps you, endured in little league, high school, or collegiate playing days. Like we mentioned before, practice makes perfect, but only when it is perfect practice!

Another perspective of which nay-sayers are usually not aware is the successes even in the smallest of programs. Any professor at any academic level and practicing sport management professionals throughout the sport business industry understand a key ingredient for gaining entry is gaining experience—early and often. Getting involved in your college's sport management majors' associations and taking on leadership roles are great starting points. Attending conferences and participating in student competitions such as the ones hosted by the Sport Marketing Association (SMA), the Sport and Recreation Law Association (SRLA), the North American Society for Sport Management (NASSM), and the American Marketing Association (AMA) can be important. Students who often win these competitions have absolutely no problem getting noticed and landing full-time positions.

In several chapters of this book, we present Time Out Interviews with professionals in the industry. Please take note of their college degrees and the institutions from which they received their degrees. This is proof that student success is not relegated to graduates of a few programs or only those with master's degrees. Many of these programs get a lot of the press for educating sport business leaders of tomorrow simply because of their size or name recognition. If you are attending a school with a quality curriculum and quality faculty and get experience early, then you too can hold a position in sport business and climb those industry ladders.

WHY A DEGREE IN SPORT MANAGEMENT AND NOT A GENERAL BUSINESS DEGREE?

A common question asked by parents and academic administrators is why should an individual seek a degree in the field of sport management versus a general business or physical education degree in order to pursue a sport business career? Additionally, why would we address this topical area in a chapter discussing experiential learning? The answers are simple. First, a sport management degree has some very unique components and among these is the experiential learning opportunities provided to students. Many degree programs in general business do not even require an internship.

Unique parameters of the sport industry itself have been addressed by many introductory and sport marketing texts for the past 30 years. But probably one of the first authors to highlight the uniqueness was Dr. Bernie Mullin (1980), who held early positions as a professor of sport management and then elected to seek key, top-level practitioner positions in sport. He has worked in professional basketball, baseball, and hockey, has been a college athletic director, and formed his own consulting business in 2008 called the Aspire Group. The Cleveland Indians and the National Hockey League (NHL) were signed as two of the company's first clients (Mansasso, 2008).

We believe there are at least seven unique parameters of the sport industry. Included in these seven parameters are concepts previously written by our esteemed colleagues in sport management (Mullin, 1980; Parks, Quarterman, and Thibault, 2007).

- **Ancillary revenue:** The majority of revenue in sport is not made from the main product—i.e., the game (Grădinaru, 2016). While revenue is realized from the sale of tickets for the event, the majority of revenue is made from sponsorships, concessions, team wear and souvenirs, parking, and media contracts (Mullin, 1980). Compare this to a particular product, large or small, where revenue is only realized from the sale of the product. Thus, understanding how to write a sponsorship proposal or understanding spectator loyalty to a particular team and how that translates into team product sales even for a losing team is important. (Yes, a losing team requires the sales team to sell the worst product in the market.) This concept knowledge is taught in many sport management programs and a generic business school class does not typically address sport sponsorships, sport sales, and all the revenue opportunities available in sport.

- **The product is pre sold:** The consumer must wait often for months at a time to experience the product—the game (Mullin, 1980). Ticket packages, group tickets, ticket sales, and the ability to predict sales based on fan loyalty are learned concepts in a quality sport management curriculum.

- **Marketing:** The sport marketer cannot predict the outcome of a sporting event (Mullin, 1980). Can you imagine a non sport business company not promising the quality of their product? This is what a sport marketer can be up against, especially when the result of the content can be drastically affected by the starting pitcher getting injured in the first inning, the star running back fumbling the ball three times, or the favored figure skater falling twice in a routine. In essence, the sport marketer cannot guarantee the outcome of an event (the product) or the quality of play from day-to-day or year-to-year.

- **Revenue sharing:** Most general businesses do not share revenue. For example, you would not catch two competing phone companies sharing revenue. However, in sport, it is not uncommon for professional sport teams to be required to share revenue realized from ticket sales or other income generating contracts. College athletic departments also share revenue when the National Collegiate Athletic Association (NCAA) issues checks to schools after one or more of a conference's teams participated in a bowl game or the Final Four. It is what keeps competition equal in many sports leagues.

- **Power and influence of sport as a social institution:** Parks, Quarterman, and Thibault (2007) believe this is an additional unique parameter and we agree. Sport parallels, contributes to, and mirrors society. Sport is utilized to open lines of communication between political leaders (Olympic Games) as well as assist in the development of troubled minors (midnight basketball leagues or games). Professional athletes establish foundations to assist with societal needs. Equal opportunity for all by providing participation opportunities that eliminate gender, handicapping medical conditions, or race as a means for participation are certainly a societal concern. Classes in sport sociology are necessary components of a sport business curriculum in order for the future sport business manager to effectively function.

We believe this parameter has escalated in importance with the growth of social media. We mentioned earlier in this chapter sport organizations are increasingly tasked with keeping up with their fan and customer base due to social media. Through digital technology, information about a country's sporting preferences and political involvement in sport is just a few keystrokes away. Fans across the globe can converse with each other minute-by-minute using the various forms of social media. We can convert foreign languages into our language of choice through computer technology in a matter of seconds. Because of these direct connections to individuals through social media and online news delivery, all countries and their citizens can learn about societal differences and political influences evolving from sport. Political involvement in sport is discussed more fully in Chapter 10.

- **Sport law and risk management:** This is an essential concept knowledge for a sport management student. While a business law class can include important generic legal vocabulary and information, it is important to learn how certain laws apply to the sport business world. For example, business law classes typically do not address Title IX, yet it is one of the most fundamental laws taught in sport law courses. It is an extremely important law to know and understand for those pursuing a career in high school or college athletics. Campus recreation programs are also affected by this law. There are many other statutes, constitutional amendments, and laws having specific application to sport and anyone working in sport should have a clear understanding of this area of study. Sport, recreation, and physical education are highly litigated areas. Risk management in sport is all about keeping spectators safe and preventing lawsuits. Furthermore, sport facilities and events (i.e., the Boston Marathon) are now terrorist targets, so possessing an in-depth knowledge of risk mitigation methods is also crucial. It is our recommendation sport management curricula have two sport law-related courses. Most will have one legal issues class that often covers constitutional and statutory law applicable to sport as well as content related to sport agents and antitrust law. However, in most of these courses, risk management is simply one chapter in a book. If one has reviewed many position announcements in event, facility, and recreational sport management, a background in risk management is now often a preferred qualification. Learning about risk management in depth including how to develop and write a comprehensive risk management plan is important experiential learning. Students taking just a business law course will gain very little understanding, if any, of the important role the law and risk management plays in sport.

The University of Southern Mississippi in Hattiesburg has recognized the importance of risk management in a very unique way. The institution developed a Center for Spectator Sports Safety and Security (NCS4). In 2015, the university created an MBA with an emphasis in sport security management (Crumpton, 2015), and individuals can now obtain a certification as a Certified Sport Security Professional (CSSP) (Crumpton, 2016). Saint Leo University has a minor in risk management where students learn firsthand about the Department of Homeland Security, receive an introduction to terrorism, learn how to write a risk management plan, and can possibly take a course in Crisis Communication.

- **Career paths:** Mullin (1980) advanced the thinking that career paths associated with sport management are not well defined. This still holds true today to some extent. The Foster Five-Step Experiential Learning Model explained earlier defines a system that can assist in predicting a more normal career path. Mullin's theory is supported when individuals gain degrees or experience in businesses unrelated to sport and then obtain a position in a sport business.

The rationalization for a sport management degree over a physical education degree is not as complicated. In our opinion, it comes down to whether you wish to enter a position focusing on business knowledge or a coaching position. Coaches may have business-related responsibilities such as budgeting, but knowledge of physiology, kinesiology, and conditioning principles can contribute to a coach's success. These concepts are best learned in quality physical education or kinesiology degree programs. In fact, when you coach, you teach, so there are some distinct advantages to the physical education degree over sport management because many sport management degrees do not educate students in teaching methodology. Yes, some sport management programs are still housed in physical education departments and require some science-related courses. However, the *Sport Management Program Standards and Review Protocol* (Sport Management Program Review Council, 2000), in their early sport management program approval process, did not require sport management programs to offer course work in education or the sport sciences, and the Commission on Sport Management Accreditation (COSMA) principles (2016) do not list any similar requirements in their Common Professional Components. Unless one works directly with an athlete in their physical or medical development, sport science courses are generally not put to good use in the majority of sport business positions.

THE FINAL BUZZER

The purpose and objectives of Chapter 1 were to provide an initial introduction to

1. the scope of the sport business industry;
2. the concept of experiential learning;
3. to describe The Foster Five-Step as a comprehensive experiential learning model built upon early experiential learning theory that can be formally or informally applied by faculty and students; and
4. to describe the importance and uniqueness of a sport management/business degree.

When vigorously applied by the student, the Foster Five-Step process provides a very successful pathway to employment. Furthermore, the intent was to dispel some myths regarding the sport business industry and provide some basic information about academic curricula in this field.

EXPERIENTIAL LEARNING OPPORTUNITIES

Classroom Experiential Learning Example: Sport Industry Exploration Portfolio

Many employment and intern positions exist in the sport business industry. Scour the internet for actual positions on team websites, in written publications (e.g., professional association newsletters, newspapers) and on employment websites such as Teamworkonline.com. Develop a notebook with separate sections for a minimum of ten industry segments. One of these can be a section on internships/graduate assistantships. Print or cut and paste these positions and place them within the section. Write a one-page summary of the position requirements and skills necessary you find for the positions in each section. You must use a minimum of ten sources.

The purpose of this assignment is to:

1. find numerous available positions in a variety of industry segments;

2. learn the variety of skills employers want in a new hire for particular types of jobs;

3. discover the enormous number of places where one can find position announcements; and

4. explore a variety of segments of the industry beyond the popular ones.

This assignment can be used in an introductory course, an early experiential learning class, as a student prepares to select an internship, or as an independent study. An added benefit to this assignment may result in a student finding apprenticeships and/or part-time positions that will specifically help their development of important skills and assist in building a quality résumé prior to the senior internship and gaining full-time employment.

Submitted by Dr. Susan B. Foster, Professor
Saint Leo University, Saint Leo, FL

Program Experiential Learning Example: Getting Involved Early

Students majoring in Sport Business are encouraged to volunteer early and often for an array of events held throughout the Tampa/St. Petersburg area. This includes serving as media assistants for the NCAA Final Four, Frozen Four, and football bowl games, working inside the ropes as a scoreboard carrier at professional golf tournaments, and serving in numerous capacities for conference, regional, and national NCAA Championship events. The Sport Business Program has a long-standing relationship with Sentry Event Services where students provide security and ushering services for events at Raymond James Stadium, home NFL games, NCAA Division I regular-season and bowl games, monster truck jams, and concerts drawing 60,000 guests. These volunteer experiences have resulted in several being selected for event and full-time career positions with these organizations.

Submitted by Mr. Phil Hatlem, Instructor
Saint Leo University, Saint Leo, FL

SUGGESTED READINGS

Albu, N., Calu, D. A., & Guşe, G. R. (2016). The role of accounting internships in preparing students' transition from school to active life. *Accounting and Management Information Systems, 15*(1), 131–153.

Alemany-Costa, J., Tornil, X. P., & Panadès-Estruch, L (2016). The impact of the EHEA on the professional internships: Interviews with the academic coordinators. *Intangible Capital, 12*(2), 420–443.

Alpert, F., Joo-Gim, H., & Kuhn, K.L. (2009). Internships in marketing: Goals, structures, and assessment – Student, company and academic perspectives. *Australasian Marketing Journal, 17,* 36–45.

Batty, K. A. (2011). *The role of motivation, perceived constraints, and constraint negotiation strategies in students' internship selection experience* (Doctoral dissertation). Retrieved from Proquest Dissertations and Theses Global. (Order No. 3576810)

Bridgstock, R. (2009). The graduate attributes we've overlooked: Enhancing graduate employability through career management skills. *Higher Education Research & Development, 28*(1), 31–44.

Council on Sport Management Accreditation (2016, May). *Accreditation Principles & Guidelines for Self-Study.* Retrieved from http://www.cosmaweb.org/accreditation-manuals.html

Dewey, J. (1938). *Experience and education.* New York, NY: Macmillan.

Divine, R. L., Linrud, J. K., Miller, R. H., & Wilson, J. H. (2007). Required internship programs in marketing: Benefit, challenges, and determinants of fit. *Marketing Education Review, 17*(2), 45–52.

Ferris, G. R., & Perrewé, P. L. (2014). Development of sport management scholars through sequential experiential mentoring: Apprenticeship concepts in the professional training and development of academics. *Sport Management Education Journal, 8*(1), 71–74.

Hoy, M. (2011). Building pathways to working collections: Can internships and student work experience help? *Australian Academic & Research Libraries, 42*(1), 29–42.

Odio, M., Sagas, M., & Kerwin, S. (2014). The influence of internship on students' career decision making. *Sport Management Education Journal, 8*(1), 46–57.

Pate, J. R., & Shonk, D. J. (2015). An experiential learning trip: Exploring student experiences and motivation for volunteering at the Super Bowl. *Sport Management Education Review, 9*(1), 11–24.

Pierce, D. A., & Petersen, J. C. (2015). Integrating an experiential client-based ticket sales center into a sport sales course. *Sport Management Education Review, 9*(1), 66–72.

Pierce, D. A., Petersen, J. C., & Meadows, B. (2011). Authentic assessment of experiential learning in sport sales. *Sport Marketing Quarterly, 20*(2), 75–83.

Popp, N., Weight, E. A., Dwyer, B., Morse, A. L., & Baker, A. (2015). Assessing student satisfaction within sport management master's degree programs. *Sport Management Education Journal, 15*(1), 25–38.

Simona, A. (2016). The role of international internships conducted during academic studies in development of entrepreneurial skills. *Bulletin of the Transylvania University of Braşov, 9*(58), 1, 169–176.

Southall, R.M., Nagel, M. S., LeGrande, D., & Han, P. (2003). Sport management practica: A metadiscrete experiential learning model. *Sport Marketing Quarterly, 12*(1), 27–31, 34–36.

Stratta, T. M. P. (2004). The needs and concerns of students during the sport management internship experience. *The Journal of Physical Education, Recreation, and Dance, 75*(2), 25–29, 33.

Tecău, A. S. (2016). The role of international internships conducted during academic studies in development of entrepreneurial skills. *Bulletin of the Transilvania University of Braşov, Series V: Economic Sciences, 9*(58),1, 169–176.

Thiel, G. R., & Hartley, N. T. (1997). Cooperative education: A natural synergy between business and academia. S.A.M. *Advanced Management Journal. 62*(3), 19–24.

Weible, R. (2010). Are universities reaping the available benefits internship programs offer? *Journal of Education for Business, 85,* 59–63.

Yarbrough, C. (2016, March-April). STEM students go abroad for research and internships. *International Educator,* 44–47.

REFERENCES

Academic degrees no longer a luxury in the burgeoning business of sport. (2008, June 9–15). *2008 Programs in Sports Business Special Advertising Section, 29.*

Andreff, W. (2006). Sports accounting. In W. Wladimir & S. Saymanski (Eds.), *Handbook on the Economics of Sport* (pp. 11–21). Cheltenham, Glos, United Kingdom: Edward Elgar Publishing, Inc.

Application of the Fair Labor Standards Act to Employees of State and Local Governments, 29 C.F.R. § 553 (2007).

Apprentice. (2010). In *Merriam-Webster Online Dictionary.* Retrieved from http://www.merriam-webster.com /dictionary /apprentice

Associated Press (2008, June 19). Strong growth in UK sports industry. *USA Today.* Retrieved from https://usato-day30.usatoday.com/sports/olympics/2008-06-19-3860996986_x.htm

Bell, J., & Countiss, J. R. (1993). Professional service through sport management internships. *The Journal of Physical Education, Recreation, and Dance, 64*(3), 45–47, 52.

Belson, K. (2009, May 27). In sports business, too many hopefuls for too few positions. *New York Times.* Retrieved from http://www.nytimes.com.

Bennett, G., Henson, R. K. & Drane, D., 2003). Student experiences with service-learning in sport management. *Journal of Experiential Education, 26*(2) 61–69.

Brandpoint (2015, April 20). Hollywood to sports stadiums, modern accountants go exciting places. *St. Joseph News-Press.* Retrieved from Proquest. Document ID: 1674559112.

Broughton, D. (2002, March 11). Dollars in sports: Methodology. *Street and Smith's SportsBusiness Journal,* p. 25. Retrieved from sportbusinessdaily.com/journal

Bush, K. A., Edwards, M. B., Jones, G. A., Hook, J.L., & Armstrong, M. L. (2016). Service learning for social change: Raising social consciousness among sport management students. *Sport Management Education Journal, 10*(2), 127–139. http:dx.doi.org/10.1123/smej.2015-0008.

Chelladurai, P. (2014). *Managing Organizations for Sport and Physical Activity.* Scottsdale, AZ: Holcomb Hathaway.

Chiari, M. (2015, October 8). Adam Silver comments of potential NBA expansion in Europe. Retrieved from http:// bleacherreport.com/articles/2577130-adam-silver-comments-on-potential-nba-expansion-in-europe

Cohen, A. S. (2013). *The impacts and benefits yielded from the sport of quidditch* (Doctoral dissertation). Retrieved from Proquest Dissertations and Theses Global. (Order No. 3607410).

Crumpton, A. (2016, November 17). National Center for Spectator Sports Safety and Security achieves ANSI Accreditation. *Southern Miss NOW.* Retrieved from http://news.usm.edu/

Crumpton, A. (2015, May 18). NCS4 announces fundraising campaign supporting new MBA, emphasis in sport security management, *Southern Miss NOW.* Retrieved from http://news.usm.edu/

Cunningham, G. B., & Sagas, M. (2004). Work experiences, occupational commitment, and intent to enter the sport management profession. *Physical Educator, 61*(3). 146–156.

Cynopsis Media (2016, October 20). eSports & gaming brief. Retrieved from www.cynopsis.com

Dabhade, A. (2016, April 26). Score high with a lucrative career: A course in sports management can open various avenues that project an upward career trajectory. *Daily News & Analysis.* Retrieved from www.dnaindia.com

DeLuca, J. R., & Braunstein-Mikove, J. (2016). An evaluation of sport management student preparedness: Recommendations for adapting curriculum to meet industry needs. *Sport Management Education Journal, 10*(1) 1–12.

Dewey, J. (1938). *Experience and education.* New York, NY: Macmillan.

Edelman, M., & Doyle, B. (2009). Antitrust and 'free movement' risks of expanding U.S. professional sports leagues into Europe. *Northwestern Journal International Law & Business, 29,* 403–438.

Employment Under Special Certification of Messengers, Learners, and Apprentices, 29 C.F.R. § 520 (2005).

Fisher, E. (2005, November 7). Baseball calls up young guns. *Sports Business Journal,* p. 1. Retrieved from http:/// www.sportsbusinessjournal.com.

Fonda, D. & Healy, R. (2005, September 8). How reliable is Brown's resume? *Time.* Retrieved from http://www.time.com.

Football Federation Australia (2015, May 5). We are football. Retrieved from http://www.wholeoffootballplan.com.au.

Gibson, H., & Fairley, S. (2014). Sport Tourism. In Pedersen and Thibault, (Eds.) *Contemporary Sport Management* (5th ed.) (pp. 266–285). Champaign, IL: Human Kinetics.

Gladden, J., & Sutton, W. (2011). Professional Sport. In Pederson, P., Parks, J., Quarterman, J., & Thibault, L. (Eds.), *Contemporary Sport Management* (4th ed.) (pp. 122–140). Champaign, IL Human Kinetics.

Glatt v. Fox Searchlight Pictures, Inc., No. 13 4478, 4481 (2nd Cir., 2015).

Grădinaru, S. (2016). Present times sport management. *Management Intercultural, 18*(1), 41–44.

Gupta, P. (2012, June 8). Jack, no more a dull boy with sports outsourcing. *Digital Learning.* Retrieved from http://digitallearning.eletsonline.com/2012/06/jack-no-more-a-dull-boy-with-sports-outsourcing/

Gupta, S. D., & Rane, G. (2016, May 3). Will my job be like Jerry MaGuire's? *Daily News & Analysis.* Retrieved from www.dnaindia.com

Heitner, D. (2015). Sports industry to reach $73.5 billion by 2019. *Forbes.* Retrieved from http://www.forbes.com.

Helyar, J. (2006, September 16–17). Failing effort. *Wall Street Journal,* p. R5.

Humphreys, B. R. & Ruseski, J. E (2009, May). Estimates of the dimensions of the sports market in the US. *International Journal of Sport Finance, 4*(2), 94–113.

Humphreys, B. R., & Ruseski, J. E (2010). Problems with data on the sport industry. *Journal of Sports Economics, 11*(1) 60–76.

Jenny, S., Manning, R. D., & Keiper, P. (2016, June). eSports: The new intercollegiate 'athlete.' Presentation at the Association Supporting Computer Users in Education National Conference. Myrtle Beach, SC.

Jowdy, E., McDonald, M., & Spence, K., (2004). *European Sport Management Quarterly, 4*(4), 215–233.

Kang, S., & Hedstrom, R. (2016, June 4). Using a step-wise career development guide to effectively mentor sport management undergraduate students. North American Society for Sport Management Annual Conference, Orlando, FL.

Kashmir Times New Service (2015, December, 20). Sports unfold unique career opportunities to youngsters. *Kashmir Times.* Retrieved from www.kashmirtimes.com.

Keen, A. J. (2012). *Digital Vertigo.* New York, NY: St. Martin's Press.

Kelly, D. R., DeSensi, J. T., Beitel, P. A., & Blanton, M. D. (1989). *A research based sport management curricular model: Undergraduate and graduate programs.* Paper presented at the International Sports Business Conference, Columbia, SC. ERIC Document Reproduction Service No. ED314404SP031899

Kerr-Dineen, L. (2016, March 4). The NFL expanding across all of Europe is a very real possibility. *USA Today.* Retrieved from http://ftw.usatoday.com/.

King, B. (2009). New lessons to learn. *SportsBusiness Journal, 12*(17), 4A–5A, 7A–10A.

Kolb. D. A., & Fry, R. (1975). Toward an applied theory of experiential learning. In C. Cooper (Ed.), *Theories of Group Process* (pp. 33–57). London: John Wiley.

Kozma, M., & András, K. (2016). A typology of international strategies for Hungarian professional sports clubs. *Management, 11*(1), 7–27.

Lambrecht, K. W. & Kraft, P. M. (2009, May). Opportunities and challenges in offering a sport management program in the B-school. Paper presented at the North American Society for Sport Management Annual Conference. Columbia, SC.

Lu, H. (2012). The economic challenge and opportunity of sport industry in Taiwan. *Modern Economy, 3,* 51–53.

Moore, A. J. (2011, March). Go for the goal: How pro sports teams score with social media. *Public Relations Tactics, 18*(3), 11.

Ninth Inning Blog (2011). 30 Unique career paths with a sports management degree. *Masters in Sport Management.* Retrieved from http://www.mastersinsportsmanagement.org/2011/30-unique-career-paths-with-a-sports-management-degree/.

Pandya, V. (2013, April, 30). Get your adrenaline pumping: Sports management is an established career world-wide and the scope in India is rising too. *Daily News & Analysis.* Retrieved from www.dnaindia.com.

Parkhouse, B. L. (1987, July). Sport management curricula: Current status and design implications for future development. *Journal of Sport Management, 1*(2), 93–128.

Pedersen, P., & Thibault, L. (2014). Managing sport. In Pedersen, P., & Thibault, L. (Eds.) *Contemporary Sport Management* (5th ed.) (pp. 6–30). Champaign, IL: Human Kinetics.

Plunkett Research, Ltd. (2015, September 30). Performing arts, spectator sports, and other live entertainment. Industry (US): Analytics, extensive benchmarks, metrics and revenue forecasts to 2022. Retrieved from http://www.plunkett research.com.

Plunkett Research, Ltd. (2016, June 10). Sports industry statistics and market size overview. Retrieved from http://www.plunkettresearch.com.

Popp, B., & Woratschek, H. (2016). Introducing branded communities in sport for building strong brand relations in social media. *Sport Management Review, 19*(2), 183–197.

Riordan, J. (2002, December 16). Epstein lights up the career path. *Sports Business Journal,* p. 35. Retrieved from http:///www.sportsbusinessjournal.com.

Ross, T., & Nelson, G. (2016, November 2). Collegiate eSports, the new frontier Presentation at the Region II National Intramural-Recreational Sports Association Conference, Atlanta, GA.

Rules. (n.d.). *US Quidditch.* Retrieved from https://www.usquidditch.org/about/rules

Sanderson, J. (2011). It's a whole new ball-game: *How social media is changing sports.* New York, NY: Hampton Press Publishing.

Sattler, E. A. (2016). *Examining the application of experiential learning techniques across sport management programs.* (Doctoral dissertation). Retrieved from Proquest Dissertations and Theses Full Text (Order No. 10164281).

Sauder, M. H. (2014). *Early experiential learning and perceived outcomes from capstone sport management internships.* (Doctoral dissertation). Retrieved from Proquest Dissertations and Theses Full Text (Order No. 3581759).

Schumann v. Collier Anesthesia, No. 14 13169 (11th Cir., 2015).

Schütz, M. (2016, March 12). Science shows that eSports professionals are real athletes. DW Akademie. Retrieved from http://dw.com.

SCSU offers new degree in sport & entertainment management. (2014, August 6). *New Haven Register,* p. T7.

Spence, K. K., Hess, D. G., McDonald, M., & Sheehan, B. J. (2009). Designing experiential learning curricula to develop future sport leaders. *Sport Management Education Journal, 3*(1), 1–25.

Sport Management Program Review Council. (2000). *Sport management program standards and review protocol.* Oxon Hill, MD: AAHPERD Publications.

Subramanian, A. (2012, May 18). Game for a career in sports sector? *Daily News & Analysis.* Retrieved from www.dnaindia.com

Sutton, W. A. (1989). The role of internships in sport management curricula – A model for development. *The Journal of Physical Education, Recreation, and Dance, 60*(7), 20–24.

United States Department of Labor, (2016). Fact Sheet: Final rule to update the regulations defining and delimiting the exemption for executive, administrative, and professional employees. Retrieved from www.dol.gov/

Vann, P. (2014). Changing the game: The role of social media in overcoming old media's attention deficit toward women's sport. *Journal of Broadcasting & Electronic Media, 583,* 438–455.

Why sports & brands want to be in esport. (2016, October 12). *Newzoo.* Retrieved from http://newzoo.com/.

Williams, J. (2002). Sport management internship administration: Challenges and chances for collaboration. *NACE Journal, 63*(2), 28–32.

Yuen, B. (2007). Sport and urban development in Singapore. *Cities, 25*(1), 29–36.

CHAPTER
2

Common Questions Regarding Sport Management Degrees

"When choosing a sport management program, it is critical to align academic needs and wants with the strengths and opportunities offered through the program. In other words, make sure you are going to be a good fit and the program you are seeking to attend caters to your strengths and interests. By doing so, the likelihood that a program's faculty and curriculum will meet your expectations increases a great deal."
—*Dr. Michael Sagas, Professor and Chair Dept. of Tourism, Recreation, and Sport Management*
University of Florida, Gainesville, FL

THE WARM UP

The content of this chapter has several purposes. It is being written for students who may not have yet selected a college major, graduate students hoping to pursue a master's degree in sport management without an undergraduate degree in the field, parents questioning the value of a sport management degree, and those who may not understand the differences among the varying degree or department titles used by different institutions. It also explains accreditation and the importance of faculty specialties, particularly at the graduate level. Many individuals unfamiliar with the sport management degree often have many questions. Thus, we hope this chapter fulfills the many queries often posed to faculty and administrators.

SPORT MANAGEMENT, SPORT ADMINISTRATION, AND SPORT BUSINESS DEFINED

Many individuals ask professors to define the difference between sport management, sport administration, and sport business. The formal answer to this question is really best provided by the educational institution offering the degree program. Sport business programs are usually tracks within a business department or college of business within a university. Saint Leo University has the Department of Sport Business, International Tourism, and Hospitality Management within their School of Business. Flagler College in Saint Augustine, Florida, has a stand-alone Department of Sport Management. As programs develop standard curricula and grow student enrollments, many programs within a college or university are able to create a specific department centered on critical mass faculty. Faculty of this order are considered critical mass due to the special need for an academic area of specialty or a specific number of full-time faculty as compared to the number of students. Many programs striving to meet accreditation standards are required to have critical mass faculty to support a designated curriculum. One may also find a sport-related program, perhaps titled sport management or sport administration, housed under department headings such as the Department of Health and Human Performance (e.g., Northwestern State University of Louisiana), Department of Kinesiology (e.g., Towson University of Maryland), or Department of Sport and Physical Education (e.g., Gonzaga University). Other departmental titles may also include such labels as sport sciences or exercise science and may house a sport management major.

Many have used management and administration synonymously. An early definition by Mullin (1980), though, provided the delineation. Dr. Mullin explained sport management as a field where the top managers were responsible for all facets of the organization including finding the money to run the organization, much as a small business would have to raise capital in order to operate. Mullin categorized this as a private sector organization. An athlete representation firm would be a good example of this.

Sport business is a relatively new term that closely aligns with the sport industry today. In most situations, but not all, those in charge of sport are running a business. (Courtesy of Big Stock)

A sport administrator was defined as an individual who was responsible for all facets of running the organization or a specific segment of an organization excluding having the responsibility for obtaining financial support. Financing comes from tax dollars, grants, or perhaps student fees if in an educational setting. The budget is provided and all individuals within the organization have to operate within their allotted budget. The best example of this is a high school or college athletic director. Coaches in an educational setting generally fall under this category as well, and this type of organization is labeled a public sector organization (Mullin, 1980).

Sport business is a relatively new term that closely aligns with the sport industry today. In most situations, but not all, those in charge of sport are running a business. This applies to professional sport, college athletics, and even to those in charge of running charitable foundations or national governing bodies. While not all individuals will be specifically charged with raising the capital to operate, most often all are involved in improving the bottom line. This even applies to most college athletic directors today. While state dollars are provided to a public institution and an athletic director manages those dollars, fundraising and sponsorships are still an integral part of their role for most in the sport industry. Simply put, sport is a business in today's world. For many, it is a multi-million dollar enterprise.

Thus, one could arrive at the conclusion that all individuals working in sport are business managers even though responsibilities may differ. Even a coach with a sport science background must often wear the hat of managing or overseeing the business affairs of a team. When considering the supervision of such an academic degree, most programs identified as sport business programs are administered through a school/college of business.

NATIONAL STANDARDS AND ACCREDITATION

A much more important factor in the program selection equation would be the recognition of authenticated curriculums. One of the requirements for employment may be that the student must have graduated from an accredited program or institution. How does one know if the chosen sport education program/curriculum is accredited or not? Fortunately, there is a professional organization to answer that very question for the prospective student. The North American Society for Sport Management (NASSM) is the umbrella organization for sport education in the United States and Canada, comprised of an international body of scholars and dedicated to the promotion and development of sport management through a broadly based scientific body of knowledge ("Constitution," 2014). One of its objectives is to protect the student seeking a sport education degree from fraudulent and innocuous academic fluff being offered at Ned's Auto Body Vocational Tech. Several years ago a research study was being conducted by Case and Dollar (2002) regarding two- and four-year curricula, and an auto mechanic trade school that offered a sport management degree was discovered. Unless you plan on being a mechanic in NASCAR, this would not be the curriculum in which you want to enroll.

A task force of early pioneers in sport management academia, chaired by Dr. Stan Brassie and Dr. Brenda Pitts, developed the first set of standards. The Sport Management Program Review Council (SMPRC) was then created to guide curriculum development for instructional programs in sport education for fourteen years (1993–2007). Called the program approval process, it served sport management administrators well during that time as program directors and faculty could follow an established and approved set of guidelines when setting up sport management curricula.

In 2007, work began for the development of a new sport management accreditation process. The Commission on Sport Management Accreditation (COSMA) was developed and the first educational program went through site visitations in the fall of 2009. Since then, over 50 institutions have gained COSMA accreditation. As the program moves forward, the number of accredited programs in sport management will increase and this will provide students, parents, and high school counselors with additional information on quality curricula.

Perhaps one of the more important decisions regarding sport management programs should be that of attending an institution with an accredited program. By doing so, a student is promised that course content and curriculum meets a national standard or guideline whereby graduates have strong core concept knowledge upon which to build successful careers in the sport industry. One can now choose from sport business, sport management, or sport administration programs, but the institution chosen should be recognized by its accredited curricula or, at the very least, a curriculum that closely mirrors COSMA's guidelines.

PARENT CONCERNS

Not all colleges are selected based upon sound rationale. Students often want to select a college their friends are attending. However, parents have a vested interest in the educational institution selection of their children. Parents and legal guardians will look at the broader scope of the college experience and, for the most part, make decisions based on sound economics, grade points, and transportation. In other words, common sense and the best education for their hard-earned dollar will be the determinants for the parents.

Parents tend to want what is best for their children and do not always understand sport management can be a rigorous educational degree program with exceptional quality. If a son or daughter indicates they wish to obtain a degree in this field, the parent may want a book report telling them what it is, what colleges offer the degree, and what one can do with it once a degree is conferred. Most parents would be very interested if the book report included some of the information in the preceding paragraphs and the rest of this textbook regarding program qualifications and accreditations. The bottom line is that if parents are interested in an appropriate college degree for their son or daughter and are paying the bill, they usually want to have a say in the institution chosen. Knowing their children, parents may feel qualified to indicate the academic fields in which the child may or may not be successful academically and socially. The overall concern from most parents is one of success in the job market upon graduation.

STUDENT CONSIDERATIONS

Hopefully, a sport management curriculum is not being pursued because of the perception that it might be an easy undergraduate or graduate degree. Preparing for a bachelor's degree should be carefully planned by the prospective student and their parents or legal guardians. Barnett (2005) found undergraduates select a sport management program based on the specific degree program, close faculty-student relationship, and specific opportunities in that order as these characteristics related to the product (the program). Barnett also found the top three factors students, and probably their parents, consider when looking at price were tuition cost, scholarship and grant opportunities, and student loan availability.

Prospective graduate students may find an institution with a more specialized curriculum. This should be one element of consideration when looking for an institution at which to pursue a master's or doctoral program. Some institutions may have specialized emphases, such as facility management or college athletic administration. If so, generally there are faculty mentors who specialize in teaching/researching this area. We do not recommend a master's student obtain a degree where the graduate curriculum mirrors the undergraduate degree. The time to specialize may be at the graduate level, but the overall educational goal of the student must be taken into account.

Choosing a career and then deciding on the institution that best fits one's plans can be a daunting assignment, but it is important to remember it's your life and your future. The sport industry is much larger than Saturday and Sunday afternoon ball games on television. Career counseling is available at all educational levels. A career counselor or academic advisor knowledgeable about the sport management field can provide you with information to follow up on your interests and, perhaps, put you on the right track toward graduation and a satisfying career. You will have to make the final decision and then follow through with the curriculum plan. The key word here is plan, and if you choose not to plan for success, then chances are your success will be limited.

FACULTY OR PROGRAM SPECIALTIES

By nature of our species, we are social animals and seek company and companionship throughout our lives. Being a student in college does not exclude one from this social dilemma. In your search for people to help you pursue your career goals, do not overlook the possibility of a professor or instructor who may serve as a role model or mentor—an academic coach so to speak. They may share a common hobby, interest, or maybe even the same hometown. This instructor or professor may become your academic advisor and, thus, take a more personal interest in your program performance and success. Many professors and instructors enjoy working with students and take personal pride when that particular student excels academically. The educators in a sport education program are usually connected to the sport industry. Quite often, they can provide expert advice on career options and access to professional contacts, and some may provide a letter of recommendation, as needed, if you perform well in the classroom.

Some universities also provide program specialties that enhance curricula with specific career niches. In these program specialties, the aspiring student can find a specific topic of interest and get an in-depth focus on a specific athletic or sport topic of interest or concern. This is truer at the graduate level, because research professors often have a specific area of interest for their research. More information on program specialties can be found in Chapter 6. We cover this topic in depth for graduate students in that chapter. However, we would like to include additional information here for the graduate student seeking a doctoral program to increase their credentials for career advancement but with no desire to teach.

THE DOCTORAL DEGREE FOR OTHER AREAS OF THE SPORT INDUSTRY

Once employed in sport, some individuals contemplate the pursuit of a doctorate with no intention of teaching. The need for a doctorate is only dictated by the organization or the demands of the industry. In Chapter 6, we discuss the master's degree, the highest applied degree and the main degree expected of a college athletic administrator. Some institutions offer free tuition as an employment benefit and, accordingly, some employees will pursue an advanced degree, law degrees included. Possessing a Juris Doctor (JD) degree may open doors not available to even those with PhD or EdD degree. Many individuals with a law degree receive strong consideration for positions as athletic directors, especially in NCAA Division I schools. More than likely, this is due to the number of contracts involved in the yearly operations of an athletic department, as well as the number of legal issues impacting such operations. Individuals with a law degree may even be considered for top positions in any sport organization without any previous sport-related experience. It does not regularly happen, but it is certainly possible.

Sometimes, individuals will pursue a doctorate because they hope to achieve the level of athletic director. Since the doctorate is the terminal degree and is associated with advanced education and learning, this degree may catapult someone to the front of the line for an athletic directorship. When applications are made for top-tier executive positions and individuals possess similar experiential backgrounds, an earned doctorate degree may be the deciding factor.

Selecting an internship based on the experience to be learned, and not the geographic location, should be a primary goal. (Courtesy of Philip Hatlem)

LOCATION: A HINDRANCE OR ADVANTAGE

Finding the best school for your undergraduate or graduate degree is now greatly facilitated by the internet and all of the information available online for making the final decision. While searching for the perfect degree program, if you were to determine the best program was in your hometown, would you be willing to travel to a lesser program? Will you be willing to leave the comforts of the hometown and travel to a better or best program? Remember, you are investing in your future.

For example, Chloe Pellican (Time Out Interview 2.1), a sport management alumnus from Europe, selected a sport management program in the United States. She was a college athlete, but also a student who was not afraid to leave her home and travel to learn about another culture in a country where she knew nobody. She interned back in her home country, was hired full-time by the same organization, and is now employed by UK Sport. A common theme throughout this book asks what are you willing to do to get your foot in the employment door of a sport organization.

Time Out Interview 2.1 with Chloe Pellican
INTERNATIONAL OLYMPIC/PARALYMPIC SPORT

Position	Sport Intelligence Officer – 1 year
Employer	UK Sport
B.S. Degree	Sport Business—Saint Leo University
Career Path	• Executive Football Analyst – Norwich City Football Club – 1 year
	• Knowledge and Insight Analyst – The Football Foundation – 1 year

Employment Recommendation

"The sport industry has so many different opportunities within it and college students must take the time to think about what they really want to do and achieve. There will be so many jobs out there that they do not know exist, and unless they do the research, they will miss out on many incredible opportunities. I would advise taking the time to do unpaid work and internships because the experience you gain will be worth so much."

Proximity to the program in which you choose to pursue your degree may be an advantage if you live in the same town as a number one program. You may have the advantage of living and eating at home, reduced concerns with transportation, being surrounded by family and friends, and generally not having to adjust to a new setting. You get to remain within your comfort zone. The only cost may be the tuition and books for the program. On the other hand, should you choose to attend school very far away from home as Chloe Pellican did, you would then have the added costs of room and board and travel-related expenses. Parents and teachers call this experience growing up. You would be cast outside of your comfort zone and have to adjust to new surroundings. Selecting an internship away from both school and home would yet again propel you into a new geographical habitat and sport organization. However, having moved to attend college away from home, another move for the internship may be less of a burden, especially if you and a roommate or fellow classmates were to intern at the same site. Sharing room and board as well as the inconveniencies of moving again might seem to be a more manageable option. Seek input from those around you who may provide some educated and sage advice (Stier, 2002). DeLuca & Bruanstein-Minkove (2016) recommend students seek advice from on-campus career centers, and we advocate making an appointment with a sport management faculty member or college admissions office. Please see Chapter 7 for a brief discussion of location as part of a six-P formula for preparation for the internship. A more in-depth discussion for selection of an internship is presented in Chapter 8.

Because most quality sport management programs require an internship (Eagleman & Mc-Nary, 2010), information about the internship program ought to be part of the decision when selecting the educational institution you will attend (Kelley, 2004). The internship is a purposeful experience, and some students would classify it as the most important part of their education. Business students in a research study by Hegert (2009) reported the internship had great value, and they appreciated the value of their internship. This is especially true when research involving sport management students has revealed high internship satisfaction is tied to commitment to entering the industry upon graduation (Koo, Diacin, Khojasteh, & Dixon, 2016). Subsequently, when selecting the educational institution or making the decision to major in sport management, inquire about all experiential learning opportunities afforded the student.

The following chapters will help you understand how to make these important decisions about the internship. If you make all of the right decisions for the right reasons, then sit back and be satisfied with your decision. You will most likely be satisfied with your institution of choice and the opportunities that will come your way.

THE FINAL BUZZER

In considering all that has been presented herein, the student should consider several parameters in the selection of the best-fit sport management program and how inquiries about experiential learning opportunities, especially the culminating internship, should be made at the same time. Be willing to invest time and review your options carefully to determine your best outcome. Ask for advice from trusted sources including professors and family. Select an internship that serves to your advantage. Do not be afraid to step outside of your comfort zone to take the challenge of new and rewarding experiences. Be adventurous!

As you read the learning examples below, think about whether the program in which you hope to enroll provides learning experiences such as the ones portrayed. Most quality sport management programs do.

EXPERIENTIAL LEARNING OPPORTUNITIES

Classroom Experiential Learning Exercise: Sport Ethics and Cross-Cultural Learning

Sport professionals do business in an increasingly global marketplace and face challenges in understanding legal and ethical parameters in cross-cultural settings. To assist students in learning about this type of environment, lectures can serve as a means of connecting eastern and western philosophies, ethical principles, and practices in a sporting context.

We incorporate experiential learning by inviting guest speakers from unique cultural backgrounds who are marketers, practitioners, and international scholars (e.g., lecturers on Turkish traditional sports, gambling issues in Taiwanese baseball, and ethical issues in disability sports). We also incorporate games (e.g., crossword puzzles for the reasons why people quit sports), activities (e.g., debate over whether esports should be considered sport), and documentaries (e.g.,

Living the Fantasy and Insanity) to facilitate an interactive environment. We also offer hands-on opportunities (e.g., field trip to UGA Special Collection Library where students can see, touch, and feel the materials that were donated by former student athletes) and to better understand course content and appreciate the culture and ethics of different countries.

Submitted by Tyreal Yizhou Qian, Instructor and Graduate Assistant
University of Georgia, Athens, GA

Program Experiential Learning Example: Community Engagement/Service Learning
Community engagement and experiential learning has been expanded throughout the Sport Management BSBA program and other disciplines across campus. During each of the four years of study within the sport management curriculum, the student is required to engage in practical experiences aligned with course content and career interests.

In the freshman year, a student must work three athletic events within a Division III venue and write a reflection paper for each experience. In the sophomore year, 75 hours in Practicum I must be completed on campus or within the community as the student begins shaping and selecting those work experiences that complement their career pathway and personal strengths. In the junior year as part of Practicum II, the student must engage in a group activity that designs and implements two one-day events for children at a local community center affiliated with a housing project. The events are developed during meetings with community partners and students so the events are appropriate for the abilities and interests of the children and meet the mission of the organization.

At the completion of study and within the senior year, the internship program is a capstone event that gives the student the option of a six credit (20 hours/week = 300 hours) or 12 credit (40 hours/week = 600 hours) work experience. The internship provides the student with a laboratory for practical learning opportunities that applies theoretical knowledge to the needs of the workforce while enhancing professional growth. We continue to customize learning by reaching beyond the classroom to better prepare our students, so we can keep up with the speed of change in the future of sport and the welfare of those in society.

Submitted by Dr. Heather Gilmour, Assistant Professor and
Executive Director of Community Engagement
Mount Ida College, Newton, MA

REFERENCES

Barnett, A. L. (2005). Marketing implications relative to factors influencing undergraduate students' choice of sport management programs in North America. (Doctoral Dissertation). Retrieved from Proquest Dissertations and Theses Global. (Order No. 3202987).

Case R and Dollar J. E. (2002). Sport management education: The case against two-year colleges. *International Journal of Sport Management, 3*(3), 171–179.

Constitution. (2014). North American Society for Sport Management. Retrieved from www.nassm.org.

DeLuca, J. R., & Braunstein-Mikove, J. (2016). An evaluation of sport management student preparedness: Recommendations for adapting curriculum to meet industry needs. *Sport Management Education Journal, 10*(1), 1–12

Eagleman, A. N., & McNary, E. L. (2010). What are we teaching our students? A descriptive examination of the current status of undergraduate sport management curriculum in the United States. *Sport Management Education Journal, 4*(2), 1–17.

Hegert, M. (2009). Student perceptions of the value of internships in business education. *American Journal of Business Education, 2*(8), 9–13.

Kelley, D. R. (2004). Quality control in the administration of sport management internships. *Journal of Physical Education, Recreation, and Dance, 75*(1), 28–30.

Koo, G., Diacin, M., J., Khojasteh, J., & Dixon, A. W. (2016). Effects of internship satisfaction on the pursuit of employment in sport management. *Sport Management Education Journal, 10*(1), 29–42.

Mullin, B. (1980). Sport management: The nature and utility of the concept. *Arena Review, 4*(3), 1–11.

Stier, W. F. (2002). Sport management internships: From theory to practice. *Strategies, 15*(4), 7–9.

CHAPTER
3

Sport Business Industry Overview: Professional Sport

"During my career, the two things I have learned that have had the biggest impact on me . . . If you love what you do, don't worry about the money . . . and embrace the workload and the hours. You won't remember your 20s or 30s, however, get ready for a roller coaster ride that never ends."

—Andy Dunn, President/Partner Vancouver Canadiens, Vancouver, Canada

THE WARM UP

In this chapter, we will begin a comprehensive review of the sport business/management industry. This review will actually span four chapters. This chapter discusses professional sport. The primary focus is on sport within the United States, although we have included a section on international professional sport. Chapter 4 is a comprehensive examination of Olympic, Paralympic,[1] and amateur sport. We realize many Olympic athletes are also professional athletes. However, we simply decided to combine these three industry segments into a single chapter. Chapter 5 will discuss areas of the industry that support the mainstream segments (e.g., event management and marketing) as well as entrepreneurial ventures in sport including small businesses started by individuals. Yes, there will be some overlap in these three chapters that cannot be prevented. Chapter 6 is a review of teaching sport management as an excellent career. We are quite sure most textbooks overlook this very important sport management occupation, and it is dedicated to all who teach those striving to enter our wonderful industry. As many of our colleagues will agree, it can be a very rewarding calling. These four chapters combined will provide an in-depth look into this rather complicated industry.

Before we begin, it is necessary to discuss one important element as it applies to the business of sport and experiential learning, and that is the seasonality of some sport industry segments.

---

[1] In late 2016, the International Paralympic Committee (IPC) announced a rebranding of its Paralympic Sports. World Para Athletics is replacing IPC Athletics. More information on this can be found in Chapter 4.

A SEASONAL INDUSTRY

When one is planning for experiential learning opportunities and, more specifically, for the culminating academic internship experience, the seasonality of sport must be considered. For example, if one is pursuing their passion to work in baseball, the best internship experiences start in January. Many major and minor league teams recruit interns to start in January when the sales season is in full swing. While some sales take place for a baseball team from October through December, this is not really the time of year that most teams start interns. Some new entry-level start dates may also be delayed to January. It is, however, a main hiring season. Many teams use the Professional Baseball Employment Opportunities website (PBEO.com) to recruit; many minor league and some major league teams will recruit via the career fair at the Baseball Winter Meetings generally held during the first or second week of December.

An internship beginning in January may not end until Labor Day weekend for those working in the baseball minor leagues. Major league internships generally end when the team's season ends. If an intern is fortunate to be working for any major league team advancing to the playoffs, the internship is often extended. Though this may upset future moves or employment plans, not many individuals would shun the chance to work for one of the two teams in the World Series. Often, divisional playoff and World Series teams offer additional incentives/perks to interns. How about a chance to earn a World Series ring? Wouldn't you want to stick around for that grand opportunity after having worked the entire season? There is no guarantee an intern would be awarded a ring, but just to have an internship end with such a spectacular event involving additional media hype and extra planning would be worth the extra month from an experiential learning perspective.

Seasonality is true for other team sport-related internships. The prime hiring season for intern positions in the National Football League (NFL) is April through July or August although some may start earlier. This is also true for the National Basketball Association (NBA), Major League Soccer (MLS), the National Hockey League (NHL), and other sport-related leagues. It is our recommendation that students not approach a team for internships toward the end of a competition season unless there is an advertised position. Application materials may go unnoticed because the team will not be looking. Wait until after the season is over for that particular team; waiting until all playoffs have ceased for the entire league should also be considered. Postseason is often when a team will begin to assess the number of interns needed for the upcoming season. Sometimes a full-time employee may move on, and the team may decide to hire one or more interns to replace that individual. If you are enrolled in an academic program that allows you to accept full-time employment and use it to satisfy an internship requirement, you have earned your first bonus. However, the organization should be informed beforehand if this is your intention. Some will allow it; others will not. After all, if they can screen your abilities and pay you internship wages for three to nine months, this is a benefit to the sport organization. While some interns may be lucky and land a full-time position for an internship, a paid internship should not be expected, especially in tough economic times.

There are exceptions to the seasonality hiring cycle as described above. The Tampa Bay Rays is one professional sport team that, as of 2016, hires interns for six-month stints. Of course, this type of hiring cycle could change when new ownership or a new human relations director is employed where they are given freedom to establish a different hiring cycle. One suggestion is to maintain constant scrutiny on job or team websites. Sometimes an annual pattern for hiring can be recognized especially for larger organizations. If the team owns the facility lease and runs events unrelated to the sport season, such activity can explain the hiring of interns throughout the year, particularly in event and facility management. Every team is different.

Quite often, positions not tied to a particular team or league are not seasonal. Organizations, such as WME|IMG (discussed later in this chapter and also known as IMG and IMG World), operate on a 12-month cycle just as any other nonsport-related business. Thus, there is no defined hiring season. This is true of marketing and event management firms; these areas will be discussed more fully in Chapter 5.

Our best recommendation is to look early and become familiar with the hiring seasons for teams or leagues of interest. It would not be too early to start this awareness process at the beginning of your post-secondary academic career or during the first semester of a graduate degree. Become familiar with where all sport organizations post position openings. Some will post openings first on their own websites. These are often found under careers, job opportunities, employment, or human resources tabs and may be hidden at the very bottom of a web page. If organizations are not successful in hiring someone through their own website or professional networking, they may post a position on one or more of the several sport-related employment websites. Small organizations tend to use employment websites a great deal for posting internships. For your convenience, a comprehensive, but never exhaustive, list of web addresses related to sport organizations and job information websites has been provided in Appendix B.

Exploring career and internship listings early, even if one is not ready to intern, gives the job seeker an additional advantage. As you progress through an academic degree, you can begin to cultivate a keen understanding of the skills and experience for which many organizations are searching simply by reading job announcements. If a particular area of the industry or even a specific team or sport is your employment objective, you may discover similar positions require a comparable set of skills. By utilizing the Foster Five-Step Model discussed in Chapter 1, specific events to work or targeted skills one hopes to acquire can be identified. The next section will explore various industry segments and provide a deeper understanding of the sport business industry.

In preparing for the internship, take advantage of all opportunities. As was indicated in the first chapter, some organizations call any volunteer experience an internship, though we clarified the differences. Regardless of the label, if you have a chance to learn anything about the operation of a sporting event or work in the offices of a sport organization, even if it means missing an important social event at your college campus, accept the opportunity. Answering the phone and filing documents still provides access to the people within the organization. These types of responsibilities are good for volunteer positions, part-time jobs, or apprenticeship learning opportunities. We do not recommend them as a sole responsibility for a culminating and/or full-time internship.

Another true story involving a student exemplifies this recommendation. An undergraduate transfer student came to campus to enroll in a sport management program. He quickly became involved in the sport management student association where the opportunity to work a variety of different sporting events was afforded to him. He worked just about every event available and ended up leading the organization as president for two years. In the course of this experience, he took it upon himself to search out organizations and events that the sport management program, to date, had not created an official connection and worked those events—passing networking information along to his peers. It did not matter if these opportunities were in amateur or professional sport or event or facility management. When he applied for his senior internship with an event management company with only a phone interview and an emailed résumé, he was offered a full-time position with benefits and the promise of an eventual company car. While this is not a regular scenario even with the most involved individuals, it does represent what can happen if one takes advantage of every possible opportunity. In the following sections, and in Chapters 4–6, every attempt has been made to provide a wide scope of information on a broad range of sport industry segments. While we could not include information about every possible position, we have included Time Out Interviews with various individuals at different levels to provide as much information as possible to ponder while you search for an internship and a career in the sport business industry.

PROFESSIONAL SPORT SEGMENTS

This section will explore the professional team and individual sport business industry. It is our recommendation students carefully explore all segments of the industry. While one may have a burning desire to be an agent or to work in a specific sport, experience has taught us as one reads, investigates, and steps into an industry segment, the beliefs and perceptions an individual brings may change dramatically. How an organization actually works on the inside seven days a week can be drastically different from the fan's perception of how the organization works on competition day.

Visiting the website of an organization and viewing an organizational chart is the best way to gain an initial understanding of the variety of positions and size of a department or organization. In fact, if available, a well-defined organizational chart should be scrutinized before interviewing for a position within the organization. A chart provides insight into departmental divisions, names of key managers, how the organization is structured, and employees that may report to more than one individual. Be aware that some organizational charts may be outdated. Attempt to find a staff listing online and compare it to any chart you may find. An employee listing with their position titles can sometimes be found within an online media guide. By learning names of key employees, an individual enters an interview with great networking information and a more comprehensive understanding of that organization.

Professional Team Sport

Professional team sport is the industry segment where many students hope to launch their sport business career. We have included a comprehensive listing of some of the more notable and not-so notable leagues—including lesser known leagues with teams in smaller towns and world-wide leagues for those interested in international sport—in Appendix B. We felt compelled to list the lesser known leagues since many of their teams are in smaller towns where universities with sport management programs exist providing additional experiential learning opportunities. We are fully aware, smaller start-up leagues often do not make it and may cease to operate during the publication of this book. Still if you can gain experience before a smaller league/team goes out of business, the networking opportunities gained may lead to sport business positions elsewhere.

Internships in professional sport are not as hard to acquire as many people may believe. Minor league baseball or positions with a minor league in any sport, such as the National Basketball Association Gatorade League (G-League) or ice hockey leagues such as the ECHL, are plentiful if one has built a résumé with several experiential learning opportunities. Entry-level positions are more difficult to find. Often the senior or graduate student internship is the optimum path to land an entry-level position with a professional team.

Positions such as football or baseball operations are not often advertised and are filled from within. Tyrone Brooks (Time Out Interview 3.1), representing baseball, stated,

> These positions can be tied to player personnel, coaching, and scouting and be labeled as player development. Fulltime responsibilities may include working with the general manager (GM) to oversee the entire operation, handling day-to-day tasks, working with rules compliance, roster management, budgeting, negotiating player and employee contracts, assisting with salary arbitration preparation, assisting with or overseeing pro or international scouting, staffing, providing scouting judgments for possible trades, and making internal evaluations within the minor league system. (personal communication, February 2, 2010)

To get into scouting, Mr. Brooks indicates a logical route is having played the game at some level, but some have broken into this side of the business simply by networking and building relationships. However, he also states a scout must be able to differentiate the different levels of play and skills needed to play the game at the highest level. Brian Hudspeth, (Time Out Interview 3.2) who has several years of NFL scouting experience states, "If you asked 100 scouts how they broke into the business, you would probably get 100 different answers" (personal communication, September 14, 2016).

Time Out Interview 3.1 with Tyrone Brooks
MAJOR LEAGUE BASEBALL

Position	Senior Director, Front Office and Field Staff Diversity Pipeline Program
Employer	Major League Baseball
B.S. Degree	University of Maryland at College Park—Accounting & Marketing (Double-Major)
Career Path	• Baseball Operations Trainee – Atlanta Braves – 3 months
	• Administrative Assistant/Scouting & Player Development – Atlanta Braves – 3 months
	• Baseball Operations Assistant – Atlanta Braves – 3 years
	• Midwest Area Scouting Supervisor – Atlanta Braves – 3 years
	• Assistant, Player Personnel – Atlanta Braves – 2 years
	• Director of Baseball Operations – Atlanta Braves – 2 years
	• Director of Baseball Administration – Atlanta Braves – 1 year
	• Pro Scout, Major & Minor League Baseball – Cleveland Indians – 3 years
	• Director of Baseball Operations – Pittsburgh Pirates – 2 years
	• Director of Player Personnel – Pittsburgh Pirates – 4 years

Employment Recommendation

"Understand your skill set and how you can immediately bring value to an organization. Network, network, network. Meet as many people as you can and learn to build an extensive network. Seek out potential mentors who can offer advice and take a vested interest in your career."

Positions within professional sport can vary from organization to organization. However, typical position titles do exist. Most job seekers can find entry-level positions within event or facility management and sales. Pete Rozelle, former but long-time NFL commissioner, started his route to success through media relations with the Los Angeles Rams (Van Riper, 2008). Roger Goodell, who began his tenure as NFL commissioner in 2006, was captain of his high school football team but never played in college due to an injury. Following his college graduation with a degree in economics, Goodell reportedly wrote to every NFL team searching for a job and landed an internship with the NFL front office followed by an internship with the New York Jets. He then was re-hired by the NFL front office and rose through the ranks ("Roger Goodell," n.d.). As you can see, even a top-level industry executive can get their start as an intern.

Time Out Interview 3.2 with Brian Hudspeth
PROFESSIONAL SCOUTING

Position	Football Scout – 8 years
Employer	Tampa Bay Buccaneers
B.S. Degree	University of Southern Mississippi—Geography, Minor in Coaching & Sports Administration
M.S. Degree	University of Tennessee, Knoxville—Human Performance & Sport Studies, emphasis in Sport Management
Career Path	• Football Operations Graduate Assistant – Univ. of TN, Knoxville – 1 year • Football Operations Assistant – Univ. of TN, Knoxville – 2 years • Player Personnel Intern – Atlanta Falcons – 1 year • Scouting Assistant – Atlanta Falcon – 1 year • Player Personnel/Football Systems Analyst – Atlanta Falcons – 1 year • Pro & College Scouting Assistant – Houston Texans – 2 years • College Scout (Southeast area) – Houston Texans – 3 years • College Scout (Southwest area) – Tampa Bay Buccaneers – 3 years • National Scout (National cross checker) – Tampa Bay Buccaneers – 2 years • College Scout (Southeast area) – Tampa Bay Buccaneers – 3 years

Employment Recommendation

"There is no specific career path to get into scouting. However, I have a simple acronym: ESPN

E - Experience – Build a football résumé through volunteering, internships, GA's, and coaching

S - Sacrifice – It's competitive; be prepared to put in a lot of hours with low pay and be willing to relocate

P - Perseverance – Understand you will hit some walls when pursuing opportunities; be patient – nobody is named GM overnight.

N - Network—Building a network of football professionals is VITAL to break in, advance or maintain employment."

Game day operations is where many get their start in the industry. This area of the industry is most closely associated with event and facility management. Events such as game-day promotions are generally run by an in-house staff. The operation of the facility will depend upon ownership and established leases. Some organizations may have an entire facility staff and their own facility manager even if they do not own the facility. However, often a team will play in a publicly owned facility where all management and maintenance functions are under control of the local government. Chapter 5 more fully discusses event and facility management and marketing as entrepreneurial careers, but all of these areas can be pursued within professional team and individual sport.

The media perform an important function in professional sport and often rely on in-house personnel to support their efforts. The role of media personnel employed by the team may involve the development and publication of game programs, writing articles within those publications, writing press releases, assisting with game and player statistics, playing host to visiting media, and coordinating press conferences. Website development and maintenance may be an additional responsibility, but some organizations will outsource this to a private company. One or more individuals may be assigned as a liaison between the organization and the television/radio media personnel. Often, one individual will be the main spokesperson for the team. Organizations are hiring individuals to manage their social media and this is where many opportunities exist for entering the sport business industry including professional sport.

Media functions may fall under a separate department, but most often they will be housed under community or public relations. Community relations often involves the foundations or fundraising functions of a team, but it also may include player appearances and other specialty programs. One such example is when a professional team sponsors a youth sport organization or develops an educational program with a local school district. All of these certainly involve public relations efforts, but some teams separate the community and public relations efforts into different departments. Later in this chapter, we discuss marketing and some organizations will hire social media personnel to handle marketing initiatives. This chapter and Chapters 4 and 5 cover media-related positions. This is necessary because of the differences between media positions within all of sport.

While many individuals will recognize the popular announcers and broadcasters seen on television or heard on the radio, many very satisfying careers in this segment can be found with smaller organizations. Sean Aronson (Time Out Interview 3.3) has been with the Saint Paul Saints for more than 11 years after having worked with three different minor league baseball teams. Even the astute baseball fan may not recognize the team name or the league in which they participate. The Saints are part of the professional independent baseball league of which the Saints have been a member since the early 1990s.

Sales are a big deal in sport. Many individuals in professional sport started with an internship in a sales department. Sales and marketing departments are structured differently throughout professional sport. In some organizations, sales and marketing may be housed in different departments. Regardless, both bring in revenue for the organization and any department that increases the bottom line often has more position openings. Each may involve ticket, sponsorship, group, and media sales. Thus, experiential learning opportunities should involve obtaining experience in all of the above if sales or marketing is the chosen specialized area of pursuit. If

Time Out Interview 3.3 with Sean Aronson
PROFESSIONAL SPORT - MEDIA RELATIONS

Position	Director of Broadcasting/Media Relations – 11 years
Employer	Saint Paul Saints
B.S. Degree	University of Colorado-Boulder—Journalism
Career Path	• Media Relations Assistant – Colorado Springs Sky Sox – 1 year
	• Director Broadcasting/Media Relations – Allentown Ambassadors – 2 years
	• Director Broadcasting/Media Relations – Fort Myers Miracle – 4 years

Employment Recommendation

"About a month after the baseball season is over you should send us your résumé. Usually when the season ends, for us in September, staff members will take their vacations and September to the beginning of October is a relaxation time. Then in mid-October we start turning our focus to the following season. Don't ever apply mid-season or a month before a season. Chances are internships are gone and applying late in the game shows that doing an internship wasn't on the top of your mind."

one chooses to pursue marketing, getting plenty of sales experience and obtaining marketing research skills are highly recommended. According to Adam Banko, Vice President of Ticket Sales for the Utica Comets minor league hockey team in Utica, New York, "Marketing is such a broad category, most minor league teams do not even have marketing positions. The sales staff is considered part of marketing. I understand many students fear sales because they associate sales with a used car dealership. The fact is, marketing is sales, and you can create an experience for someone at a game they never would have had before" (personal communication, November 1, 2016). Adam began as an intern with the Tampa Bay Lightning in group sales and, as of 2017, had worked for four different professional sport teams in three different states.

Because so many entry level jobs and internships in professional sport begin with sales, we have included two Time Out Interviews from individuals who have made their careers in sales. Mike Stanfield (Time Out Interview 3.4) provides us with his career ladder crisscrossing the industry geographically and within industry segments. His amazing career path started in part-time sales as a stadium food vendor and confirms Adam's comments from above regarding the marriage of marketing and sales. While very unique, his current position requires him to oversee sales for two professional teams in the same city, New Orleans.

Time Out Interview 3.4 with Mike Stanfield
PROFESSIONAL TEAM SPORT

Position	Senior Vice-President of Sales
Employer	New Orleans Saints and Pelicans
B.S. Degree	Saint Leo University—Sport Management
Career Path	• Vendor—Tampa Stadium – 4 months
	• Cincinnati Reds – Spring Training – 4 months
	• Assistant GM – Clinton Giants, Clinton, Iowa – 1 year
	• Ft. Lauderdale Strikers – Director of Marketing – 3 years
	• Ft. Lauderdale Yankees – Director of Marketing/Sales – 2 years
	• Florida Marlins – Ticket Sales – 2 years
	• Miami Heat – Director of Ticket Sales – 2 years
	• Detroit Vipers – Director of Sales – 1 year
	• Detroit Tigers – Director of Ticket Sales – 2 years

Employment Recommendation

"Work hard and then if you are already working hard, work harder. When taking a job, think about how you're going to get the job after the job you're about to start.

Will the people you are working for really help you with your career and get you to the next level? It does not hurt to be the first person in the office and the last one to leave four days a week."

Bill Mauger's (Time Out Interview 3.5) career path has been quite different. He began as a ticket sales intern with the Orlando Magic and has never left the team. Both of these individuals have worked more than 20 years in the industry.

Financial positions are also available and may include accountants and controllers. Individuals in these positions may have little or no sport-related experience before being hired. According to Van Riper (2008), individuals filling these jobs are sometimes hired from a team's or organization's auditing company. Thus, finding an entry-level position may be difficult but definitely not impossible. Internships might be more likely found if you have a strong background with numbers. Good grades in general or sport-related finance and accounting courses are a strong indicator of one's skills in this area.

Analytics is currently an area in which many teams and organizations are searching for well-qualified individuals. In baseball, this area is better known as sabermetrics. Many of you may have read the book or seen the movie *Moneyball*. According to Baumer and Zimbalist (2014), after the book was published in 2003, whole departments were created by baseball

Time Out Interview 3.5 with Bill Mauger
PROFESSIONAL SPORT/BASKETBALL

Position	Assistant Director, Ticket Operations – 1 year
Employer	Orlando Magic
B.S. Degree	Western Carolina University—Sport Management – Professional Sport Concentration
Career Path	• Box Office Representative – Orlando Magic, three years • Sr. Box Office Representative – Orlando Magic – 5 years • Fan Relations Manager – Orlando Magic – 5 years • Assistant Director, Ticket Services – Orlando Magic – 5 years • Assistant Director, Ticket Operations – Orlando Magic – 6 years

Employment Recommendation

"Working in the sport industry is a lot of hard work, a lot of hours and spending time in the office during nights, weekends, and holidays. There is a dedication to the organization, to your department, to your co-workers, and to the fans that is needed to succeed in your career. There are many benefits to being in the industry, including having the joy of following the success of the team on the field or court. Be aggressive in trying to find a team that can utilize your passion to work in sports and, when you get the opportunity, show your organization and department they are better off with you being a part of their daily operations. Always show a willingness to work whatever hours are required. Go above and beyond what is asked of you. Establish as many relationships around the organization as possible, not limiting those to just inside your department. Don't hesitate to job shadow other areas of the organization to get the best feel possible for all that goes into running a franchise. Just understand many individuals are watching you so make the very best impression you can at all times."

organizations for sabermetrics. Michael Lewis, the author of *Moneyball,* wrote the story basically to explain how small money teams could use sabermetrics to beat the rich teams who simply go out and buy talent. Billy Beane, the 2002 general manager of the Oakland A's, used sabermetrics to analyze talent, select players, and win 103 games with bargain-priced players (Barra, 2013; Baumer and Zimbalist, 2014). Today, analytics is an area where students who choose to learn and gain experience using analytics can get their foot in the door of a variety of sport-related organizations. According to Valerdi (2013), economists have used analytics to analyze penalty kicks in soccer. The Sports Facilities Advisory, a facility development and management company based in Clearwater, FL, uses analytics to develop and plan all types of recreation and sport facilities. So, even though analytics is better known for baseball, it is being used by many professional teams and other sport organizations.

Guest services, often called customer service or customer relations, is not always a separate position in many separate organizations. However, the Tampa Bay Lightning have made it their mission and passion to be an industry leader in this category. Mary Milne (Time Out Interview 3.6) indicates the Lightning have received a lot of recognition for their high scores on fan experience. In 2016, EPSN ranked the Lighting #1 in pro sports based on fan relations, stadium experience, ownership, affordability, bang for the buck, and players (personal communication, April 24, 2017).

Positions also exist in working with volunteers. Managing a corps of volunteers for a professional sporting event can be a very challenging position. Just think about it. Volunteers do not have to show up even after they trained to fill a much needed position for an event like the Super Bowl or a professional golf tournament. Dependent upon an organization's structure and lease agreements, on any game day, there can be a wide variety of functions filled by volunteers. A position may exist for an individual solely responsible for selecting, training, and supervising these volunteer groups. A Super Bowl organizing committee will recruit thousands of volunteers for the pregame week of festivities, half-time shows, and more. For game days within a season, one of a manager's functions may be the oversight of concession stands staffed by community

Time Out Interview 3.6 with Mary Milne
PROFESSIONAL SPORT

Position	Vice President, Guest Experience
Employer	Amalie Arena, Tampa Bay Lightning, Tampa Bay Storm
B.S. Degree	Health and Physical Education—Longwood University
M. Ed. Degree	Athletic Administration—Eastern Kentucky University
Career Path	• Graduate Assistant Field Hockey Coach – Eastern Kentucky University – 1 year • Head Field Hockey Coach, Head Softball Coach, Assistant Athletic Director – Catholic University – 5 years • Head Field Hockey Coach – Ohio University – 10 years • Front of House Manager – The Ice Palace – 2 years • Director of Event Operations – St. Pete Times Forum – 5 years • VP, Event Operations – St. Pete Times Forum – 3 years • VP, Operations – TB Times Forum – 3 years

Employment Recommendation

"Get involved. Accept opportunities even if they are outside your field. Be willing to try new things."

organizations volunteering as a fundraising group and collecting a percentage of the income for their organization. Professional golf tournaments cannot be run without a large corps of volunteers who often pay for their uniform. Thus, a student who may have gained experience by volunteering and observing how volunteers are recruited and managed could end up finding employment in this area of sport.

Soccer is growing in the United States and is becoming the often cited fifth major sport. Along with the four major team sport leagues—the NFL, MLB, the NBA, and the NHL—there are also opportunities in soccer. In Chapter 4, we include a Time Out Interview with Vincent Wiskowski who works for United Soccer League (USL). This organization sponsors youth to professional teams and the Tampa Bay Rowdies recently relocated under their umbrella. Luke Mohamed (Time Out Interview 3.7) also made his way to professional soccer after gaining experience by working with other organizations.

Time Out Interview 3.7 with Luke Mohamed
PROFESSIONAL SPORT

Position	Manager, Corporate Partnerships – 18 months
Employer	D.C. United
B.S. Degree	Robert Morris University—Sport Management & Accounting
M.B.A. Degree	University of South Florida—Sport Business
M.S. Degree	University of South Florida—Sport & Entertainment Management
Career Path	• Marketing & Development Coordinator – Dick's Sporting Goods Pittsburgh Marathon – 2 years • Development Manager – Dick's Sporting Good Pittsburgh Marathon – 1 year • Sales Development Coordinator – IRONMAN Triathlon – 1 year • Graduate Assistant – Tampa Bay Sports Commission – 9 months

Employment Recommendation

"Think outside the major professional leagues. There is a wealth of opportunities with events, leagues, and other sports organizations that are not regularly found on the highlights of ESPN. True of all sports jobs, but particularly professional, the demand for jobs greatly exceeds the supply—you have to set yourself apart. Be open to any opportunity. Focus more on what you will be doing and learning, versus the name and notoriety of the organization. Some of the best internships are with lesser known organizations and teams."

The moral of the story? A larger professional sport team (e.g., the MLB) may employ over 100 individuals on a year-round basis. Seasonal positions with teams are also available, but many are subcontracted to other organizations thus reducing the overall staff size. Looking for employment with the subcontractors creates additional opportunities. Entrepreneurial positions providing support to the industry are discussed in Chapter 5.

Professional Individual Sport

Positions in professional individual sport may be more difficult to find than within professional team sport. This is mainly because individual sports are often set up as tournaments or meets and can be hosted by local organizing staffs. These tournaments usually rotate weekly from site to site, such as in golf and tennis. Positions will exist in marketing, event management, public relations, and other analogous departments. However, working with an individual sport may actually be categorized as more exciting depending on one's point of view. In any segment of the sport industry, each day can present a different scenario with varied responsibilities. With individual sport, a new champion may be crowned weekly and event sites can change from year to year, so crisscrossing North America or the world geographically may be a typical responsibility. For example, the LPGA's 2016 schedule started in the Bahamas with 12 additional stops in foreign countries and 19 sites in the United States from Hawaii to New Jersey from January through mid-November. A similar scenario can be experienced within the purview of other individual sport schedules. However, this does not mean every employee travels to every event. Individual responsibilities can dictate the travel schedule, if any travel is expected at all.

Professional golf or tennis tournaments and other large individual sport events are excellent experiences where one can learn about the incredible amount of detail it takes to run a three- to four-day or longer affair and the number of different organizations involved. For example, professional golf recruits large corporations to sponsor their events. The tournament income pays the local organizing group's full-time employees, covers expenditures for running the event, and is the source of the prize money for the competitors. However, a great deal of the income also goes to numerous charities that have been designated recipients. In many individual sports, the event or tournament is owned/operated by someone else beyond the governing offices. Each event may have its own local event director and staff. The home office definitely consults and sends staff to work and control specific segments of the event, but entire office staffs and managers do not travel on a weekly basis. For example, the Valspar Championship is one of the PGA TOUR's annual events. The paint division of the Valspar Corporation is the title sponsor. Copperhead Charities owns the rights to this tour event and contracted with Pro Links Sports to serve as the management company. Pro Links employs and pays these individuals. Contract and part-time staff are paid through Copperhead Charities from sponsorship income (Labbe, personal communication, December 22, 2016).

For the PGA Tour, and possibly other individual sport governing bodies, each tour stop would have their own independent websites that may contain staff listings. On the PGA Tour website, a schedule of events can be found, which lists each tournament. Selecting the tournaments will redirect you to the specific website. According to Zachary Labbe, the director of tournament operations for the Valspar Tournament in Palm Harbor, FL, this would be the easiest way to learn about employment opportunities for each individual tournament and discover more information about host organizations and charities supported (personal communication, December 22, 2016).

For example, Erin Mazurek (Time Out Interview 3.8) works in the professional tennis industry. She served two internships gaining event management and tournament organization experience. Tournaments with successful sponsorship deals may determine longevity in a position whereas the failure to obtain a title sponsor may mean the loss of a tournament stop and require you to search for employment with a new tournament in a different location. Obviously, flexibility in your geographic location is a key requirement.

Time Out Interview 3.8 with Erin Mazurek
PROFESSIONAL SPORT

Position	Tournament Director – 2.5 years
Employer	United States Tennis Association (USTA)
B.B.A. Degree	Northwood University—Business Administration/Entertainment Sports Promotion & Management
Career Path	• Internship – Detroit Metro Sports Commission – 3 months • Internship – Dow Corning Tennis Classic (USTA Pro Circuit) – 3 months • Tournament Assoc. – Dow Corning Tennis Classic (USTA Pro Circuit) – 7 years • Event Sales Manager – Detroit Red Wings/Olympia Entertainment – 1 year • Event Sales Director – Detroit Red Wings/Olympia Entertainment – 4 years

Employment Recommendation

"Start at a small enough tournament that allows you to get your hands in all areas of the business so you can learn all sides. Figure out how the tournament operates inside and out, how sales are made, what the value proposition is, current players, field etc. Starting small and getting a feeling for each side of the business also lets you figure out what you're good at."

An individual interested in any professional sport could actually work for an athlete's foundation. Lee Greely (Time Out Interview 3.9) does just this. Many athletes establish a foundation to raise money for specific charitable causes and hire a staff to run their foundation. Lee's sales background in other professional sports, no doubt, played a role for him in securing this position.

Extreme or action sport is a segment of the industry where internships have not been explored as often as other individual sports. Additionally, there is not complete agreement as to what constitutes an extreme sport. Extreme sport is defined as any athletic endeavor considered more dangerous than others . . . often featuring a combination of speed, height, danger, and spectacular stunts ("Extreme Sport," 2014). Wikipedia also calls extreme sport an action or adventurous sport and defines it as certain activities having a high level of inherent danger ("Extreme Sport," 2016). This segment of the industry is extremely popular with many students living or attending college in colder climates who may be interested in snowboarding or other winter action sports,

Time Out Interview 3.9 with Lee Greely
PROFESSIONAL INDIVIDUAL SPORT

Position	Sales Manager, Quicken Loans National – 1 year
Employer	Tiger Woods Foundation
B.A. Degree	York College, York, PA—Sport Management
Career Path	• Sales Intern – Ripken Baseball – Aberdeen IronBirds – 2 summers • Account Representative – Ripken Baseball – Aberdeen IronBirds – 3 years • Group Sales Manager – Ripken Baseball – Aberdeen IronBirds – 1 year • General Manager – Ticket Sales – IMG Learfield Ticket Solutions / Univ. of Akron – 1 Year • Training & Sales Coach – Ripken Baseball – Aberdeen IronBirds – 2 years

Employment Recommendation

"Experience, networking, and hard work. These are three HUGE aspects to individuals with whom I have seen been successful within the sports industry. Gaining valuable experience, whether it be through internships, volunteer work or during their time in college—all of those experiences gained within the sports industry will help to get a leg up over other applicants within the industry. Networking is another very important factor. I am in my current position thanks to connections I have within the industry, and continuing to stay in touch with any and all contacts I have made. While experience is great, the only way to stand out among other interns and applicants is to work harder than everyone else."

but it does not preclude others from investigating possible internships with extreme sport governing bodies, tour hosts, or geographical regions where extreme sporting events are held. In 2016, the Dew Tour hosted events featuring BMX, skiing, snowboarding, and skateboarding. The Dew Tour is the main professional tour for extreme sports. The X Games, an ESPN created and owned event, involves televised events including some of the sports mentioned above as well as motor cross and surfing. Medals and prize money are awarded.

If you have a passion for sport in any of the industry segments listed above, there certainly are numerous positions. This is one area where it is quite easy to volunteer in order to learn first-hand how individual sporting events are run. A student living in an area where professional events are taking place could work events in successive years in different positions and gather a great deal of experience. When volunteering, one would have to focus on the responsibilities given, but it is very possible to meet key individuals and develop a network of contacts. For example, if you volunteered for the Valspar Championship mentioned above, you could possibly meet individuals from the PGA TOUR, Copperhead Charities, Suncoast Golf, Inc., Innisbrook Resort, their food concessions supplier, any one of a number of golf equipment suppliers, the Golf Channel, and more. Thus, volunteering and networking are probably the two most prominent ways to learn about individual professional sport.

Professional Motor Sports

Motorsports is truly a very popular professional sport in many areas of the United States. Powerboat racing, snowmobile racing, otherwise known as snocross, and all-terrain vehicles (ATV) racing have professional circuits. The American Power Boat Association (APBA) sanctions events mostly from February through November in locations across the United States. The snocross season spans the winter months and are typically held in various locations from South Dakota to New York. The ATV circuit has events sprinkled from March through October across the United States. The National Association for Stock Car Auto Racing (NASCAR) sponsors a variety of truck races throughout the United States. However, this section will focus on car racing.

Several professional auto racing circuits exist; this includes the more popular ones such as NASCAR, the IndyCar Series, the National Hot Rod Association (NHRA), and Formula One. NASCAR, the largest of these motor sports associations, is headquartered in Daytona Beach, FL, with offices in four other states and two countries. Within the NASCAR family are the individual NASCAR teams. While there have been single and multiple car teams, the trend seems to be with multiple car teams where individual drivers sign with a team. For example, Joe Gibbs Racing (JGR) had, as of 2016, eight professional drivers in their organization ("The Team") and employed over 500 individuals. Marketing, licensing, sponsorship acquisition, and public relations are certainly mainstays of the organization. Internship listings could not be found on the JGR website, but it did allow for an individual to submit a résumé. An examination of the biographies of the 12 top executives on their website (including two sons of Pro Football Hall of

Fame coach Joe Gibbs) revealed a closely networked group of individuals. Although his two sons seemed to have started at the proverbial bottom by serving on pit crews or in auto maintenance, only one executive started as an intern (with "The Team"). The racing industry, including JGR, is considered a family business. With JGR, nine of the 12 executives have been involved in some aspect of racing for over 20 years (Turner, 2016; "Executives," n.d.). Thus, the employment entry door is more tightly secured in this segment of motorsports. Checking with NASCAR and other parent organizations, contacting a marketing company that handles motor sport clients, and networking are potential paths for entry. Living in or near a hot bed for racing, such as the piedmont area of North Carolina, may also prove beneficial. Stephanie Harris (Time Out Interview 3.10) confirms that one needs to be networking to get their foot in the door in professional motor sport. According to Harris, internships are available at NASCAR.com (personal communication, September 13, 2016).

According to the Fédération Internationale de l'Automobile, the governing body for international world motor sport, there are 238 motoring organizations in 140 countries. Thus, the opportunity to work in motorsports is far reaching (Federation Internationale De L'Automobile, 2016). Several of the more popular international automobile motorsports associations include

Time Out Interview 3.10 with Stephanie Harris
PROFESSIONAL MOTOR SPORT

Position	Senior Manager, Integrated Marketing/Racing Communications – 3 years
Employer	NASCAR
B.S. Degree	Saint Leo University—Sport Management & Business Administration
Career Path	• Promotions Coordinator – Coastal Bend Aviators – 1 year • Promotions Coordinator – Christi Rayz – 7 months • Promotions Coordinator – Saint Paul Saints – 2 years • Admission Counselor/Tennis Coach – Hamline University – 1 year • Sports Information Director – Hamline University – 5 years • Digital Marketing Manager – Crown Automotive Group – 1 year • Senior Manager, Content Communications – NASCAR – 3 years

Employment Recommendation

"Don't be afraid to talk to anyone or ask for help. This is a competitive, fast-paced field with a lot of outgoing people, but it's also like a family. You need to make connections to get your foot in the door and to be successful on a day-to-day basis."

American Le Mans Series; Conference of Australian Motor Sport, Federation International Association, Formula1, Indy Racing League, International Hot Rod Association, International Motor Sports Association, Motor Sports Association, and Score International Off-road Racing.

Athlete Representation Firms/Sports Agents

Becoming a sports agent is an early goal for many sport management majors. The role of an agent can include many functions in today's sports landscape. While an agent is often viewed as the individual who negotiates a player's or participant's contract, they are also referred to as athlete agents, contract advisors, or player representatives and can perform a variety of roles. These include, but are certainly not limited to, providing legal advice, financial services, and insurance/tax planning; coordinating travel arrangements; handling personal errands or tasks; and more. An athlete may hire more than one representative given the broad range of roles listed. There are two main reasons an athlete may sign with a large representation firm. First, it is because the firm may be better equipped to handle a broad range of responsibilities. Second, talent agencies are now representing athletes, and, according to Oyoung (2012), this has somewhat muddied the waters because there are some differences between the laws that govern talent agents vs. athlete agents.

The path to actually signing an athlete to a contract can be difficult and, often, not well-defined. Different sports mandate different routes, and different states have different certification requirements for agents. For example, in Florida, an agent must be certified, provide fingerprints, and have a thorough background investigation conducted by both the Florida Department of Law Enforcement (FDLE) and the Federal Bureau of Investigation (FBI) (Athlete Agents, 2016). While the state of Florida only requires a prospective athlete to be 18 years of age, the NFL requires an agent to have an advanced degree beyond the bachelor's ("How to," n.d.), but this is not true for all sports. Many agents got their start because a fraternity brother or college roommate was a scholarship athlete and wanted a trusted friend as their agent. According to Masteralexis, Masteralexis, and Snyder (2013), in some sports, all one needs to become an agent is to have a client. However, a solid business background and knowledge of contracts are important credentials. Todd Crannell, owner of Q2 Sports and Entertainment, indicates he uses quantitative and qualitative learned strategies to determine fair market value for athlete services (Wulterkens, 2008). Learning the art of negotiation is also a critical skill. For this type of career, a sport-business curriculum can provide good academic preparation because of the combination of business and sport-related courses. Some sport management programs have faculty who also are attorneys/agents. If this is your desired career path, finding one of these programs to obtain your master's degree would give you great insight, possibly experience, and certainly a network. Chapters 2 and 6 discuss the selection of a graduate program.

Kerryann Cook's (Time Out Interview 3.11) progress to her current legal career was first highlighted in Chapter 1. She has some general tips about basic skills needed for a career in the industry, but Kerryann also states,

> A regular part of our business is dependent on the friendships and professional relationships I developed working while an undergraduate, graduate, and post-graduate student. With agencies, your reputation is everything. The more people you know that trust you, the better chance you have of breaking into the industry. Quality contacts will always trump quantity of marginal contacts. (personal communication, September 1, 2016)

Time Out Interview 3.11 with Kerryann M. Cook, Esq.
SPORTS AGENCY—ATHLETE REPRESENTATION

Position	Co-Founder, MK Sports & Entertainment Group
Employer	MK Sports and Entertainment Group, New York McGivney & Kluger, P.C., New York
B.S. Degree	Sport Management, Western Carolina University
M.B.A. Degree	University of Tennessee, Knoxville
J.D.	University of Memphis (TN)
Career Path	• InterIntern, Compliance Department – University of Tennessee, Women's Athletic Program – 6 months • Graduate Assistant, Development – University of Tennessee, Women's Athletic Program – 2 years • Post-Graduate Intern – University of Memphis – 1 year • Research Assistant, Faculty Athletics Representative – University of Memphis – 1 year • Advocacy Coordinator – Women's Sports Foundation (NY) – 9 months • Attorney – McGivney & Kluger – 13 years • MK Sports & Entertainment – Co-Director – 2 years; Co-Owner – 3 years

Employment Recommendation

"Make sacrifices to gain experience. It's rough early on; the long-term rewards are worth it. With internships and entry-level positions, employers know you likely do not have a lot of experience. Therefore, control the things over which you have absolute control and are not related to your level of experience—effort, professionalism, responsiveness, follow-through, and spelling/grammar.

Spend time thinking about why you would be great at the job for which you are applying. Do not get hung up on being a perfect match for the job—be realistic and qualified, but do not limit yourself to only "perfect matches.""

As with all industry segments, getting your foot in the door is extremely important. This is perhaps more important in the area of athlete services, because actually signing an athlete may only happen after you have worked with experienced agents or if you start your own agency as Kerryann Cook did. Landing volunteer or part-time work experiences with an agent or a small law firm is a good place to start. Some agents hire and train runners. Runners are individuals hired as independent contractors or employed by an agent to make contacts with athletes in situations where an agent is denied access. A runner can infiltrate a college campus and befriend an athlete (Payne, 2011; Viltz, Seifried, & Foreman, 2014; Willenbacher, 2004). In unethical situations, a runner is often the one that violates NCAA rules or the law, perhaps even unbeknownst to them. If this is the line of work you desire, educate yourself on the laws and NCAA's rules regarding runners and agents, and only accept placement with an agent or agency that upholds the law and operates in an ethical manner.

Large athlete representation firms or sports agencies can be a great place to start a career in this business. Agencies such as IMG and Octagon are recognizable names, but there are many other athlete representation firms and talent agencies. According to Belzer (2015), Creative Artists Agency was the most valuable athlete representation firm as of 2015. That year, they were managing $2.6 billion in NFL contracts alone, and their MLB and NHL contracts were highly ranked as well. The Boras Corporation was ranked second overall in 2015 primarily due to their representation of MLB players. The 2015 rankings included 47 different agencies. Most agencies specialize in specific sports, but some can be sport-specific. One example of this is Gestifute, a Portuguese agency representing soccer players and number seven on the list. To make this list, agencies were ranked based on maximum commissions mainly because agents in different sports make their income differently. You can Google this topic each year and find updated listings of agencies if you choose to enter the athlete representation business, but do not neglect your geographical living area as your current location could have a firm willing to hire interns to assist you in getting into the business. Undergraduate students have found agencies willing to mentor them.

Octagon specializes in sport marketing and sponsorships, event management, and athlete representation. The company owns some of the largest golf and tennis events and has over 800 employees worldwide with a strong footprint in Australia and many Asian countries. Thus, the student is presented with an organization worth studying if athlete representation is the desired career. Obtaining an internship or entry-level position in event management could lead to an internal transfer to the athlete representation side of the firm. Octagon represented six of the Cubs players and Manager Joe Maddon from the 2016 World Series championship team. They also represent broadcasters, other talent divisions, teams, and team owners. Their website claims they invest in mentorships, learning opportunities, and career development and have a trainee program open to students ("Culture," n.d.).

Global Athletics & Marketing, Inc., founded in 1993, is an example of an athlete representation firm that specializes in running events, specifically operating track and field meets

("About," n.d.). While much smaller than IMG or Octagon, this type of firm specializes in a specific sport. Working events with them may also lead to a representation career for runners throughout the world. Employment opportunities in event management are more fully discussed in Chapter 5.

Internships are not as easy to obtain in this area so finding an athlete representation or law firm willing to take you on as a volunteer early in your academic career might be a starting point. Thus, obtaining this type of position in a summer leading up to a culminating senior internship, during graduate school, or immediately following graduation would be a recommendation. To be qualified for an agency internship, one should consider gaining experience in sales, marketing, event management, website development, or public relations, as different divisions of some large firms include positions in these areas. Focusing law or graduate school studies on licensing and merchandising could create great content for an application and résumé. This could be a back door entry into athlete representation, because one could possibly meet and network with agents working in different firms.

Many believe the life of an agent to be an easy route to wealth. While some agents make a great deal of money, particularly those that sign the first round draft picks every year, this does not represent a true lifestyle for most agents. Compensation varies for agents depending upon the sport. NFL player agents cannot make more than 3–5% of the athlete's contract. Professional baseball player agents are not as restricted, but compensation rules do apply. With individual sports, there are no player unions. The amount an agent makes depends on market forces but is typically around 20% for marketing the athlete (T. Crannell, personal communication, October 12, 2009). The real money in athlete representation often comes from endorsement or marketing deals (Oyoung, 2012).

Finally, law school or obtaining a masters of business administration (MBA) degree are the optimal routes to becoming an agent, especially if one wants to represent NFL players. The NFL regulations for agents requires an undergraduate and postgraduate degree (master's or law) to apply for certification. There are provisions that allow an individual without an advanced degree to sit for the required examinations if one can prove they have seven years of negotiating experience. This information must be documented to be considered in lieu of the advanced degree ("How to," n.d.).

The requirements for becoming a certified agent for other sports vary. For example, to represent a professional baseball player, the MLB simply requires an application, certification, and payment of the appropriate fees. In order to become certified, the individual must take and pass a written exam. The Major League Baseball Players Association (MLBPA) does provide a seminar and materials to help with passing the exam. While MLBPA is the sole bargaining agent for all players, any player can select an individual to be their representative to negotiate or assist the player in negotiating a contract (Fennel, 2016).

Certified representation of professional basketball players in the National Basketball Association (NBA) and the Women's National Basketball Association (WNBA) is similar to that for baseball, including passing a written proctored exam. One difference regarding basketball is that the agent must possess a four-year degree or other qualifying experience (Crain, 2015; National Basketball Players Association, 1991; WNBPA, 2000).

The NCAA also has rules governing an athlete's relationship with an agent. Any agent should become very familiar with these rules, because a student-athlete could be ruled as ineligible to participate in college athletics if these rules are violated. Familiarity with state laws or certification requirements is important as well. The Uniform Athlete Agents' Act (UAAA) allows an agent's certification to be valid in any state that has adopted the Act provided certain regulations are met. According to the NCAA website, 41 states, Washington, DC, and the Virgin Islands have adopted this law, and three other states have laws regulating agents or impending legislation ("UAAA Laws," n.d.). The Sports Agent Responsibility and Trust Act (SPARTA), passed in 2004, is another federal law that was enacted to govern the conduct of sports agents. The law controls deceptive practices and is regulated by the Federal Trade Commission.

Before accepting any position with a sports agency or agent, one should research the organization very carefully. Historically, there have been agents who violated NCAA rules and federal and state laws and landed in jail or became embroiled in lengthy lawsuits. Maintaining a strict ethical code should be a priority for any agent; the laws enacted for the governance of agents target ethical and illegal actions.

INTERNATIONAL OPPORTUNITIES

There are many international sport opportunities in other countries of which students in the U.S. may not be aware. Thus, we felt a need to discuss additional international opportunities separate from what we have previously presented.

Professional sport in other countries has seen tremendous growth and often has an alternative purpose. Sport is endorsed as a national symbol of pride and a way to cement international relations. The 2016 summer Olympics and Paralympics brought great notoriety to Rio de Janeiro, Brazil. Many may know the most popular sport in Brazil is soccer and the country's team has won the FIFA world cup five times. It is the only country to qualify a team for every World Cup. The Beijing Olympics was a prime example of a country using sport to boost its image, and Schrag (2009) indicated the media described the image boost as a logistical success.

Leagues, traditionally confined to a single country, are increasingly crossing borders. The Premier League (EPL) is something the UK claims it does quite well. It generates money worldwide in the billions of dollars and, according to Chadwick (2014), the British government claimed just the national insurance and income tax was worth 1.3 billion European pounds annually. It has a worldwide live television audience and participation in fantasy sports. We are all aware of the NFL's and the MLB's tradition of beginning their seasons overseas. Thus, a single sport or league can be truly without borders.

Morocco hosted the sixth round of the world's richest Arabian horse race called the HH Sheikha Fatima Bint Mubarak Ladies World Championship in 2015. Al Asri Al Dhaheri, the ambassador of the United Arab Emirates (UAE) to Morocco, claimed the event exhibited the strong relations between UAE and Morocco (UAE, 2015).

Canada hosted the world championships for orienteering in October 2014. Orienteering is very popular in Europe. So allowing this major championship to cross the Atlantic Ocean signals the desire to gain a larger athlete population for both amateurs and professionals. Orienteers from Switzerland, France, Sweden, New Zealand, the United Kingdom, and other countries joined athletes from the United States and Canada (Arnpior, 2014).

Australia hosted The Victorian Open with more than 100 professional squash players from 15 countries in 2015 ("Squash Steps," 2015, p. 38). The World Karate Kickboxing Championships in Dublin in 2014, the World Table Tennis Championships in Kuala Lumpur, Malaysia, in 2016, and the Ice Hockey World Championships in Russia also in 2016—the list goes on and on.

International professional sport can have a very different meaning in countries outside North America. Badminton, squash, and table tennis are wildly popular in many Asian countries and dominate television airwaves. In the US, with the addition of many international channels on some cable providers, professional tournaments involving these individual sports can be found. Professional sport, however defined in a particular country, is growing. It is not surprising that, according to a 2011 study conducted by SMG/Yougov involving 2,582 respondents, soccer was by far the number one sport in 16 countries in the Middle East and North Africa.

The World Baseball Classic, begun in 2006, is globalizing professional baseball. Developed by Major League Baseball, Kelly (2007) claims baseball scholars refuse to label it a global sport. This is understandable as only 20 different countries have qualified for the four Classics through 2017 and the host sites have been limited to Asia and Central and North America. Regardless, professional baseball seems to be growing internationally, particularly in Central and South America. In terms of establishing a career in professional baseball management, this is a positive step, especially for bilingual students.

Dorschner reported in 2006 the world had caught NBA fever, and it was the number one sport in the Philippines. The NBA developed NBA China to grow its brand and the sport in that country ("China's Market," 2009). The NBA began doing many things to capture the international market. By changing Sunday playing times in the US with 12:30 p.m. start times, the European market can view games in early to mid-evening times, and the approximately 100 international players from 37 countries fosters an interest in the sport in their countries (Badenhausen, 2016; Groves, 2015).

Australian football may be quite confusing to a student studying in North America because the Australian description of football does not relate to the NFL or Canadian football, and the term could be used to describe rugby, soccer, or a combination thereof. Australia has four football codes—better understood as governing rules—and each involves professional, semi-professional, and development systems (Skinner, Zakus., & Edwards, 2008).

Although gaining some momentum, cricket, a sport nearly nonexistent in the United States, is fiercely popular in many countries including Australia, England, India, and New Zealand. It has tremendous popularity in the Caribbean nations as well (Sinclair, 2005). According to Holden (2008), "there was a shift of wealth and power within the game towards India" (p. 337), and in 2016, India hosted the world's richest cricket tournament (Tomlinson, 2016). International students coming to America to study can bring knowledge and interest for the sports popular in their countries. Evidence of this is found by visiting university and campus recreation websites and by searching for the wide variety of sport clubs available to students. While this does not constitute professional sport, sport clubs are often elevated to a varsity sport, and the next logical step is the creation of professional sport tournaments although they may be very small. Additional evidence for cricket becoming more popular in the US lies in the addition of a staff member at the National Intramural-Recreational Sports Association (NIRSA) in charge of the National Cricket Program on U.S. college campuses.

We have just discussed a few examples of professional sport in other countries, but they are just a few of the more popular ones. What one needs to be aware of is that international professional sport is often managed or governed differently than the professional sport system observed in the United States. Some countries, including those within the European Union, discuss sport within their national constitutions due to its sociological and societal importance; several governments provide financing while many believe in self-governance by sporting unions (Parrish, 2008) and financing through private grants or sponsorships. After Hong Kong's retrocession to China in 1997, the government abolished a Sports Development Board because of the board's use of venues and high salaries paid to directors (Scott, 2006). In 2015, Zimbabwe's government confirmed a cricket tour to Pakistan. In Pakistan, the government must approve all sport tours, mostly to assure safety of the teams (Ali, 2015). In November, 2016, China and Germany signed treaties involving a football (soccer) trade deal (Nicholson, 2016). Can you imagine the U.S. government signing deals covering player, coach, and referee training?

Professional or amateur sport can be used as a political staging ground (Van Tuyckom, Bracke, & Scheerder, 2011) or to resurrect an understanding of a country's social or policy environment (Ruseski & Maresova, 2014). The "constructive use of sport in politics began with the ancient Greeks . . . when athletes were paid . . . to enhance the prestige of their city-states" (Abisha, 2016, p. 119), but most countries have provocatively claimed that politics is not the purpose behind their country's involvement in sport. In an era of international political unrest, incidences to the contrary abound. Abisha (2016) discusses how Zimbabwe "controls sport through their Ministry of Sport" (p. 121) and recalls how 20 countries boycotted the Montreal Olympics in 1976 over Apartheid. In an article published in early 2009, the United States Federal News Service stated that "athletics should unify people across cultural divides and international sporting events should not be used as venues for bigotry and prejudice" (para. 2) when Dubai announced it was prohibiting the participation of an Israeli tennis champion in a Women's Tennis Association (WTA) tournament in its country. As a result of Dubai's actions, the *Wall Street Journal* pulled its sponsorship of the event.

Even in the US, Zirin (2013) discusses extensively political issues and sport, and one only has to remember how the NBA All-Star Game was pulled from North Carolina in 2016 over First Amendment issues. These discussions are but the tip of the iceberg regarding political and government involvement in professional sport, especially when the United Nations began proposing in 2004 that sport be implemented as a tool "to promote nationhood, health, education, peace, and development" (Abisha, 2016, p. 122).

Intertwined with politics, some of the differences of how professional sport is organized in different countries can certainly be based upon tradition and culture. Truyens, De Bosscher, and Sotiriadou (2016) reported that countries organize resources in very different ways. Structure, the development process of elite athletes, allocation of resources, centralization of training programs, and the prioritization of specific sports have been identified as policy drivers for some governments. Also found in this study is that just because a country may have the resources does not mean that country will have a competitive advantage.

There is no doubt professional sport is growing internationally (Emmett, 2010; Papaloukas, 2012; Yang, Sparks, & Li, 2008). Thibault (2009) and Papaloukas (2012) reminded us the Fédération Interationale de Football Association (FIFA) was larger than the United Nations with respect to member countries, and, as of 2016, that was still true with 211 countries holding membership in FIFA and 197 countries holding membership status in the United Nations. However, neither this book nor this chapter can investigate international professional sport in the depth it deserves. One main purpose of this section is to assist students who are contemplating a career in sport to understand the immensity of sport on a global landscape. Professional sport has existed in many countries for a long time; in others, it may just be developing. What is necessary to comprehend is that sport governance, policy, and structure can be very different from country to country. Countless positions are available internationally, and similar paths to internships and employment are possible when properly studied, planned, and pursued.

Cathy Griffin (Time Out Interview 3.12)—owner of The Griffin Network, an executive recruitment, marketing, and project management consulting firm—has extensive international experience and specializes in industries that cross sport, entertainment, and consumer products. Some of her clients have included Visa International; U.S. Track & Field; the ATP, WTA, and USTA; the California Speedway; the California Special Olympics; Time, Inc./Sports Illustrated;

Time Out Interview 3.12 with Cathy Griffin
INTERNATIONAL SPORT

Position	CEO and Founder – 14 years
Employer	Griffin Network
B.A. Degree	Business Marketing, Florida State University
Career Path	• Intern – Pepsi-Cola – 3 months
	• Substitute Spanish Teacher – 1 Year
	• Manager, Sports Promotions – Pepsi-Cola Company – 4 years
	• Manager, Sports Merchandising – Sports Illustrated – 4 years
	• Assistant to the Publisher, Sports Illustrated – Four years
	• Vice-President, Ticket Marketing – Soccer World Cup 4 – years
	• Vice-President, Business Development – Zing Interactive TV – 1 year
	• Marketing Consultant – Nike – 2 years
	• Vice President – AT Kearney Executive Search – 1 year
	• Managing Director/Partner, Head of Sports – Korn/Ferry International – 3 years

Employment Recommendation

"Your first few jobs are like getting a MBA or Ph.D. at Harvard. I call them 'Academy Companies'. You want to be a sponge and learn from the best in the business so you can market it later. You want to build a network of contacts that will be accomplished and support each other in years to come. It will all come back to you. Once you build a résumé with accomplishments at great companies, you will be able to sell yourself later in life to go where you want to be."

and two California universities. In order to get to a point where she opened her current consulting firm, Cathy honed her craft by working with key sport-related clients including NASCAR, Nike, the United States Olympic Committee, the United States Soccer Federation, Fox, and CBS. She served as the global vice president for one of her former employers and reported to that company's managing director of global media (personal communication, December 14, 2016). Many of these companies obviously have an international outreach, and Cathy's international career tied to sport began by accident when she was hired by Pepsi for a sport-related marketing position. In order to get involved in international sport, Cathy recommends creating an opportunity to work in another country and that knowing the culture and learning the language is a definite asset (personal communication, January 26, 2010). Her background is a wonderful example of how a career can be woven in and around sport, both in the United States and internationally.

In order to create an international opportunity, our first recommendation is to find an experiential opportunity (e.g., volunteering or apprenticeship) state-side with global connections that would allow you to work with individuals who are key executives with international responsibilities. The Women's Tennis Association is one such example. An internship with this organization in the past allowed a student to work closely with tennis tournaments in Dubai, a major business hub of the United Arab Emirates (UAE) and the Middle East. While it is not the same thing as actually being there, it does provide an up-close look at how sporting events are operated in another country and the types of sponsorships solicited. Often, religious beliefs or customs can impact events hosted. As mentioned before, international sport can be drastically different from sport governance and structure in the United States.

A second recommendation involves student memberships in professional organizations. International sport business conferences are on the rise. Geneva, Switzerland; London, England; Bangkok, Thailand; and Sydney, Australia are just some of the cities that have recently hosted major sport business conferences. All of these opportunities support the growing nature of professional sport on the global stage and the increasing possibilities for networking and employment in the sport industry. Graduate students are often able to take advantage of these opportunities by co-presenting a paper with a faculty member.

Our third recommendation to students is to locate a sport-related study abroad program. Most are available during the summer semesters. Some sport management programs sponsor these programs. As one example, StudyAbroad.com has the Sport Management Professional Program in London. While available courses are subject to change, some offerings have included sport promotion and sponsorship, major event management, international business decision-making, e-business, and internships. A second organization to review would be the Sports Travel Academy. By studying abroad, it is quite possible to make networking connections that could lead to international employment and to a full-time internship as discussed in the next paragraph.

Our final recommendation would be to search for a capstone internship with an international sport organization. Earlier in the chapter, we provided links to many international leagues that may host interns. However, do not fail to search leagues dedicated to a single sport in any country or smaller sport organizations fitting your specific interests. In our experience, most international internships have led to full-time job offers.

THE FINAL BUZZER

The intent of this chapter was to expand a student's awareness to the seasonal nature of the professional sport segment of the industry, provide some insight into gaining entry with a professional sport organization, and introduce the breadth of possible career opportunities from a global perspective. By interviewing individuals in actual positions, researching organizational websites, and presenting information learned about the segments, additional insight can be gained into careers and career paths. Just as each segment presents different employment responsibilities and foci, we felt the information presented in the comments and Time Out Interviews should reflect the experiences of the individuals involved and highlight interesting information and aspects of the segment not found in many textbooks.

There is no way we could introduce all professional team sport organizations and leagues, in the United States or across the globe. Hopefully, your sport business/management program will assist in expanding your knowledge in other ways regarding the enormous size of our industry.

EXPERIENTIAL LEARNING OPPORTUNITIES

Classroom Experiential Learning Exercise: Ticket Sales Boot Camp

Have the students read any number of sales-related books as an introduction to the topic. One recommendation is a quick read by Zig Ziglar titled *Selling 101.* Bring in a guest speaker who works directly in ticket sales to provide insight. Students are then introduced to the Sales Game, created by the Sales Huddle Group, which is an online training platform that incorporates role play situations to engage students in the sales process. Students work on a sales script as a homework assignment that is critiqued by the instructor.

Next, the students participate in a Meet the Bruins night, which is the promotional kick-off to the basketball season, through our athletic department. While it is a free event, students are tasked with selling the event as a fun family night with free giveaways and other promotions. As part of the boot camp, students spend two class periods prior to the promotion in our on-campus call center calling past ticket buyers. Students gain practice in delivering their pitch and closing the deal. For this activity, closing the deal is obtaining email addresses from the person they are calling to send them additional information. During the event, students work a promotional booth and ask individuals to sign up for a free giveaway, whereby the information gathered is used later to evaluate the event and for a special ticket promotion for the athletic department. The entire experience gives students an introductory but realistic look into the much-needed skill of selling.

Submitted by Dr. Ted B. Peetz, Director of the Sport Administration Graduate Program
Belmont University, Nashville, TN

Program Experiential Learning Example: Internship Fair and Networking Event

St. Ambrose University has a sport industry networking event as part of their senior capstone course. At the beginning of the semester, students submit a résumé and cover letter for a position on one of the three committees: marketing, sales, and event operations. They are interviewed by professors within the sport management program and then assigned roles based on their experience and interests.

The students work within their committees to plan and implement a networking event at the end of the semester. They are tasked with securing sport industry practitioners to serve as panelists, as well as sport organizations to participate in an internship fair. Sponsorship packages are developed and the students actively sell these packages to local businesses. The students then market the event to area students, practitioners, and community members through both traditional and digital media forms.

At the culminating event, the senior students, as well as other sport management students in the program, are encouraged to connect with the sport industry practitioners in attendance, thus providing additional experiential learning opportunities.

Submitted by Dr. Liz Sattler, Assistant Professor
St. Ambrose University, Davenport, IA

REFERENCES

Abisha, M. (2016). Separability and inseparability of sport and politics. The reality in Africa today. *Journal of Arts, Science, and Commerce, 7*(2), 119–125.

About GA & M. (n.d.). *Global Athletics & Marketing.* Retrieved on from http://www.globalathletics.com/about.php

Ali, R. (2015, May 15). Pakistan cricket chief says Zimbabwe official confirms tour. *AP English Worldstream.*

Arnpior, Carp hosts world championship of orienteering. (2014, October 9). *Arnpior Chronicle-Guide & Weekender.*

Athlete Agents, The Florida Statutes, Chapter 468, Part IX, §§ 468.451-468.457 (2016). Retrieved from http://www.leg.state.fl.us/Statutes/index.cfm?App_mode=Display_Statute&URL=0400-0499/0468/0468PartIX-ContentsIndex.html&StatuteYear=2016&Title=-%3E2016-%3EChapter%20468-%3EPart%20IX

Badenhausen, K. (2016, January 20). New York Knicks head the NBA"s most valuable teams at $3 billion. *Forbes.* Retrieved online at http://www.forbes.com/

Barra, A. (2013, September 24). Forget 2002 – This year's Oakland A's are the real Moneyball team. *The Atlantic.* Retrieved from http://www.theatlantic.com

Baumer, B., & Zimbalist, A. (2014). *The sabermetric revolution: Assessing the growth of analytics in baseball.* Philadelphia, PA: University of Pennsylvania Press.

Belzer, J. (2015 September 23). The world's most valuable sports agencies 2015. *Forbes.* Retrieved from http://www.forbes.com/

Chadwick, S. (2014, August 14). Hard evidence: How much is the premier league worth? *The Conversation.* Retrieved from http://theconversation.com/

China's market for sport is growing rapidly but state controls are holding back potential (2009, October 5). *The Wire.* Retrieved from http://bx.businessweek.com/

Crain, D. L. (2015, August). Sports agency – Process to player. *Houston Bar Association.* Retrieved from http://www.hba.org/wp-content/uploads/2015/09/2015-08-11-Updated-Sports-Agent-CLE-dlc-August-2015-svf.pdf

Culture. (n.d). *Octagon.* Retrieved from http://www.octagon.com/careers

Dorschner, J. (2006, June 15). World catches NBA fever: The NBA has made basketball into a truly international sport as 38 teams come to Miami to broadcast the finals worldwide. *Miami Herald.* Retrieved from www.miamiherald.com.

Emmett, J. (2010). Fighting its way to the mainstream. *SportsPro, 2*(17), p. 87.

Executives. (n.d.) *Joe Gibbs Racing.* Retrieved from http://joegibbsracing.com/

Extreme Sport. (2014). In *Dictionary.com.* Retrieved from http://www.dictionary.com/browse/extreme-sport.

Extreme Sport. (2016, October 7). *Wikipedia.* Retrieved from https://en.wikipedia.org/wiki/Extreme_sport

Federation Internationale De L'Automobile. (2016). Members. *Federation Internationale De L'Automobile.* Retrieved from http://www.fia.com/members

Fennel, J. (2016, August 31). The MLBPA: What we do. *Major League Baseball Players Association.* Retrieved November 22, 2016 from http://www.mlbplayers.com/ViewArticle.dbml?DB_OEM_ID=34000&ATCLID=211157446

Groves, R. (2015, December 12). Why the NBA will eventually overtake the NFL in popularity and why it matters. *Forbes.* Retrieved from http://www.forbes.com/

Holden, G. (2008). World cricket as a postcolonial international society: IR meets the history of sport. *Global Society, 22*(3), 337–369.

How to become an agent. (n.d.). *NFL Players.* Retrieved from https://www.nflpa.com/

Kelly, W. W. (2007). Is baseball a global sport? America's 'national pastime' as global field and international sport. *Global Networks, 7*(2), 187–201.

Masteralexis, J., Masteralexis, L., & Snyder, K. (2013). Enough is enough: The case for federal regulations of sport agents. *Jeffrey S. Moorad Sports Law Journal, 20,* 69–105.

National Basketball Players Association (1991). NBPA regulations governing player agents. *NBPA.* Retrieved at http://www.nbpa.com/downloads/NBPA_Regulation.pdf

Nicholson, P. (2016, November 28). German and Chinese governments sign pact to develop world's biggest market. *Inside World Football.* Retrieved from http://www.insideworldfootball.com

Oyoung, M. (2012). Renegotiating the role of athlete agents. *McGeorge Law Review, 43,* 528–537.

Papaloukas, M. (2012). Political considerations in the sports establishment. *International Sports Law Review, 9*(3–4), 410–412.

Parrish, R. (2008). Access to major events on television under European law. *Journal of Consumer Policy, 31*(1), 79–98.

Payne, A. (2011). Building the prevent defense: Why unethical agents continue to score and what can be done to change the game. *Vanderbilt Journal of Entertainment & Technology Law, 13,* 657–694.

Roger Goodell biography. (n.d.). *Biography.* Retrieved from http://www.biography.com/people/roger-goodell-011316

Ruseski, J. E., & Maresova, K. (2014). Economic freedom, sport policy, and individual participation in physical activity: An international comparison. *Contemporary Economic Policy, 32*(1), 42–55.

Schrag, D. (2009). 'Flagging the nation' in international sport: A Chinese Olympics and a German World Cup. *The International Journal of the History of Sport, 26*(8), 1084–1104.

Scott, I. (2006). The government and statutory bodies in Hong Kong: Centralization and autonomy. *Public Organization Review, 6*(3), 185–202.

Sinclair, D. (2005). Sports education – a priorty for Caribbean sports tourism. *International Journal of Contemporary Hospitality Management, 17*(6/7), 536–548.

Skinner, J., Zakus, D. H., & Edwards, A. (2008). Coming in from the margins: Ethnicity, community support and the rebranding of Australian soccer. *Soccer and Society, 9*(3), 394–404.

SMG/Yougov Sport Marketing, (2011). Popularity and participation of sport in the Middle East and North Africa. *SMG Insight Limited.* Retrieved from http://www.revolutionsports.co.uk/news/wp-content/uploads/2011/11/SMGI-Middle-East-North-Africa-Report-180911final.pdf

Sports Agent Responsibility and Trust Act, 15 U.S.C.A. §§ 7801, 7802, 7803 (2004).

Squash steps into sports spotlight. (2015, July 28). *Bayside Leader,* p. 38.

The team. (2016). Retrieved from http://www.joegibbsracing.com/team

Thibault, L. (2009). Globalization of sport: An inconvenient truth. *Journal of Sport Management, 23*(1), 1–20.

Tomlinson, H. (2016, April 8). Indian cricket branded a 'criminal' waste of water. *The United Kingdom Times.* Retrieved from http://www.thetimes.co.uk/

Truyens, J., De Bosscher, V., & Sotiriadou, P. (2016). An analysis of countries' organizational resources, capacities, and resource configurations in athletics. *Journal of Sport Management, 30*(5), 566–585.

Turner, J. (2016, February 4). Joe Gibbs Racing announces changes to executive team. *Fox Sports.* Retrieved from www.foxsports.com

UAAA Laws in the 50 states. (n.d.). *NCAA.* Retrieved from http://fs.ncaa.org/Docs/ENF/UAAA/map/index.html

UAE Ambassador hails organization of the 6th edition of Sheikhai Fatima bint Mubarak Ladies World Championship (2015, April 9). *Arabia 2000,* 2(17), 32.

United States Federal News Service (2009, February 27). Lawmakers respond to Dubai's ban on Israeli tennis player peer by proposing professional sports anti-discrimination law in New York. Document ID: 1652852211.

Valerdi, R. (2013, November 1). Is game theory the new sabermetrics? *Industrial Engineer, 45*(1), 24.

Van Riper, T. (2008, July 29). How to get a job in pro sports. *Forbes,* Retrieved from http://www.forbes.com

Van Tuyckom, C., Bracke, P., & Scheerder. J. (2011). "Sports:Idrott: Esporte: Deporte: Sportovní. The problem of equivalence of meaning in comparative sports research." *European Journal for Sport and Society, 8*(1/2), , 85–97.

Viltz, R., Seifried, C., & Foreman, J. (2014). An Analysis of sports agent regulation in intercollegiate athletics: A call for cooperation. *Journal of Legal Aspects of Sport, 24,* 62–77.

Willenbacher, E. (2004). Regulating sports agents: Why current federal and state efforts do not deter the unscrupulous athlete-agent and how a national licensing system may cure the problem. *St. John's Law Review, 78*(4), 1225–1255.

WNBPA regulations governing player agents. (2000, January 1). *WNBPA.* Retrieved from http://wnbpa.com/agent-information/

Wulterkens, J. (2008). Todd Crannell. *Sports Agent Blog.* Retrieved from http://sportsagentblog.com/interview-with-the-agent/todd-crannell/

Yang, X. S., Sparks, R., & Li, M. (2008). Sports sponsorship as a strategic investment in China: perceived risks and benefits by corporate sponsors prior to the Beijing 2008 Olympics. *International Journal of Sports Marketing & Sponsorship, 10*(1), 63–78.

Zirin, D. (2013). *Game over: How politics has turned the sports world upside down.* New York, NY: The New Press.

CHAPTER
4

Sport Business Industry Overview: Olympic, Paralympic, and Amateur Sport

"Internships are great ways, not only to get introduced to the Olympic and Paralympic family and learn how to plan, prepare, and execute for Team USA, but also for Team USA to get a chance to know you. Demonstrating that you can apply the information learned in your university program to the real world, while also showing a great work ethic and willingness to learn and grow on the job, is an invaluable experience."
—*Christine Bolger, Associate Director of Education, United States Olympic Committee, Colorado Springs, CO*

THE WARM UP

This chapter will explore industry segments generally considered Olympic, Paralympic,[1] or amateur in nature. For simplicity, sports that may not be included in the Olympics, but have a recognized national governing body are collectively discussed in this category. Many of them are included in the Pan American (Pan Am) and Para Pan Am Games held every four years, the year before the Olympics and Paralympics. We recognize some Olympic athletes receive compensation through endorsements and other competition prize money and may be more properly identified as professional athletes. Not all countries, including the United Kingdom, pay their Olympic athletes, and some pay more than others. Some countries provide grant monies to assist their athletes to offset expenses incurred during training (C. Pellican, personal communication, December 16, 2016).

This book does not focus on the professional careers of the competing athlete. Instead, our focus is on the careers of the individuals creating, organizing, and conducting the events and managing the organizations. Intercollegiate and interscholastic (high school) athletics,

---

[1] In 2016, the International Paralympic Committee announced it was changing some of their terminology. They are now using Para Athletics and Para Sport. Paralympic is not changed in how it is used with respect to the Paralympic Games.

recreational, and youth sport are all being included under the broad category of the chapter title.

In the last chapter, we discussed seasonal sports for the purpose of clarifying the posting of positions. Seasonality of job postings may also apply in these categories. Positions not tied to a particular team, league, or competition season may be advertised at any time in a calendar year. These organizations operate on a twelve-month cycle just as other nonsport-related businesses. Once again, as with the previous chapter, we are attempting to provide a wide scope of information but, of course, cannot explore every type of available position.

SPORT SEGMENTS EXPLAINED AND EXPLORED

Governing Bodies

Sports falling under the umbrella of Olympic, Pan American, or Paralympic sport have a governing body administering their affairs. A national governing body (NGB) can be charged with coordinating competitions, fundraising, team selection processes, and management of national and international competitions. Grassroot (local) level branches or events tied to a particular sport may also be an assigned responsibility. There are 47 Olympic sports (winter and summer), 25 Paralympic sports, 48 Pan American sports, and 17 Para Pan Am sports as of the writing of this textbook. Some sports share the same governing organization. Additionally, there are more than 30 affiliated organizations that hold membership on the Multi-sport Organization Council (MSOC) ("Fact Sheet," 2016).

The United States Olympic Committee (USOC) has steadily increased the number of training facilities throughout the years, and, as of 2017, there were three Olympic/Paralympic training centers and 18 training sites ("Fact Sheet," 2016). The training sites are often specialized for one particular sport.

There are many other NGBs for sport in the United States. Just about every Olympic/Paralympic sport has an NGB that governs its day-to-day operations. Relocating to Colorado Springs, CO, would put you in the main hub of many of the central headquarters for sport governing bodies such as U.S. Figure Skating, U.S. Basketball, and the United States Fencing Association (USFA). These are examples of sport organizations that have full-time positions with fencing, a relatively minor sport, posting a full-time staff of 16 individuals in 2016.

John Potts (Time Out Interview 4.1) did not have a traditional degree or career in the sport industry. However, like many, he volunteered for events and eventually found his way to the United States Association for Blind Athletes (USABA), the NGB that governs some sports for the visually impaired. John's position used to be a volunteer position labeled as chair of coaches and officials committee. Thus, one can eventually work their way into a sport organization, possibly creating a position where there is an observed and obvious need.

Let us just focus quickly on one sport to further emphasize the breadth of sport NGBs in the United States. U.S. Softball was founded in 1933 as the Amateur Softball Association (ASA)

Time Out Interview 4.1 with John Potts
PARALYMPIC SPORT

Position	High Performance Director – 11 years
Employer	United States Association of Blind Athletes
B.S. Degree	Management – Troy University
M.S. Degree	Management – Troy University
Career Path	• Air Force – 30 years (Related positions included Morale, Welfare, & Recreation – Human Resource Mgmt.)

Employment Recommendation

Anyone entering this field must be willing to be flexible and love what they're doing since the hours can be long. There can be paperwork during the week and often at nights, and you may manage sports events over weekends when people are most available to participate. Pay can be minimal as well, but the intrinsic value in the work can be great. I believe the Paralympic side of sport provides a unique opportunity for anyone considering a profession in sport or sport administration. This side of sport is still in a developing stage. Opportunities are great for anyone who wants to conduct research and use those outcomes to make a contribution to enhancing this segment of sport. Because much is still new and untapped, those who like to think "outside the box" will enjoy their work.

---

and was appointed the official national governing body of softball in the United States by the USOC in 1978. It officially rebranded as U.S. Softball in November 2016, dropping the long recognized ASA name. It is one of the country's largest sports organizations. Among its many roles is the regulation and sanctioning of competition, assurance of equal opportunity, sponsorship procurement, equipment oversight, and rule development. With a membership of over two million, you can possibly understand that many jobs are created by this one organization. They also register over 25,000 umpires annually and are the leader in the industry for training of softball umpires. Under U.S. Softball alone, there are over 165,000 teams playing both fast and slow pitch, and they sanction competition in every state through 70 local associations. According to Codi Warren, the managing director of communications at their headquarters in Oklahoma City, OK, U.S. Softball employs approximately 25 full-time staff members and generally hires two to three paid interns per year (personal communication, December 7, 2016).

So, let us delve a little deeper into the governance of this one sport in the United States. U.S. Softball is not the only softball governing body. The United States Fastpitch Association (USFA) sponsors girls fast pitch softball and is headquartered in Panama City Beach, FL. USFA has over 1,125 member teams in 16 states and growing and hosts its own World Series every July. The United States Specialty Sports Association (USSSA), headquartered in Melbourne, Florida (as of 2017), was founded as the United States Slow Pitch Softball Association and changed its name in 2005 to sponsor other sports. However, it still has a softball division that hosts world and national tournaments.

Additional softball governing bodies in the US include the National Softball Association (NSA), headquartered in Nicholasville, KY, and the International Senior Softball Association (ISSA), headquartered in Manassas, VA—a very large organization with men's and women's divisions starting at age 35 through 70+ competition divisions.

By just looking at softball, think about all of the other sports, NGBs, teams, and tournaments that probably exist just in the US. This further emphasizes that the number of existing full-time positions grows exponentially with each sport. It would be extremely difficult to count all of the governing bodies tied to sport in the United States and even more difficult to count the number of employment opportunities, even though smaller organizations may only have one or two full-time positions and a handful of part-time slots.

Beyond sport governing bodies, professional organizational governing bodies exist and may have large office staffs. The National Intramural-Recreational Sports Association (NIRSA), headquartered in Corvallis, OR, is the governing body for campus recreation professionals and boasts a professional staff of 32 ("NIRSA Team," 2017). One might think professional positions may come across as desk jobs, but many are very far removed from this. NIRSA employees oversee and work in departments such as marketing, conferences, membership recruitment, and more, and a very satisfying career can be found with these types of associations. Many individuals working in organizations such as NIRSA may be running events and national championships or traveling to select sites for upcoming national conferences.

Other NGBs exist for coaching organizations such as the Women's Basketball Coaches Association (13 employees) headquartered in Lilburn, GA, and for fitness-related associations such as the National Strength and Conditioning Association (10 members on just their leadership team) ("Our Staff," 2016; "About Us," 2016). Many of you may be members of these types of organizations when you become employed in the industry, so make sure your search for internships and full-time positions includes a professional organization related to your specific interests.

All of the organizations previously mentioned reflect national-level organizations, and the numbers are not all-inclusive of jobs in sport tied to local Boys and Girls Clubs, YMCAs, Jewish Community Centers, and more. Additional governing bodies will be highlighted as they pertain to some of the sections below.

INTERCOLLEGIATE SPORT

Most people are very familiar with college athletics. However, understanding its depth is crucial to the prospective intern. While television gives one a first-row view of most major college programs, positions with smaller post-secondary institutions, as well as with conference offices, are available. Additionally, it is often easier to climb the ladder and rise to the top of your field within a smaller organization. In fact, in hard economic times when states are cutting budgets, internships will often increase as a means of hiring interested and qualified individuals at a lower rate than would be offered to a full-time employee.

If you desire a career in collegiate athletics, the National Collegiate Athletic Association (NCAA) is the largest NGB for this segment. It boasts nearly 1,100 member schools ("Our Three Divisions," 2017). Thus, employment at its headquarters in Indianapolis, IN, or any one of its member schools opens the door for many career positions, but do not stop your search there. Individuals interested in a career in college athletic administration should also check for available positions with the following:

- National Christian College Athletic Association (NCCAA) and its 95+ member schools (Headquarters in Greenville, SC);
- the National Association of Intercollegiate Athletics (NAIA) and its 250+ member schools (Headquarters in Kansas City, MO);
- the National Junior College Athletic Association (NJCAA) and its 330+ member schools (Headquarters in Colorado Springs, CO);
- the United States Collegiate Athletic Association (USCAA) and its 75+ member schools (Headquarters in Norfolk, VA);
- University Athletic Association (UAA) and its eight member schools (Headquarters in Rochester, NY); and
- Canadian Collegiate Athletic Association (CCAA) and its 66 + French organizations (Headquarters in Corwall, ON).

Within most governing bodies for college athletics, member schools are divided into divisions. The responsibilities of employees generally vary based on the size of the school. For example, the NCAA has traditionally divided its schools into three major divisions, with Division I housing the largest programs in two different subdivisions—Divisions I-A and I-AA. In 2006, for football, these subdivisions were renamed to the Football Bowl Subdivision (commonly known as the BCS) and the Football Championship Subdivision (FCS), but the NCAA still identifies its entire membership under the three major divisions ("Our Three Division," 2017).

Positions in college athletics vary widely especially at the larger schools. Individuals employed in this setting tend to work within one department with responsibilities focused solely in that area. It is recommended, if you are targeting this career field, to explore different niche areas. One does not start out as an athletic director. Climbing the ladder usually begins with a position in sports information, facility management, sales or marketing, compliance, athlete academic advising, or coaching. Gaining a graduate assistantship position (see Chapters 1, 2 and 6) in one of these departments or with a team is often the best course to pursue. In order to become an athletics director (AD), Ryan Erlacher (Time Out Interview 4.2), the associate director of athletics at Flagler College in St. Augustine, FL, states, "Don't be afraid to take on additional responsibilities and wear as many hats as you can, especially early on in your career. You want to make yourself indispensable, so seeking different ways to get involved will help you build your administrative skills and give you a tremendous background in a number of different areas" (personal communication, September 6, 2016).

An AD at a Division I institution must accept the responsibilities of fundraising, public relations, facility development, a hefty travel schedule, and more. Thus, many may prefer holding other positions in college athletics and at smaller institutions that keep individuals directly in touch with the athletes.

A sports information director (SID), although specialized in the media area, may hold the title of an assistant or associate athletic director as in the case of Doug Ireland (Time Out Interview 4.3). In the college athletic environment, the responsibilities are similar to those of a public relations director in professional sport, but most departments are labeled sports information instead of public relations. The title of communications director is becoming more widely used for individuals in this area as well. Often, SIDs must be familiar with a wide variety of sports

Time Out Interview 4.2 with Ryan Erlacher
COLLEGE ATHLETICS

Position	Associate Director of Athletics - 7 years
Employer	Flagler College
B.A. Degree	Sport Management—Flagler College
M.S. Degree	Sport Administration—Florida State University
Career Path	• Director of Basketball – Stetson University – 1 year
	• Athletics Assistant – Florida State University – 1.5 years
	• Assistant Athletic Director – Northwood University – 3 years
	• Associate Athletic Director – Newman University – less than 1 year

Employment Recommendation

"Don't rely solely on your education. You must intern, volunteer, and gain experience in the industry. People underestimate the value of volunteering for positions. Early on in your career, look for positions and organizations that provide you a lot of opportunity for growth. I've always been a big believer in working for organizations that do things the right way and are highly sought after places for employment. Organizations like these usually treat their employees well and offer tremendous growth potential. The industry is constantly changing; try positioning yourself to keep up with, or if possible, stay ahead of the times.

Time Out Interview 4.3 with Doug Ireland
SPORTS INFORMATION

Position	Assistant Athletics Director/Sports Information Director – 28 years
Employer	Northwestern State University
B.A. Degree	Broadcast Journalism—Northwestern State University
Career Path	• Assistant SID – University of Louisiana at Lafayette – 4 years
	• Sports Editor – Natchitoches Times – 2 years
	• Consultant – Northwestern State Sports Info – 3 years
	• Graduate Assistant SID – University of Louisiana at Monroe – 1 year
	• Sports Writer – Alexandria Town Talk – 3 years

Employment Recommendation

"Dive in. Immerse yourself and get all the experience possible in every facet of athletic communications. Be able to do a public address. Broadcast a game, host a luncheon or press conference, and speak to broadcast reporters without verbal crutches. Stay on pace with evolving media trends and social media skills. Be able to shoot and edit video. Learn basic publication design skills and hone them. Some of this requires you being involved in an SID office; some of this you can get from student media involvement, or even in some cases, in classes. All of this will set you up for success in life, not just in this industry. It is important to realize. with the vastly different needs of various levels of institutions, opportunities constantly are available somewhere. Many of the people who advance to top jobs began at small schools, "doing it all." If you have interest in working in pro sports in the communications field, you can get the experience and skill set needed in college sports."

and computer programs, especially those involving game statistics. They will write press releases for websites. Many will contact hometown newspapers of their institution's athletes and submit articles covering the athlete's successes. In larger athletic programs, they are often tasked with the responsibility of protecting the student-athlete and coach from the outside media. Good writing and people skills are a must.

Another specialty area many may not know about is athletic academic advising, now commonly called academic support services. This is a great area to enter if you were a good, well-organized student and time manager, like Toni Kay Oliverio (Time Out Interview 4.4). Having been an athlete may also help you enter this area. This is an area where there is not as much competition for employment, especially when compared to marketing, sales, and coaching. It would be one of those great areas to enter and wear one of those hats as Ryan Erlacher mentioned. Learning as much about college athletics as a whole is a good conceptual skill to have if you aspire to be running an athletic department one day.

Time Out Interview 4.4 with Toni Kay Oliverio
ATHLETE ACADEMIC SUPPORT SERVICES

Position	Assistant Director of Student Athlete Development – 2 years
Employer	West Virginia University Intercollegiate Athletics
B.S. Degree	Exercise Science—West Liberty State College
M.S. Degree	Sport Administration—University of Louisville
Career Path	• Assistant Women's Basketball Coach/Head Women's Tennis Coach – Salem International University – 1.5 years • Graduate Teaching & Research Assistant – University of Louisville – 2 years • Sports Information Director Intern – Louisville – 1 year • Conference Commissioner Intern – Mid-South Conference – 1 year • Assistant Sports Information Director/Academic Coordinator – WVU Tech – 2 years • Sports Information Director – Mid-South Conference – 1 year • Assistant Athletic Director/Sports Information Director – WVU Tech – 6 months • Director of Women's Basketball Operations – West Virginia University – 7 years

Employment Recommendation

"Network as much as possible and gain as much experience as you can before looking for your first full-time position. The more you know and the more people you know, will make you more marketable to a prospective employer. Take the opportunity to work in and learn about all aspects of collegiate athletics. Being able to see things from multiple angles will give you the ability to offer a unique perspective and place you as a front runner for a position in the future."

College Coaching

Many aspire to enter college athletics through the coaching ranks. Entry strategies may vary depending upon the level of the institution. The best way to get your foot in the proverbial door of any level of college athletics, especially Division I, is through a graduate assistantship (GA) defined in Chapter 1. The first step is to choose the school athletic program and coach under which you like to work, and then choose the respective Master's degree. The NCAA publishes GA position offerings by member institutions at ncaamarket.ncaa.org.

Graduate assistantships at smaller schools may be actual coaching positions. For the athletic program, it is a less expensive way to hire head coaches, coaching assistants, and other staff members. At the same time, it is a great way to get a master's degree and gain experience at the same time. More information on GAs and graduate school can be found in Chapter 6.

At any institution, teaching may be part of a coach's responsibilities. Often a coach may teach sport skills classes, coaching theory courses, or other classes that fit their undergraduate degree. Some may be assigned teaching responsibilities for freshmen experience classes as well. Thus, anyone wishing to start a career in coaching may want to take a few education courses if there is room for electives within a sport business or business administration degree program. Of course, getting an education degree is a good option as well because a physical education or kinesiology program is an excellent route for coaches. If one already has an undergraduate degree in one of these areas, a master's degree in sport management/business and/or higher education administration is a great compliment to round out the educational background.

Many believe that college playing experience is a prerequisite for getting into coaching. There is no doubt that having been a collegiate athlete allows an individual an upfront and personal view of the pressures placed on athletes and the team environment. This experience also exposes you to a wide variety of game strategies and operations. However, according to Saint Leo University Head Men's Lacrosse Coach Brad Jorgensen, playing experience means less and less the further one gets away from their playing days, but it might help one get that first coaching position. Playing experience only gets one so far. Coaches are evaluated on their current coaching abilities and professionalism, and this is what keeps one in the coaching profession (personal communication, December 12, 2016).

At a smaller institution, coaches may wear many hats across traditional departmental boundaries. In addition to teaching, coaches may also hold responsibilities in areas such as facility maintenance, sports information, in a fitness center, or intramural sport programming. At any size school, it is not uncommon for a coach's educational minimum requirement to be a master's degree, particularly if teaching in the academic program is required. If coaching is part of your future goals, talk to your academic advisor about getting some experience in teaching. You hear a lot in the media about million dollar salaries for coaches. However, this is definitely not the norm at smaller schools, so teaching is a way to supplement one's income.

The responsibilities of a college coach vary widely. A head coach is often delivering presentations, meeting with alumni groups, attending dinners, participating in golf or other sport-related outings, traveling to meet with parents and recruits, and, of course, coaching. They are very much an organizational figurehead and an extension of an institution's public relations staff. A head coach of a major sport is also a manager of a sizeable staff, thus management and organizational skills and a people-friendly personality benefit one tremendously. For example, Erin Kinberger (Time Out Interview 4.5) used her skills to move up in the coaching ranks.

While all coaches may have some budgetary accountability, a coach at a smaller institution is likely to have more hands-on responsibilities in this area and perhaps other office duties. Their support staffs are not likely to be large. They may drive the team van, organize races and meets,

Time Out Interview 4.5 with Erin Brunt Kinberger
COLLEGE COACHING

Position	Head Softball Coach – 3 years
Employer	Saint Leo University
B.A. Degree	Elementary Education—Saint Leo University
M.S. Degree	Health and Human Performance—Fort Hays State University
Career Path	• Graduate Assistant Coach – Saint Leo University – 1 year
	• Assistant Softball Coach – Fort Hays State University – 3 years
	• Head Softball Coach – Fort Hays State University – 3 years

Employment Recommendation

"Be prepared to work your way into the career. You will most likely have to live off minimal income if you want to eventually earn a living by coaching college athletics. Too often, I hear young coaches (ages 24–27) complaining they do not "make enough" and all their friends and family are making much more. Eventually, they talk themselves out of coaching just as they are approaching opportunities to move up to higher paying positions."

set-up their facility's venue, and even direct the maintenance crew. Thus, event management skills and knowledge of current facility technology, flooring, and field turf maintenance are necessary core skills. A coach at a smaller institution is very much a do-everything, know-everything type of person for their sport. The institution counts on them and their abilities to direct support staff in these areas.

INTERSCHOLASTIC SPORT

Individuals wishing to pursue a career as a high school's AD may elect sport management as their college degree field. Rising to this type of position usually begins with a coaching and/or teaching position. However, caution is warranted. Many states or school districts may require a specific degree in education with the appropriate teaching certifications. Some sport management programs are housed in an education department (i.e., physical education), but this alone may not qualify an individual to obtain teaching certifications in certain states. Additional education courses may be necessary. Private schools and certain school districts may have different requirements and may be able to hire an individual with a non-teaching sport management degree if they obtain a teaching certification in a designated number of years after being hired.

The responsibilities of a high school athletic director traditionally require accountability in a variety of areas including coaching, facility maintenance and management, eligibility compliance, game supervision, hiring and discharge of sport coaches, teaching, budget development, and management. Because a high school athletic director may supervise a large staff of coaches and other related personnel with little support staff, being an organized manager and a great people person are strong assets. A high school athletic director must also understand risk management. Creating a safe environment for athletes, coaches, and spectators and understanding the legal liabilities involved in supervision of facilities and people are of utmost importance. ADs are often involved in the design and management of new sport facilities, and all athletic directors are event managers. Many curricula in physical education do not have separate courses in any of these areas, so it is a strong recommendation for interested individuals to seek out sport management courses on these topics if pursuing an education degree and teaching certification. As with many positions in sport, a traditional 8 a.m. to 5 p.m. workday is not the norm. With teams playing in the evenings and on weekends, an AD must accept flexibility in their schedule, long hours, and time away from family. Because of the multitude of responsibilities of a high school athletic director, some schools/school districts may not allow an AD to hold a coaching position at the same time. According to Erick Timko (Time Out Interview 4.6), the life of a high school AD can be very rewarding, but you must be able to multitask and do whatever it takes to be successful (personal communication, August 23, 2016).

Our interview with Erik Timko displays a wide variety of responsibilities throughout his career. Note that he was an athletic director in a previous position, and his current title is activities coordinator. A title, such as this, can mean the individual is still the athletic director, but added responsibilities may involve other activities within the school. For example, Kellie Doucette (Time Out Interview 4.7) holds the position of director of athletics for the Florida High School Athletic Association (FHSAA), a state-level NGB. Kellie rose through the teaching/coaching ranks to achieve her current position and offers some great comments regarding taking advantage of opportunities, a common theme throughout this text.

RECREATIONAL SPORT MANAGEMENT

Careers in recreational sport management are often overlooked by those pursuing a sport management degree. Sometimes people believe a degree in recreation is best, and others just simply have not explored this very satisfying employment area. This section is strictly devoted to recreational sport management and does not pertain to positions that may include such responsibilities as arts and crafts, story time, and other non-sport leisure pursuits.

College Recreational Sport

A comprehensive career in this industry segment can be found on most college campuses under the department of campus recreation. In today's higher education organizational structure, most campus recreation programs are aligned with a division of student affairs. Several decades ago, the most likely place to find this type of department was under athletics, and some institutions still operate in this manner. A quality campus recreation program houses a multitude

Time Out Interview 4.6 with Erik Timko
HIGH SCHOOL ATHLETIC ADMINISTRATION

Position	Activities Coordinator
Employer	Palmetto Ride High School, Collier County Public Schools (FL)
B.A. Degree	Elementary Education—Michigan State University
M.B.A. Degree	MBA Concentration Sport Business—Saint Leo University
M. Ed. Degree	Educational Leadership—American College of Education
Career Path	• High school American History & Economics teacher – 2 years; Football Coach – 4 years; Basketball Coach – 1 season (Some positions concurrent)
	• Middle school social studies teacher – 2 years concurrent with high school JV baseball coach – 5 years
	• CCAC Chairman – Collier County Public Schools – 1 year
	• Activities Coordinator – Palmetto Ridge High School – 4 years
	• Head Baseball Coach – Palmetto Ridge High School – 1 year
	• Teacher- Geography – Collier County Public Schools – 1 year
	• LCAC Chairman – Lee County Public Schools – 3 years
	• Athletic Director – North Fort Myers School – 4 years

Employment Recommendation

"The best way to get your foot in the door is to begin getting involved in a school district. That includes volunteering, coaching, teaching, etc. From what I have found, most schools/school districts do not hire from outside when selecting a new AD. They want someone who has been invested in the lives of their student-athletes of their district. Once beginning to be involved, try to get as much experience as you can by volunteering or even getting paid as a worker. Learn what it takes to put on a Friday night football game or a cross country meet on a Saturday. There is usually much more to the event (and planning) than what meets the eye."

of recreational pursuits, and most relate to fitness or sport. A typical department will house intramural, extramural, club, fitness, and aquatic programming. Non-credit instructional programming, such as aerobics, dance, martial arts, and basic sport skills development classes, are customary. On large campuses, it is not uncommon to have a large (200,000 square feet or more) facility housing multiple team and individual sport courts, one or more areas dedicated to fitness, swimming pools, climbing walls, an outdoor equipment check-out station, and even athletic training and physical therapy facilities to treat and rehabilitate the recreational athlete. One of the largest collections of campus recreation facilities in the United States is located at

Time Out Interview 4.7 with Kellie Doucette
STATE GOVERNING BODIES

Position	Director of Athletics – 3 years
Employer	Florida High School Athletic Association
B.S. Degree	Elementary Education—University of Central Florida
M. Ed. Degree	Education Leadership—Stetson University
Career Path	• Teacher/JV Cheer Coach – Volusia County School – 3 years
	• Teacher/Varsity Cheer Coach – Flagler County Schools – 8 years
	• Cheer Camp Manager – Varsity Spirit – 7 years

Employment Recommendation

"Be patient and don't overlook an opportunity because it may not fit into your vision. Your dream job may not fall into your lap the day you graduate and you may have to take a route to your goal that you weren't planning on taking. Opportunities that you may not have considered sometimes present themselves in the least likely places and they can lead to unexpected advancements that you may not have previously considered."

The Ohio State University. Five indoor recreational sport facilities and 70 acres of outdoor recreational space adorn this sprawling urban campus. First opened in 2005, the Recreation and Physical Activity Center (RPAC) cost $140 million and has a total square footage of 568,459. It houses the following:

- a welcome center;
- an aquatic pavilion with a competitive pool and diving area;
- dive and leisure whirlpool spas;
- a meet management area and wet classroom;
- a recreation natatorium with three pools;
- two saunas;
- a jogging track;
- three aerobics/multipurpose rooms;
- 10 racquetball/squash courts;
- a wellness center;
- 25,000+ square feet of weight, fitness/cardio areas, massage areas, and fitness suite for personal training;
- four gymnasiums;
- an indoor golf area with simulator with putting and chipping areas;

- an athletic training room; and
- ancillary support areas for lounging, babysitting and kids zone, food service, offices, locker rooms, massage areas, kitchen, a juice bar, amphitheater, and pro shop ("Recreational Sports," n.d.).

Their $7.5 million dollar, 87,000 square foot indoor Adventure Recreation Center houses:

- indoor turf fields;
- basketball courts;
- a climbing center;
- a fitness center;
- locker rooms; and
- a rental equipment guest services counter ("Recreational Sports," n.d.).

There is also an Outdoor Adventure Center housed in a glass cube for visibility. The Center includes:

- a climbing center with over 4,000 square feet of climbing surface;
- a bouldering cave;
- storage space for kayaks, canoes, and other equipment; and
- restroom, trip room, service desk, offices, and a resource center ("Recreational Sports," n.d.).

Other outdoor facilities spread out over five distinct campus areas include:

- 43-acre state of the art park (which includes some of the areas listed below);
- four softball diamonds plus eight softball/baseball shared fields;
- five flag football/ultimate disc fields;
- 11 basketball courts;
- a synthetic turf field shared with the marching band;
- 17 total grass fields for various sports;
- a tennis center with 15 tennis courts and a practice wall court;
- A roller hockey rink;
- seven sand volleyball courts;
- a 1.1 mile jogging path and a pad with fitness stations;
- two picnic shelters and a playground;
- a cricket pitch and a skate park;
- an 18-hole recreational disc golf course;
- restrooms, drinking fountains, storage, and equipment check-out areas; and
- plans to build a leadership challenge course that will include high and low ropes courses, a rappelling tower, and confidence course ("Recreational Sports," n.d.).

Why would we bother listing everything above? How many full-time positions would you believe are needed to run OSU's facilities and programs in campus recreation? Can you picture managing over 50 sport clubs, 800 basketball teams, 500 flag football teams, and countless more recreational sport teams along with several fitness centers? OSU also includes family activities and embraces an inclusive philosophy that incorporates a wide array of programming and events for participants with disabilities. What would you imagine the operational and staff budget to be? Let us add to your understanding of the magnitude of this one department. Seventy-six full-time employees, 14 graduate administrative assistants (GAAs), and 850 students are employed. The annual operating budget is in excess of $18 million.

Many graduate assistantships are available in this field and expect to see a master's degree as a preferred requirement for a full-time entry-level position. JR Rathjens, the associate director of campus recreation at Ohio State, states "the average starting salary for an entry-level coordinator's position at Ohio State in 2016 was between $40,000 and $42,000" (personal communication, December 14, 2016). J. Michael Dunn, influential NIRSA member and long-time director at OSU, who was instrumental in the early stages of the design of RPAC, in building many of the current facilities, and improving others, recommended the following for anyone exploring a career in campus recreation:

- Join and be active in NIRSA by attending conferences, submitting presentations for any of NIRSA's conferences or workshops, and serving on committees.
- Get involved in conducting research with faculty or staff.
- Begin looking for graduate schools as early as your junior year. One way to narrow your choice is to find institutions heavily involved in NIRSA and with a history of preparing and supporting young professionals.
- Maintain an undergraduate GPA of 3.0 or above.
- Meet and develop a professional relationship with a minimum of three to six mentors from other campuses that would support you in a mentee/mentor relationship.
- Develop a consciousness that is open to change. Adopt a forecasting mentality of possible changes in higher education and in recreational sport that will have a short- or long-term impact on your career. Reading the *Chronicle of Higher Education* on a regular basis can assist in the understanding of changes affecting higher education. (personal communication, September 1, 2009)

If you are not lucky enough to be enrolled at a strong NIRSA institution for your undergraduate experience, or are not offered a graduate assistantship at one, work harder and smarter in other areas and take advantage of all opportunities (M. Dunn, personal communication, August 31, 2009). Of course, finding an internship at a NIRSA member institution is highly recommended. For example, JR Rathjens (Time Out Interview 4.8) has been working in campus recreation since his undergraduate internship. JR thought he ultimately wanted a career in

Time Out Interview 4.8 with JR Rathjens
COLLEGIATE RECREATIONAL SPORT MANAGEMENT

Position	Associate Director, Programs – 3 years
Employer	The Ohio State University Department of Recreational Sports
B.A. Degree	Sport Management—Flagler College
M.A. Degree	Sport Management—The Ohio State University
Career Path	• Intern, Recreational Sports – The Ohio State University, Columbus – 5 months
	• Graduate Assistant, Recreational Sports – The Ohio State University, Columbus – 2 years
	• Coordinator of Recreation and Athletics – The Ohio State University, Mansfield – 2.5 years
	• Assistant Director/Associate Director, Campus Recreation – Towson University – 7.5 years

Employment Recommendation

"Make sure you get exposed to as many different positions and areas of sport management as possible. This will help narrow down what it is you want to do while building your network. Make sure you pay attention to the material covered in your academic coursework. I consistently use a lot of the information covered in my Sport Law and Facility/Event Management classes specifically."

college athletic administration. His first full-time job was tied to small college athletics and recreation, but he decided to go back into campus recreation full-time after two and a half years.

City or County Recreational Sport

Recreational sport management positions can also be found within city and county recreation departments and nonprofit organizations such as a YMCA. Some positions may be solely dedicated to the operation and management of sport leagues and tournaments. Thus, these positions also fall under this employment category. Any municipal recreation department most likely has at least one full-time position dedicated to sport-related management. These other categories are explored more fully in the paragraphs below.

Working for a city or county recreation department can include an entire career involving sport programs of all types and for all ages thus allowing more variety in position responsibilities when compared to high school or college athletics. Sport offerings depend largely on available facilities and local or regional sport interests. The 2016 National Parks and Recreation Association (NRPA) annual survey indicated nine out of 10 Americans agree parks and recreation services are important, 75% of Americans support increased government spending for park and recreation agencies, and, on average, respondents visited their local park and recreation facilities about 29 times a year (National Parks and Recreation Association, 2016). These numbers show strong support for employment opportunities in this sector of the industry.

To emphasize the sport management side of recreation, running tournaments is an exciting responsibility for many, and some recreation departments are known for running numerous tournaments every year. Larger departments submit bids to host national championships. Even though there are computer programs to assist the manager to set up tournament brackets, Wi-Fi or a computer are not always available at tournament sites. Thus, knowing the different types of tournaments and formulas for setting up single elimination, double elimination, and round robin tournaments would be a great skill to have and put on a résumé. When dealing with seeding and byes, this can be very helpful. Thus, tournament organization is an important sport management skill to possess along with other event and facility management knowledge to round out enormous responsibility under this employment umbrella.

As in all areas of sport, there are many ways to come up through the recreation ranks. David Schmitz (Time Out Interview 4.9) got his start as an aquatics superintendent and is now the director of parks and recreation in College Station, TX. He states, "The variety of activities and positions holds opportunities for just about everyone…the job never gets old" (personal communication, September 14, 2016).

Time Out Interview 4.9 with David J. Schmitz
PUBLIC RECREATIONAL SPORT MANAGEMENT

Position	Director of Parks and Recreation – 7 years
Employer	City of College Station, Texas
B.S. Degree	Public Recreation—South Dakota State University
Career Path	• Aquatics Superintendent – City of McAllen, TX – 12 years
	• Recreation Superintendent – City of McAllen, TX – 6.5 years
	• Parks and Recreation Manager – City of Bryan, TX – 8.5 years
	• Assistant Director of Parks and Recreation – City of College Station, TX – 2.5 years

Employment Recommendation

"Search the NRPA website, your state association website, and any city websites for which you are interested in working. Be active with your community parks and recreation department and develop a relationship with them so that when the time is right you are ready!"

Military Sport Management

Military sport and recreation often falls under the Morale, Welfare, and Recreation (MWR) division. MWR offerings depend very heavily on the base location and size as well as the military branch (Miles, 2013b). Many bases have scaled back the amount of offerings. Miles (2013a) explained that fitness centers, physical and emotional health, and stress reductions programs are tied to readiness of soldiers and retention of military families. MWR does poll active duty and reserve members and past surveys have indicated respondents wanted money to go to fitness centers and programs (Garamore, 2014). Thus, the government continues to fund these facilities. Other facilities such as golf courses, bowling alleys, and campgrounds exist but must be self-sustaining. Some bases have begun to outsource these programs to fitness centers or civic recreation programs as many military personnel and their families live off base and can find facilities in their local neighborhoods. The downside to this is that volunteers are assisting in the operation of some facilities due to fewer military personnel being assigned to work in MWR facilities/ programs (Miles, 2013a). However, the outsourcing to private fitness centers or organizations opens the door for jobs in the private sector.

Some military bases sponsor major events. The Bethesda, Maryland MWR office has held events such as the Dr. Martin Luther King, Jr. Basketball Tournament, a Great Inflatable Raft Race, a 12-day Winter Swim Challenge, and even a Reindeer Run. This last event is a 5k/10k virtual race where individuals can run on a treadmill or on their own during a three-day span after which participants take pictures and post them on social media. Ugly sweater shirts are offered for the first 50 who sign up ("Events," n.d.). What a fun and unique event to stage!

Beyond individual base military programs, the Department of Defenses' Armed Forces Sports (AFS) programs are where tournaments and events for a variety of different sports are hosted. Besides your typical team sport offerings, rugby, golf, bowling, and judo can dot the AFS event calendar, but events for 17 sports are listed on their website. Officially established in 1948, the AFS is the culmination of each military branch's sports and fitness program. Personnel compete at the unit level and can advance to national and international competitions. AFS also provides the opportunity for personnel to compete in the Olympics and Paralympics ("About the U.S. Armed Forces," n.d.).

The U.S. Military All-Stars (baseball) operates a Red, White, and Blue Tour where off-duty military personnel play baseball and cover their own expenses. The tour visits about 45 states and 12 foreign countries and makes nearly 150 appearances annually to promote their mission of raising awareness of the sacrifices of the United States Armed Forces. Part of the team's tour travels includes games against minor league teams. ("What We Do," n.d.). Internships have been offered, and Saint Leo University senior Jeff Gray interned with the Tour in 2012 as associate general manager. Following his 10-month stint, he was hired as the GM of the Bluefield Blue Jays—making him the youngest GM in baseball at the age of 22. This is testimony to taking advantage of opportunity even if it was not a first choice internship.

On a larger scale, the International Military Sports Council or the Conseil International du Sport Militaire (CISM) has 134 member countries making it one of the largest multidisciplinary organizations in the world (International military sports council, n.d.). CISM organizes 20 world military championships for approximately 30 different sports. Every four years, there is a CISM Military World Games. Sport for peace and solidarity is their main purpose.

All of these military programs represent the possibility of full-time positions and/or opportunities for gaining terrific experience, especially if you live close to a military base. When the U.S. military forces were first deployed to Iraq in Operation Desert Storm, job postings appeared for non-military individuals to run recreational sport programs for the troops in Iraq and Saudi Arabia. According to Chris Corcione, who served six tours and was stationed in Iraq, Afghanistan, Saudi Arabia and Kuwait from 2003–2015, larger deployment areas had MWR tents that would have game rooms with ping pong, play stations, and computer set-ups inside and volleyball nets outside for recreational play. They would also set up and organize trips to neighboring countries and military personnel could sign-up during time off (personal communication, December 13, 2016). Furthermore, a creative programming idea was published in a NIRSA publication many years ago regarding the modified rules for playing softball on an aircraft carrier. Thus, regardless of where the U.S. troops are located, the possibility exists for employment in recreational sport management via military bases and their programs.

For military veterans returning to the classroom and looking for employment opportunities, the NRPA partnered with the Coca-Cola Foundation to support the employment of veterans in recreational facilities. Since veterans are often very fit, involved recreation centers have hired them to instruct fitness classes and run fitness programs. The program called Troops for Fitness has thus far received rave reviews and more than 75,000 participants have been recorded in 12 communities across the country (Collum, 2016).

Other Non-Profits and Private Recreational Sport Programming

Local and national organizations exist that cater to communities through outreach programs and house fitness centers and sport leagues. The Young Men's Christian Association (YMCA) was actually founded in London in 1844 to provide a place for rural men to live while working jobs in larger cities at the end of the Industrial Revolution. Today, the Y is a strong and impressive organization that focuses on four pillars of which sports, recreation, and healthy living initiatives play a major role ("National Impact Report," 2015). The first YMCA in the United States was established in Boston in 1851. The 1880s saw a boom in the building of new and larger YMCAs, and pools, gymnasiums, and bowling alleys were made part of the new YMCA environment. The sports of basketball, volleyball, and racquetball were started at YMCAs. By the close of World War II, many Ys were admitting women, and, soon, people of all races and religions were welcomed. Because the Y actually held classes at many of their facilities, by the 1950s, the organization was operating 20 colleges ("History," n.d.).

Today, YMCA's exist in over 119 countries, with over 2,700 YMCAs across the United States. Thus, it is logical to assume a large number of positions exist that fall under the recreational sport category due to 19,000+ full-time staff positions reported by the organization and the involvement of other sponsoring sport organizations such as the NBA ("National Impact Report," 2015). With a traditional focus on health and wellness, recreational sport has always formed a strong nucleus for many community programs involving individuals of all ages. Social justice, an area in which many sport management professionals desire to be involved, is a strong value promoted by the Y. In 2014, it launched Togetherhood, a signature program for social responsibility ("National Impact Report," 2015). Holding a job at a YMCA will give you an inside track to other YMCA positions throughout the world. Thus, unlike professional sport organizations where new ownership can result in immediate staffing changes in some departments leaving previously very dedicated employees without jobs, the support network for finding full-time employment within the Y network is incredible. It is definitely a great place to establish a career that includes recreational sport management. Ys are known to heavily recruit from within and, every two weeks, alerts are sent to employees about position openings.

The Boys and Girls Clubs of America (BGCA) has also grown into a haven for youth to become involved in organized sport and positive personal growth. It, too, has a long history with its first club organized by women in 1860. The name Federated Boys Clubs was adopted in 1906, eventually evolving into the Boys and Girls Clubs of America in 1990. Recreation has always been part of its core foundation (Boys & Girls Clubs of America, n.d.). Some of its current sport-related programs include:

- All-Stars, co-sponsored by BGCA and Buffalo Wild Wings, is a program to assist in establishing youth sports leagues in flag football, basketball, and cheerleading with a focus on building life skills and self-confidence.
- Reviving Baseball in Inner Cities (RBI), sponsored by Major League Baseball, to expand boys baseball and girls fast-pitch softball leagues.
- Jr. RBI, also sponsored by Major League Baseball, focuses on teaching baseball and softball fundamentals to children ages 5–12.
- Wanna Play? is a third program sponsored by Major League Baseball and encourages youth ages 6–12 to increase fitness and health by participating in physical activities, improving nutritional education, and learning baseball and softball skills.
- PGA Sports Academy, co-sponsored by the Professional Golfers' Association of America (PGA) and the United States Golf Association (USGA), introduces youth ages 7–13 to golf and assist in building character and healthy lifestyles.
- Triple Play, sponsored by Coca-Cola, supports games and sports clubs (Boys & Girls Clubs of America, n.d.).

This organization, obviously, can open the doors for a long and lasting career related to recreational sport management. While only one glimpse in time, when we looked at this organization's career opportunities, there were 71 available positions across the United States (Boys & Girls Clubs of America, n.d.).

Our third nation-wide recreational sport organization we are highlighting is The Jewish Community Centers Association (JCC). This organization is a well-known and a very connected group that promotes sports, aquatics, fitness, and wellness at over 156 JCCs in North America. Additionally, one can find a JCC day, overnight, or summer camp that offers traditional sports. In 2014, it began hosting a Maccabi Sports Camp in Atherton, CA, that offers youth a chance to advance their sport skills in seven different sports. This is in support of the annual JCC Maccabi Games, which is currently the second largest gathering for Jewish teens in North America. Competition is held in 15 different sports. This event celebrated its 31st anniversary during the summer of 2016 with over 6,000 athletes ages 13–16 participating. In recent years, this event has been held at three to four host sites each year, and several major corporate sponsors support the Games ("About," n.d.; "Camps, n.d.; "Find a JCC," n.d.).

Other private organizations provide sport programming for youth and adults. The Amateur Athletic Union (AAU), headquartered in Orlando, FL, has a long history. Its staff runs sports programming in over 30 sports and host national championships. The Amateur Athletic Union reports a staff of 10 with five additional official officers ("National Leadership," n.d.). As of 2016, the president of this association was paid $175,000.

I-9 Sports has over 100 locations and 200,000 members and uses the motto "helping kids succeed in life through sports" ("The i9 Story," n.d.). The website features mostly part-time opportunities, but I-9 and AAU might be a place to gain experience in sports officiating or programming even as a college student. I-9 part-time jobs can possibly serve as apprenticeships/practica depending upon your sport management academic program requirements. However, the I-9 website offers franchising opportunities. If one has or can find start-up funding, what a great chance to start your own business.

The National Alliance for Youth Sports, headquartered in West Palm Beach, Florida, was founded in 1981 with a mission of providing "educational programs and resources to improve youth sports programs worldwide" ("Missions and History," n.d., par.1). If you are looking for an organization to gain coaching and officiating experience, this may be a valuable resource. They provide training and resources for concussions, emergency action plans, bully prevention, and background screening for hiring of volunteers. The organization also offers the Academy for Youth Sports Administrators, an annual Youth Sports Congress, and sponsors the National Youth Sports Administrators Association (NYSAA). They sport a full-time staff of 17.

The United Soccer League (USL), headquartered in Tampa, Florida, is an example of sport programming involving a unique opportunity for soccer enthusiasts. The USL has a unique organizational structure. The USL sponsors leagues from the youth to professional levels but has quickly become known as a minor league for professional soccer due to a partnership entered with Major League Soccer (MLS) in 2013. Specifically, they sponsor a very large youth division called the Super Y League, which is made up of over 500+ teams within 95 separate clubs for ages 10–18. These clubs are located in 19 U.S. states ("Leagues," n.d.). Vincent Wiskowski (Time Out Interview 4.10) interned in the USL's youth division, was offered full-time employment at the completion of his internship, and quickly rose to the position of director of social media. Vincent played collegiate soccer and runs his own soccer academy in his home country of Panama. The USL offers him a wide variety of career options because of the marriage of youth and professional teams under one organizational umbrella. The USL website reports a full-time staff of 39, with the possibility of full-time positions and internships across the country ("USL Executive Team," n.d.).

Youth leagues are not the only place to gain valuable full-time, part-time, or volunteer experience or to establish a long career in the industry. In addition to city and county recreational leagues and offices, there are private organizations sponsoring adult recreational offerings. One example of programming involving adult leagues is within an organization called Tampa Bay Club Sport in Florida. This organization runs leagues and tournaments for 10 sports/recreational activities including traditional team sports, kickball, and cornhole. They also host special events including poker and bar game tournaments and social events such as a New Year's Eve party, and

Time Out Interview 4.10 with Vincent Wiskowski
YOUTH AND PRO SPORT/LEAGUE ORGANIZATION

Position	Director, Social Media – 1 year
Employer	United Soccer League
B.A. Degree	Sport Business—Saint Leo University
Career Path	• Olympic Development Program Intern – United Soccer League – 6 months
	• Manager Youth League Operations & Video Production Assistant – United Soccer League – 6 months
	• Social Media Manager – United Soccer League – 4 months

Employment Recommendation

"The sport industry is a very tough and extremely competitive market; everyone considers themselves to be a suitable candidate since they happen to be a "fan". I would recommend making the jump into sports as soon as you can. Starting outside the industry and expecting to come back in a higher role is going to be much tougher than climbing the ranks from within."

their staff will plan corporate events for organizations. As one example, Carly Houman (Time Out Interview 4.11) originally interned with Disney Sports and worked in event management on a part-time basis before finding her niche with this organization.

We hope we have convinced you there are plenty of full-time positions in this segment of the industry. We want to satisfy your hunger even more. Employment is just around the corner. Google amateur adult sports or amateur youth sports, and find a league or association in your locale.

Time Out Interview 4.11 with Carly Houman
PRIVATE RECREATIONAL SPORT MANAGEMENT

Position	Vice President of Operations – 3 years
Employer	Tampa Bay Club Sport
B.S. Degree	Sport Business—Saint Leo University
Career Path	• Vice President of Operations – Tampa Bay Club Sport – 3 years
	• Director of Operations – Tampa Bay Club Sport – 5 years
	• Leagues Director – Tampa Bay Club Sport – 2 years
	• Event Support – Disney Wide World of Sports – 8 months (Internship and post internship)
	• Assistant Event Director, Let it Fly (Flag Football Tournaments) – 4 months

Employment Recommendation

"Volunteer to find what you really like to do. Have a lot of patience. It takes a while to find a good fit for yourself and to get paid what you would prefer. Work hard in any position within a company. The bosses notice this and you will hopefully have more opportunities to move to another position you may prefer. When you work with youth, you also work with parents. Customer service is a must!"

THE FINAL BUZZER

The intent of this chapter was to introduce the sport management student to career possibilities in Olympic, Paralympic, and amateur sport. While many are somewhat familiar with college and high school sports, key information was presented to broaden an individual's understanding of where internship opportunities and full-time positions might exist with national governing bodies, governmental and private organizations, and youth and adult amateur sport opportunities. Career positions are truly unlimited in these areas if one is willing to move to where the career positions exist. Speaking with a faculty advisor or major professor to initiate contact with one of these agencies is a good place to start a career in this segment of the industry.

EXPERIENTIAL LEARNING OPPORTUNITIES

Classroom Experiential Learning Exercise: Tournament Scheduling

As the sports coordinator for the city recreation department, you have 107 entries in your wallyball tournament. You have 10 leagues of eight teams and three leagues of nine teams. You have courts reserved for five weeks and will be able to play Monday through Thursday. In order to finish this tournament in the allotted time, how many games must be played per day? Utilize your tournament scheduling formulas to show your work.

Yes, there are computer programs used to set up tournament brackets. Do students know the different types of tournaments beyond single and double elimination? What if a tournament coordinator is on-site and teams don't show up? Do they just forfeit or does the tournament coordinator know how to quickly redo the tournament bracket using simple algebraic formulas to redraw an appropriate and fair bracket?

Submitted by Dr. John Dollar, Department Head & Associate Professor
Northwestern State University, Natchitoches, LA

Program Learning Exercise: Sport Administration Society

The Lock Haven University (LHU) Sport Studies Program and their student-run Sport Administration Society (SAS) offers an experiential learning assignment that requires students to organize and administer a 5K run/walk for a local or national charity selected through student research and a student vote. Student learning in several professional components includes marketing, sponsorship, event and venue management, leadership, and fundraising. This annual program emphasizes the practical implications of incorporating experiential class assignments in the classroom and the benefits they have for students as employers in the sports industry are continually looking for graduates with real-world experience.

Submitted by Dr. Justin Wartella, Assistant Professor
Loch Haven University, Loch Haven, PA

REFERENCES

About. (n.d.). *JCC Maccabi Games.* Retrieved from http://www.jccmaccabigames.org/about/

About the U.S. armed forces sports program. (n.d.). *Armed Forces Sports.* Retrieved December 12, 2016 from http://armedforcessports.defense.gov/About/

About us. (2016). *National Strength and Conditioning Association.* Retrieved from https://www.nsca.com/about-us/

Boys & Girls Clubs of America. (n.d.). Our mission & story. *Boys & Girls Clubs of America.* Retrieved from http://www.bgca.org/about-us/our-mission-story

Camps. (n.d.). *JCC Camps.* Retrieved from http://jcccamps.org/camps/

Collum, M. (2016). Troops for fitness engages military veterans in community health and wellness programs. *Parks and Recreation, 51*(11), 34–35.

Events. (n.d.). *NavyMWR Bethesda.* Retrieved from http://www.navymwrbethesda.com/events

Fact sheet. (2016). *United States Olympic Committee.* Retrieved from http://www.teamusa.org

Find a JCC near you. (n.d.). *Discover JCC.* Retrieved from http://www.discoverjcc.com/home/find-a-jcc-near-you/

Garamore, J. (2013, May 14). Morale, welfare, recreation customer survey rolls out. *American Forces Press Services*. Retrieved December 12, 2016 from http://www.af.mil/News/ArticleDisplay/tabid/223/Article/484754/morale-welfare-recreation-customer-survey-rolls-out.aspx

History. (n.d.). *YMCA of the USA*. Retrieved from www.ymca.net/history

International military sports council. (n.d.). International military sports council. Retrieved from http://www.mil-sport.one/

Leagues. (n.d.) *Super Y League*. Retrieved from http://www.sylsoccer.com/syl-leagues

Miles, D. (2013a, August 21). Innovative programs keep MWR relevant. *American Forces Press Services*. Retrieved from http://www.af.mil/News/ArticleDisplay/tabid/223/Article/466924/innovative-programs-keep-mwr-relevant.aspx

Miles, D. (2013b, August 22). Air Force offers potential model for future MWR programs. *American Forces Press Services*. Retrieved from http://www.af.mil/News/ArticleDisplay/tabid/223/Article/466940/air-force-offers-potential-model-for-future-mwr-programs.aspx

Mission and history. (n.d.). *National Alliance for Youth Sports*. Retrieved from http://www.nays.org/about/about-nays/mission/

National impact report. (2016). *YMCA of the USA*. Retrieved from http://www.ymca.net/sites/default/files/National%20Impact%20Report%202015.pdf

National leadership. *Amateur Athletic Union of the United States*. Retrieved from http://www.aausports.org/District-Articles/ArtMID/3489/ArticleID/681

National Recreation and Park Association. (2016). Americans engagement with parks survey. *National Recreation and Park Association*. Retrieved from http://www.nrpa.org/publications-research/research-papers/engagement/#.WFAon9mbWz0.email

NIRSA team at headquarters. (2017). NIRSA. Retrieved from http://nirsa.net/nirsa/contact/headquarters-staff/

Our staff. (2016). *Women's Basketball Coaches Association*. Retrieved from https://wbca.org/about/our-staff

Our three divisions. (2017). NCAA. Retrieved from http://www.ncaa.org/about/resources/media-center/ncaa-101/our-three-divisions

Recreational sports. (n.d.). *The Ohio State University*. Retrieved from https://recsports.osu.edu/

The i9 sports story. (n.d.). *i9 Sports Corporation*. Retrieved from http://www.i9sportsfranchise.com/research/the-i9-sports-franchise-story

USL executive team. (n.d.). *United Soccer League*. Retrieved from http://www.uslsoccer.com/executives

What we do. (n.d.). *US Military All-Stars*. Retrieved from http://usmilitaryallstars.com/.

CHAPTER

5

Sport Business Industry Overview: Support and Entrepreneurial Careers

"If you are contemplating a move from an employee to a business owner, consider taking on a few contracts while still an employee. Clearly define your niche and where your expertise sets you apart from everyone else, then, figure how to market it. Be prepared for the inevitable ups and downs that come with owning your own business."

— *Amy Perkins Mallett, College Sport Regulatory Consultant, The Compliance Group, Lenexa, KS*

THE WARM UP

Entrepreneurs, those starting their own company within the sport business industry, are often thinking outside the box when their product or service satisfies an essential need of a sport organization. Convincing a company your service fills a current void for them can be your ticket into the sport business industry. Do you have a new idea? Do you abhor the idea of working for someone else when you believe you can be your own boss, at least at some point after gaining experience? This chapter presents several ideas and incorporates Time Out Interviews from many of those who sat in the same college seats you are occupying right now.

Being an entrepreneur and wanting to start your own business is a great way of getting into the sport business industry. Creativity, business and organizational skills, and finance and budgeting knowledge can all pave the way for an exciting career. Individuals even start their own businesses while in high school or college, sometimes with the financial backing of their parents or another family member. To launch a sport business and be successful before one finishes a degree is truly a gift. As Amy Mallett recommended in this chapter's introductory comment, learn what sets you apart from others and build your network before resigning a position with an employer (personal communication, October 5, 2016). Work for successful individuals and/or organizations to learn specific skills within a business, and save money before venturing out on one's own path. A group of European students participating in an intense international touring practicum to Italy, titled Counseled Student-Excellent Future Employee (p. 171), reported learning extremely valuable entrepreneurial skills simply by meeting with industry executives. Through this unique experiential learning opportunity, students learned about economic activity and the labor practices of another country, marketing strategies, and how to write successful business plans. The experience also changed their attitudes about business and influenced their vision of the future (Tecău, 2016), both of which can be important for budding entrepreneurs.

As discussed in Chapter 1, in the 11 components of the sport employment model, there are many services sport organizations need. Media, food services, apparel, event management, marketing, fitness/athletic training, and others could come under the heading of support careers, and these are just the tip of the iceberg for ways a knowledgeable individual could launch a new business and pave their way into the sport business industry. Any entrepreneurial venture can become a year-round business if marketed well. Marketing and event management firms and many sport facilities host events throughout the year. Geography may also play a role. It only makes sense that an event management firm in Florida may operate throughout the year while the same type of organization in a colder climate may only contract with entrepreneurs during the warmer times of the year.

SUPPORT AREAS OF THE SPORT BUSINESS INDUSTRY

Event Management

Event management is popular among students, and positions exist in all employment fields. College athletic departments may employ an event manager to handle the logistics of half-time shows, meetings, recruit visits, camps, and more. Even though an individual's actual title may not be that of an event manager, a closer look at job responsibilities of some positions may reveal the handling of the logistics of an event. One might even want to search under logistics for an event management position. The word logistics is defined as "the planning, implementation, and coordination of the details of a business or other operation" ("Logistics," n.d.). Thus, managing logistics is event management. Sport facilities, professional sport teams, recreation departments, sports commissions, halls of fame, and even sport marketing firms have individuals who setup and run events. All of them might not include a sporting event, but careful planning, establishment of a timeline, other event logistics, and more can be the responsibilities of an event manager.

Claire Lessinger (Time Out Interview 5.1) is director of special events for the Tampa Bay Sports Commission. During her tenure with this organization, she has worked a multitude of events including the NCAA's Women's Final Four basketball tournament, the Frozen Four men's ice hockey tournament, the national championship football game, and other NCAA events including sports festivals, bowling tournaments, and more. Her route may not be typical for an event manager, but as a college coach, one is always assisting in running games and

Time Out Interview 5.1 with Claire Lessinger
EVENT MANAGEMENT

Position	Director of Special Events – 3 years
Employer	Tampa Bay Sports Commission
B.S. Degree	Exercise Science concentration in Sports Management—University of Florida
Career Path	• Internship – Tampa Bay Juniors Volleyball Club – 1 year
	• Assistant Volleyball Coach – Boston College – 1 year
	• Assistant Volleyball Coach – University of South Florida – 2 years
	• Associate Head Volleyball Coach – University of South Florida – 3 years
	• Head Volleyball Coach – University of South Florida – 8 years
	• Sales and Events Manager – Tampa Bay Sports Commission – 2 years

Employment Recommendation

"Event management should be a labor of love. In order to be great at it, you have to enjoy rolling up your sleeves and being in the trenches."

---

tournaments. According to Claire, if you have the following, you were born to be an event manager: great interpersonal skills, a diverse skill set, energy, flexibility, a calm demeanor, the ability to handle pressure, creativity and a knack for innovation, attention to detail, time management skills, passion, and leadership skills (personal communication, August 29, 2016).

Event managers must work very closely with facility managers, and the information in the next section can also apply to event management. Every sporting event must have a facility. The facility for a road race can be a street, and an event manager must take into account the logistics that come into play (e.g., police, road condition and closures).

Facility Management

Like event management, facility managers are needed in many of the industry segments. While most turf management positions require specialized certifications to take care of well-manicured golf courses and most professional and collegiate playing fields, there are many other positions in this area. Getting experience in facility management is easier at a larger school where you might have numerous sports and larger facilities as well as athletic department personnel who may hold membership in the International Association of Venue Managers (IAVM). There are also many well-qualified NIRSA members (see Chapter 4) who specialize in facility management employed on college campuses. Working with these professionals would give you the opportunity to gain some very good experience with the management of indoor and outdoor facilities. For those attending smaller schools, seeking apprenticeships or other experiential learning opportunities with similarly qualified individuals at any arena, stadium, convention center, or facility hosting sporting events will assist you in gaining much needed hands-on experience. Even working in a small nonsport facility in your hometown may expose you to an understanding of front-of-the-house ticket sales, customer service, and more.

While there may not be a great deal of top-level executive positions at any given venue, small to very large staffs are employed at different types of facilities. There are many stadiums, arenas, and convention centers for the multitude of sports in small and large cities, counties, and unincorporated areas. The responsibilities for those working in this area can be very broad. Management, maintenance, understanding and drafting contracts, budgeting, understanding facility systems, and/or becoming a certified pool operator (CPO) could make one's skill set quite unique, as could having a strong background in risk management (RM) or knowing how to write comprehensive RM plans.

The size of the facility affects the number of full-time positions available, but often some roles are contracted to outside firms. This is especially true for the areas of security; concessions; lighting; and heating, ventilation, and air conditioning (HVAC) control and maintenance. Additionally, any local sport facility can be a very good place to gain part-time experience in facility management as an usher, security official, supervisor, or concessions worker. In one five-month span between October 2008 and February 2009, the Tampa Bay area hosted the American League Divisional Playoffs, the American League playoffs, the World Series, and the Super Bowl. For the Super Bowl alone, 1,500 security personnel were needed. Selection and training began in August 2008. Good thing, because when the Tampa Bay Rays surprised everyone and made it to the playoffs, additional security was already available from the same security company, Sentry Event Services, that was the outside contractor for all events. Local college students, faculty members, and citizens from surrounding counties were called upon to fill many volunteer and paid positions for these events. While one might consider these to be event management positons, it is often the facility manager or a facility management company charged with selecting and training the individuals needed to pull off these events.

John Lee (Time Out Interview 5.2) has worked in facility management nearly his entire career. He recommends getting experience through an internship and a graduate assistantship (personal communication, September 2, 2016). This recommendation is especially important for any position in collegiate athletics or recreation.

Sport Marketing

Many sport organizations have a self-contained marketing department. In Chapter 3, we touched on marketing in professional sport. College athletic departments may also have sport marketing

Time Out Interview 5.2 with John Lee

FACILITY MANAGEMENT

Position	Associate Director, Campus Recreation – 15 Years
Employer	Wichita State University
B.A. Degree	Economics—Creighton University
M. Ed. Degree	Sports Administration—Wichita State University
Career Path	• Graduate Assistant – Wichita State University – 2 years
	• Assistant Director, Facilities – Wichita State University – 3 years
	• Assistant Director, Intramural Sports – Wichita State University – 5 years

Employment Recommendation

"Join a professional association related to facility management. By doing so, you can develop contacts and network with other professionals in the field which could be beneficial when you apply for your first facility management position. A degree in sport management or a related field is important, but it is just as important to work in facility management during your time in school."

---

personnel under the athletic department umbrella where promotion of events, sponsorship procurement, and ticket and advertising sales are the most prominent functions. This segment of sport marketing will focus on this function as a support role for the sport business industry.

Bill Gieseking (Time Out Interview 5.3) has worked in sales/marketing for his entire professional career at a beer distribution company in Tampa, FL. Bill's role helps support many community events, and his company is a major sponsor of most large sporting events and facilities in the Tampa Bay region. Thus, his company falls under the corporate segment of the Sport Employment Model in Chapter 1. His company, Pepin Distributing, markets through sport as discussed in the next paragraph.

Private sport marketing firms can vary in size and function. Some will solicit the business of teams, events, or other sport-related businesses. Their functions may include the design and implementation of a media or advertising campaign, the design or development of organizational brochures, the development and writing of a marketing or business plan for a client, and much more. Sport marketing functions can also be distinguished by the marketing of sport or marketing through sport. The marketing of sport typically involves the promotion of a team, event, or that of a sport-related product. An organization that has nothing at all to do with sport may hire a sport marketing firm if they desire to promote an aspect of their company through sport. One very good example where this is practiced on a regular basis is the Susan G. Komen Breast Cancer Foundation that often uses road races to raise money for research. The Race for the Cure

Time Out Interview 5.3 with Bill Gieseking
CORPORATE SUPPORT FOR SPORT BUSINESS INDUSTRY

Position	Director of Marketing – 23 years
Employer	Pepin Distributing Company
B.S. Degree	Marine Science—University of Tampa
Career Path	• Sales/Promotions – Pepin Distributing – 5 years
	• Sales Supervisor – Pepin Distributing – 5 years
	• Sales Manager – Pepin Distributing – 3 years

Employment Recommendation

"One needs strong people skills and be willing to commit to many hours. Be very flexible. Be community mindful and have social media skills. Be passionate!"

event certainly uses sport to raise awareness of the main purpose for their existence. Thus, if the foundation hires a sport marketing firm to design all race-related events, brochures, and media campaigns, this practice would be labeled outsourcing. Outsourcing a service is now a common phenomenon within the sport industry, and, according to Burden and Li (2009), outsourcing is a main reason for the loss of marketing positions within sport organizations. As a result, the entrepreneurial sport marketing firm becomes a primary need for many organizations. Research by Ratten & Ratten (2011) confirmed there is an "enormous potential" for entrepreneurial opportunities in sport marketing.

Public Relations/Sports Media/Social Media

In Chapter 3, we briefly discussed the placement of media within a professional sport organizational structure. In Chapter 4, we examined the role of the media in college athletics and provided an interview with a sports information director. In this section, we will cover other positions one could obtain in this area.

The role of media personnel working for independent television and radio stations and for the various media outlets or companies can be rewarding and, at the same time, exhausting. Travel can be a major responsibility of these individuals, especially for those who must travel large distances to cover major sporting events. Writing and broadcasting skills are both extremely important. Often, the role of photographer must also be assumed. The sport business major may have an inside track to some of these positions because of knowledge of a variety of sports. However, if the courses required for the major do not include courses in broadcasting or other desired media skills, it would behoove one to take additional electives, obtain a minor in journalism or digital media, and/or attend a sports broadcasting camp such as Play by Play

Sports Broadcasting Camps, Sports Broadcasting Camp, and Triangle Sportscaster Camp. Understanding and knowing how to record statistics for a variety of sports can qualify one to obtain entry-level positions in this area.

However, sport media goes far beyond taking statistics and getting in front of the television camera. Social media plays a major role for most organizations by engaging fans, assisting in marketing efforts, reporting scores, live streaming events, and much more. Individuals can also play a major role by developing their own media company. Megan Hueter (Time Out Interview 5.4) makes her living working in social media for WME/IMG, an international company mentioned earlier in the text.

Time Out Interview 5.4 with Megan Hueter
SOCIAL MEDIA

Position	VP, Digital/Social Media – 1 year
Employer	WME | IMG
B.S. Degree	Bachelor of Science, Health & Exercise Science— The College of New Jersey
M.A. Degree	Digital Communications—Johns Hopkins University
Career Path	• Intern – Ovarian Cancer National Alliance – 3 months • Freelance Writer – TheFinalSpring.com, HesFit.com – 2 years • Membership Director – DC Cancer Consortium – 1 year • Account Executive – Edelman Digital Public Affairs – 2 years • Senior Account Executive, Digital – Catalyst Public Relations – 2 years • Account Supervisor, Digital – Catalyst Public Relations – 2 years • Director, Digital – Catalyst Public Relations – 2 years • Director, Digital – WME | IMG – 1 year

Employment Recommendation

"In my company, there are a variety of different businesses you can get into ranging from talent representation, media rights, licensing, event operations, fashion, brand strategy/consulting, original content, etc. You really need to know what it is you want to do, and then focus on how you're going to get there by networking and constantly applying for open positions. Networking is typically the most valuable way to get in. My suggestion is to build your résumè with interesting case studies, and walk into interviews with a point of view on current topics and debates within the industry. Know who it is you're talking to and do your research. Confidence is key. I love meeting smart candidates that ask me as many questions as I ask them."

Laura Walden (Time Out Interview 5.5) owns her own communications company called Sports Features Communications, Inc., and her company fills a niche by focusing on the Olympics and Paralympic games. Laura runs her company out of central Florida but travels the world as a consultant assisting local organizing bodies in securing successful bids to host the Games. While both working in sports media, Megan and Laura followed very different career paths to their positions.

In order to obtain an understanding of this industry segment, one can gain extraordinary experience before graduating by volunteering for your college athletic department's sports information office, an on-campus radio or television station, your school newspaper, a sport business association newsletter, or related social media opportunities. You can also gain experience working at the media area for major events and/or writing if you possess excellent writing skills.

This can be a particularly difficult segment of the industry to enter and honing a complete set of skills is crucial. It is also recommended that students purchase a student membership in any related professional organization and attend one of their workshops or conferences.

Sports Commissions/Authorities

A sport commission or authority is usually a governing body made up of influential people nominated or selected by government officials. The purposes of such a governing body can be many, but, in most cases, these bodies are created for countries, states, counties, or local municipalities to foster the development of sport programs and facilities and increase tourism. While the building of facilities to house sporting events can be a tax burden on the local residents, bringing in or creating large events for the purpose of establishing income for local hotels, restaurants, and other businesses is the primary purpose of their existence. Promoting the image of a geographical region to what is now being coined major league or big league is another primary purpose. The term is generally used to classify large cities that have been able to attract and retain major sport franchises. A sports commission can play an immense role in attracting events and teams if the facilities exist to host large events. In fact, the majority of major sporting events are hosted in conjunction with some type of sports commission (Bradish, 2003). The National Association of Sports Commissions assists governmental bodies and/or privately funded authorities in the entire process for attracting sporting events with a goal of putting heads in beds—in other words, bringing individuals to town to increase the income of local hotels. Other businesses such as stores, gas stations, and restaurant owners enjoy the additional dollar in their bottom line as well. One of the midwestern cities reaching major league status was Oklahoma City after the Seattle Supersonics were purchased and subsequently moved in 2008, becoming the Oklahoma City Thunder. They built the Ford Center to house the team, and, according to Mayor Mick Cornett, the facility changed everything including the quality of life, pride, and employment (Luschen, 2009). A new, 20,000-seat, debt-free minor league baseball stadium, trails, parks, and a river sports facility called the Chesapeake Boathouse were also built contributing to the transformation (Moore, 2013).

Time Out Interview 5.5 with Laura Walden
COMMUNICATIONS

Position	Director/Owner – 15 Years
Employer	Sports Features Communications, Inc.
Technical Degree	Fashion Merchandising—Barbizon School of Fashion Merchandising and Modeling
Career Path	• Editorial Assistant – Pandora News & Press Features, Rome, Italy – 2 years
	• Managing Editor – Journal of Experimental & Clinical Cancer Research, Rome, Italy – 10 years
	• Freelance, Film and Television Translator & Script Reconstruction, Rome, Italy – 3 years
	• Secretariat & Editorial Assistant – SportEurope Official Magazine, European Olympic Committees (EOC) – 11 years
	• French & English Editor – International Labor Sports Federation (CSIT) – 4 years
	• Assistant to Mario Pescante – Rome 2004 Olympic Bid, Turin 2006 Olympic Bid – 3 years
	• Partnership – Sportcal, London, United Kingdom – 2 years
	• Managed Media and PR – Dr. Jacques Rogge IOC Presidential Bid, Rome, Italy – 2 years
	• Media, PR & Editorial – World Olympians Association (WOA) – 5 months
	• Olympic Media Consultant – Wyland Foundation – 5 months
	• Director Media Relations, Back Softball – International Softball Federation (ISF) – 9 months
	• Olympics Sports Consultant – Buckner Law – 8 months
	• International Media Advisor – PyeongChang 2018 Olympic Winter Games, PyeongChang, South Korea – 4 years

Employment Recommendation

"Research sports organizations in which you are interested and volunteer if needed to get a foot in the door. If the organizations stage sports events, attend their meets, and try to network and meet as many key people in the sectors for which you are interested in working. Take plenty of personal business cards and prepare a quick USB drive with your résumé and portfolio of updated work so you have it on hand when the opportunity arrives to pitch yourself for a job opening."

Every course in sport governance should include content on sport commissions or sport authorities. Through the study of these organizations, one can learn a great deal about government, public and private organizations, and politics. Yes, politics. An examination of a variety of news articles covering sports commissions, authorities, or other governmental entities elicited a great deal of information about their political makeup and issues with which these boards have dealt. Topics revealed in the articles examined included appointment or dismissals from boards; financing/development/hosting of services, events, or facilities; development, dissolution, investigation, or reform; and cutting deals to teams. However, these issues are not isolated to the United States (see Suggested Readings for this chapter). Religion has become a major international issue whereby governments acting as their countries sports authority interject control over image, participation, uniform, and gender.

This all sounds as if these specialized bodies are only wrought with problems. This often happens if individuals are only hired or appointed because they will have an inside tract with the opportunity to rub elbows with rich, famous, and well-connected sports figures and top-level executives. However, if these commissions are ethically run with the main purpose for which they were intended, résumés of the well-qualified sport managers should be at the top of the stack. Having an understanding of politics would add to one's experiential background.

Sports commissions can provide tremendous opportunities for volunteer, part-time, and full-time positions when they bring major events to a municipality. Thus, future sport managers should consider these positions as major opportunities to work in event management when they provide the local citizenry with sport programming and facilities or attract major events such as the Super Bowl, college bowl games, NCAA events of all kinds, and other professional and amateur sport national championship or annual events.

Sport Tourism

As defined in Chapter 1, sport tourism is traditionally defined as active (travel to participate in sport) and passive (travel to watch sport) (Gibson & Fairley, 2011). However, we believe there is another neglected component of this description. Sport enthusiasts, including sport management professors, often travel to tour facilities and often have on their bucket list the goal to visit every facility for a particular league. Regardless, sport tourism is on the upswing. Hinch and Higham (2011) state the "scale, complexity, and potential of sport tourism along with the expanding mutual interests of sport and tourism industries that have developed as a consequence, demand that academic and industry expertise be directed towards this field" (p. 3).

A short review of literature found researchers are writing sport tourism articles on cycling, surfing, golf, windsurfing, horse riding, scuba diving, baseball, the Olympic/Paralympic Games, winter sports, and more (see Suggested Readings for this chapter). Sport tourism has been happening for centuries. It is now being recognized as a more targeted segment of the industry in which to gain employment. We provided the above topics simply to exhibit a small sampling of how much opportunity exists for a sport tourism entrepreneur. One could partner with a trained travel agent and create all kinds of prospects for a long and satisfying career.

Sporting Goods/Apparel

A career within the sporting goods or sports apparel industry can be widely varied. One can work within the retail industry where stores are often located in malls or shopping centers. This can be a great part-time job while in high school or college, though work hours are often unpredictable and can be quite long during holiday seasons. A manager must often fill in for less responsible employees who do not show up. However, the rise to the position of store manager can be quick (generally from 18 months to two years) and financially rewarding if this type of environment is suitable to the individual's career interests. The manager must be very astute to the problems surely to be encountered revolving around human resource management and shoplifting. If working with a large sporting goods chain, a promotion to regional sales manager where you may supervise other store managers is often the next step up the corporate ladder. Extensive travel can be involved.

If the retail store is not your choice for a career work environment, working as either a manufacturer's or independent sales representative can be quite lucrative. Many individuals prefer this environment if they like sales because the work schedule is typically flexible. However, to be successful here, one needs to be a very good time manager and a self-starter with a great deal of motivation for success.

A manufacturer's representative represents a single company or several companies. Most often, an individual in this type of position is self-employed and may be an independent contractor for large companies. When an individual represents a single company, they are generally assigned a specific territory. Caren Fiorillo (Time Out Interview 5.6) indicates her position in the sales industry is all about networking and relationship building (personal communication, September 15, 2016).

Companies operate differently, but a career involving this industry can be very profitable for the individual who is an effective self-starter. It is recommended to start in retail sales and learn as much as possible about individual products, because product knowledge is extremely important to develop a life-long career in this segment of the industry. The positions mentioned above are not the only ones that exist in this industry, but it is a typical snapshot of what one may experience in getting started.

ENTREPRENEURIAL CAREERS

Many individuals look to start their own business related to sport. A sport business can be tied to anything and, often, consulting represents some aspect of the business. Many small sport businesses are tied to event management, sport marketing, athlete representation, and consulting. Taking a class in entrepreneurship or one that assists you in walking through the step-by-step

Time Out Interview 5.6 with Caren Fiorillo
SPORTING GOODS

Position	Sales Pro – 3 years
Employer	BSN Sports
B.S. Degree	Sport Management – Flagler College
Career Path	• Intern – Nancy Lieberman Enterprises – 9 months • Assistant WBB Coach – Lees-McRae College – 3 years • Assistant WBB Coach – University of Maine – 2 years • Assistant WBB Coach – Indiana/Purdue University-Fort Wayne – 2 years

Employment Recommendation

"It is not just about selling Nike and Under Armour or field equipment. It is about creating relationships, networking and creating a great atmosphere for the student athletes and coaches."

---

process for starting a new business is especially helpful. Some institutions offer major or a minor in entrepreneurial management.

Before starting a business, get experience by working with one or more sport organizations. Learning how others handle the day-to-day operations of different types of business or responsibilities can be very insightful. You can hone your skills and obtain a network of individuals that can attest to your business acumen and abilities. An entrepreneur generally develops expertise in one or more areas before beginning their own business venture. It is not uncommon to work 10 or more years to develop the necessary skills and business knowledge before venturing into the world of business ownership.

Other skills a business owner should possess would be acute attention to detail, organizational skills, knowledge of business plans, and the ability to obtain business financing. Understanding accounting procedures would also be extremely important unless you can afford to hire a personal accountant. It is also recommended that an attorney be hired to make sure business paperwork is in order and to establish contracts, including waivers and other legal paperwork needed for different types of businesses. Of course, attorneys are not a required hire, but one skilled in business law can assist the new business owner in making sure everything necessary is covered.

When starting a business, a full stable of employees is not always needed. Immediate staffing will depend upon the business type and its initial size, personal organizational skills, and more. Brian Hoek (Time Out Interview 5.7), president of Pinstripes Media, LLC in Rockville, MD, runs his advertising business by himself, but outsources certain tasks depending upon the current project. His recommendation when running a business on one's own is to not take on

Time Out Interview 5.7 with Brian Hoek
SALES & ADVERTISING

Position	President – 13 years
Employer	Pinstripes Media, LLC
B.S. Degree	Sport Management—Western Carolina University
Career Path	• Intern – Albany River Rats – 3 months
	• Account Executive – Baltimore Bandits – 1 year
	• Director of Ticket Sales – Chesapeake Icebreakers – 1 year
	• Director of Corporate Sponsorships – Chesapeake Icebreakers – 1 year
	• Senior Account Executive – Home Team Sports/SportsNet Marketing Manager – 5 years

Employment Recommendation

"Don't be too hyper-focused on a straight-line path from Point A to Point B based on where you think you want to be down the road in future years. Have an open mind when it comes to what an opportunity can offer you—it may not immediately be apparent. I could not have anticipated I would be doing what I am doing today and loving every minute of it. Although I am not working for a sports team/organization, I am engaged with many of them through a client's product and a role I fulfill that allows me to represent Pinstripes Media. This has me engaged with athletic trainers of professional and college teams, directly with professional athletes in the NHL, MLB, NFL, and Arena Football League, and with media organizations nationwide (the product is Boost Oxygen)."

I would also recommend any entrepreneur watch the CNBC show The Profit. It's an incredible show that focuses on Marcus Lemonis, the CEO of Camping World, and how he invests his own time and money in helping small entrepreneurial businesses.

---

too many projects simultaneously so you do not become overwhelmed. In other words, when running a one-person business, the size and length of a project will dictate how many projects can be concurrently handled. Finding reliable companies and individuals to hire as independent contractors, when a particular project dictates assistance will be necessary, is extremely important and can lead to additional income (personal communication, September 15, 2016).

Marketing personal skills and knowledge and the pricing of those skills and talents can be a tricky task, especially at the outset of a new venture. Trial and error, as well as market demands for your services, will be prime factors in establishing a pricing structure. Entrepreneurs charge either on an hourly or per project basis. Obviously, pricing a project on an hourly rate will require more documentation and personal time than establishing a project fee.

Marketing your services can be accomplished through advertising or networking. Once again, the size of your business, as well as the existence of competing companies offering the same or similar product, will be relevant determining factors for the amount or type of marketing a business will need to maintain sustainable growth and a comfortable level of financial income. Word-of-mouth and networking can be great marketing and advertising methodologies at very little cost to the business. A one-person business that relies on networking and a satisfied clientele will take a business in sometimes unfamiliar or unexpected directions, leading to beneficial learning, partnerships, and relationships. Every person met can have a potential impact on your professional future. They can become trusted friends or partners that assist in those larger projects (B. Hoek, personal communication, February 12, 2017).

Risk management (RM) in sport is a newer type of entrepreneurial venture. A risk manager's main role is to prevent injuries by keeping facilities and sporting events safe. However, there is, oh, so much more. According to Monica Rusch, the senior director of risk management for the Houston Astros,

> One objective of RM is to understand and manage risk versus eliminating risk and volatility. RM is proactive and forward looking, whereas problem management is reactive. It is the process by which we systematically identify, educate, train, measure, and manage various types of risk inherent within the sports industry. Prepare, plan, and communicate are the three critical functions for successful risk management programs. Managing risk in the sports industry is important in identifying risk factors, communicating those risk factors to assist in decision making—ultimately improving the bottom line. (personal communication, January 13, 2017)

Risk managers in sport very often work for insurance companies and conduct audits for clients who own sport facilities. However, since large sporting events and venues are now high-level terrorist targets, risk management consultants can play a very important role in assisting organizations in writing comprehensive risk management plans. While many teams do not have dedicated or advertised positions in RM, Ms. Rusch has observed more teams adding individual RM positions, but the responsibilities of a risk manager may also be housed under finance or human resources (personal communication, January 13, 2017). We have also observed an increase in the number of sport-related job announcements, particularly in recreational sport, asking for risk management knowledge and skills.

The Department of Homeland Security runs workshops for sport facility professional associations and law enforcement agencies as both play important roles in maintaining safe facilities, but terrorism has only heightened the knowledge and importance of having a detailed and practiced RM plan. Any sport-related facility, foundation, camp, youth agency, or other organization running events must have a well-written and documented RM plan to make events and facilities safe and prevent injuries, thus curtailing lawsuits. Foster and McPhee (2017) are proposing a comprehensive 10-step model for use in writing sport-related risk management plans for organizations.

Risk management is one of those areas where you have to identify and sell your skills as a consultant to the sport business industry. Ian McGregor (Time Out Interview 5.8) has done a very good job of making RM his life career, particularly as it relates to the recreational sport management segment. His experiential background while working on his academic degrees introduced him to college athletics and recreational sport management that threw him into the fire for running sporting events and managing sport facilities. Just like Amy Mallett commented that one must get experience before becoming a consultant, so, too, Ian McGregor states, "You first need to build up sufficient knowledge and experience so you can claim you have 'sat in the chair' and have the expertise to share" (personal communication, August 24, 2016).

Time Out Interview 5.8 with Ian McGregor
RISK MANAGEMENT CONSULTING

Position	President – 12 years
Employer	McGregor & Associates
B.S. Degree	Chemistry—University of Aberdeen
Ph. D. Degree	Chemistry—Simon Fraser University
Career Path	• Graduate Assistant – Simon Fraser University – 5 years
	• Chemistry Instructor – Capilano University
	• Intramural Coordinator – Simon Fraser University – 4 years
	• Director of Recreation – Simon Fraser University – 6 years
	• Director, Athletics & Recreation – St. Mary's University – 5 years
	• Director, Athletics & Recreation – University of Toronto – 5 years
	• Director, Athletics & Recreation – Dominican University – 6 years

Employment Recommendation

"Get a ton of experience before embarking on a consulting career. You need credibility to survive in the consulting world, and the best way to achieve this is get broad-based experience in the area of managing risk in the field you have chosen, e.g., campus recreation, municipal recreation etc."

Amy Mallett (Time Out Interview 5.9) intertwines college athletics and the law and exhibits how skills and knowledge obtained can transfer into an exciting and fulfilling consulting career. Amy Perkins Mallett obtained a law degree after playing collegiate volleyball. She worked for college athletic departments, the Big East Conference, and the NCAA. Her responsibilities primarily involved athletic compliance, membership services, and athlete academic support. She was able to eventually use this background to obtain her current position where she works as a consultant for a firm who contracts with athletic departments often working on Title IX investigations.

Time Out Interview 5.9 with Amy Perkins Mallett
CONSULTANT/ COLLEGE SPORTS REGULATORY

Position	Consultant – 2 years
Employer	The Compliance Group
B.A. Degree	St. Thomas University School of Law
Career Path	• Law Clerk – Law offices of Tacher and Fee – 2 years
	• Assistant Athletic Director for Compliance – American International College – 3 years
	• Assistant Commissioner for Compliance – Big South Conference – 2 years
	• Assistant Director of Membership Svc – NCAA – 3 years
	• Assistant Commissioner for Compliance – Big East Conference – 1 year
	• Senior Associate Athletic Director – University of South Florida – 9 years

Employment Recommendation

"The fastest way to gain the confidence of clients is to speak to them about their challenges and empathize with their struggles. I don't spend much time on it, but I will share an example or two from my past that demonstrates to them they are not alone and there is a solution we can get to without too much heartache for anyone. Of course, this is for a job that is to fix or resolve an issue. A contract designed to help a client build from scratch is focused more on setting the vision, but still with some example of how that vision can be translated into a functional reality."

THE FINAL BUZZER

The intent of this chapter is to assist students in their exploration of some nontraditional careers many may not have considered. While some only think of major teams or individual sports for employment, this chapter adds to the initial premise introduced in Chapter 1 (i.e., the size of the sport industry is unfathomable to most people). This chapter supports many categories displayed in the Sport Employment Model (Figure 1.1). From the highlighted risk management consulting businesses to the entrepreneurial spirit displayed in founding Sports Features Communications and Pinstripes Media, opportunities available in this industry are created one business at a time. Fortunately, for many aspiring interns and entry-level employees, sport-related businesses are created every day.

EXPERIENTIAL LEARNING OPPORTUNITIES

Classroom Experiential Learning Exercise: Marketing/Event Class Project

Students are required to develop a proposal for executing a half-time performance/event at a men's basketball game. In the proposal, an element of competition and showcasing the game-day sponsor throughout the planned event must be incorporated. Each group has 30 minutes to present, followed by a 10-minute question and answer period. The assistant athletic director (AAD), who oversees marketing, fundraising, and community engagement for the university, is invited to class to listen to all presentations and make the final selection of the group that will be awarded the opportunity to execute their event.

All presentations must include specific details as to how the event will be executed including applicable music, time frame, materials needed for the event, set-up, break-down, etc. Students whose proposals are not selected assist with the event's execution and are given direction by the winning proposal team. After the event, a follow-up meeting is held that includes the AAD where the main purpose is to discuss the execution and success of the half-time event. This gives everyone a chance to evaluate the event and project.

Submitted by Dr. Dené Williamson, Assistant Professor, and
Dr. Leon Mohan, Associate Professor
Saint Leo University, Saint Leo, FL

Program Experiential Learning Example: Field Trips

The Department of Sport Management provides a variety of immersion experiences for the students during the academic year. These include trips to Lake Placid, NY; Los Angeles, CA; New England; Europe; Ireland; and Australia. Leading up to each of the immersion trips, students are required to do significant research on the current issues within the industry as well as the organizations and individuals with which they are meeting at the respective location.

A spring break trip to Los Angeles, CA, includes tours and lectures of over 30 sport organizations including the LA Lakers, LA Clippers, Staples Center, Rose Bowl, Stub Hub Center, Fox Sports, CAA, AEG, UCLA, and more. Students are exposed to all facets of the sport industry during this week-long trip including event management, marketing, sponsorship, media, agency, and facilities. A second trip to Boston, Massachusetts, at the end of the spring semester is also sponsored. Students have the opportunity to learn from industry leaders during this seven-day trip that includes stops at Boston Celtics, New England Revolution, TD Garden, Kraft Sports Group, Gillette Stadium, Team Epic, and ESPN. During both of these trips, students have an opportunity to network with and learn from industry professionals, resulting in several internships.

Submitted by Dr. Gina Arlene Pauline, Associate Professor and Undergraduate Director
Syracuse University, Syracuse, NY

SUGGESTED READINGS

AFP. (2016, April 9). Saudis take action against footballer hairstyles deemed 'anti-Islamic'. *Daily Sabah*. Retrieved online from http://www.dailysabah.com/asia/2016/04/09/saudis-take-action-against-footballer-hairstyles-deemed-anti-islamic

Alan, S. (2004, December 14). Sports authority approves Tampa Bay Lightning tax break. *Tampa Tribune*. Retrieved from tampatribune.fl.newsmemory.com

Almond, E. (2016, November 29). College Cup returns to San Jose after NCAA abandons North Carolina. Retrieved from Newspaper Source Plus. (Accession Number: 2W62743087536).

Booth, T. (2016, October). Investment group offers to foot cost of Seattle arena. *Spokesman Review*. Retrieved from http://www.athleticbusiness.com/stadium-arena/investment-group-offers-to-pay-full-cost-of-new-seattle-arena.html

Brown, G. P., Hixson, E., & McCabe, V. (2013). Privileged mobility: Employment and experience at the Olympic Games. *Journal of Sport Tourism, 18*(4), 265–286.

Buning, R. J., & Gibson, H. J. (2016). Exploring the trajectory of active-sport-event travel careers: A social world's perspective. *Journal of Sport Management, 30*(3), 265–281.

Danielson, M. N. (1997). *Home Team: Professional Sports and the American Metropolis*. Princeton, NJ: Princeton University Press.

Davis, A. C. (2015, October 18). Big money in Congress, and now in D.C. politics. *Washington Post*. Retrieved from www.washingtonpost.com

Drakakis, P., & Papadaskalopous, A. (2014). Economic contribution of active sport tourism: The case of four sport activities in Messinia, Greece. *Journal of Sport Tourism, 19,* (3-4), 199–231.

Getz, D., & McConnell, A. (2011). Serious sport tourism and event travel careers. *Journal of Sport Management, 25*(4), 326–338.

Hammond, J. (2012, May 7). Bureau may host events a la sports commission. *Regional Business News*. Retrieved from Regional Business News.

Hauslohner, A. (2015, April 23). Mayor picks lobbyist to chair convention and sports authority. *Washington Post*. Retrieved from www.washingtonpost.com

Hinz, G. (2011, December 19). State politics ain't beanbag; It's baseball. *Crain's Chicago Business, 34*(51). Retrieved from Regional Business News.

Hodeck, A., & Hovemann, G. (2015). Destination choice in German winter sport tourism. *Polish Journal of Sport and Tourism, 22*(2), 114–117.

Hussain, M. (2015, February 16). Muslims and Islam in sports. *Gatestone Institute*. Retrieved from https://www.gatestoneinstitute.org/5207/muslims-islam-sports

Kaiser, S., Alfs, C., Beech, J., & Kaspar, R. (2013). Challenges of tourism development in winter sports destinations and for post-even tourism marketing: The cases of the Ramsau Nordic Ski World Championships 1999 and the St. Anton Alpine Ski World Championships 2001. *Journal of Sport Tourism, 18*(1), 33–48.

Kotlarsky, S. (2013). What's all the noise about: Did the New York Yankees violate fans' First Amendment rights by banning Vuvuzelas in Yankee Stadium? *Jeffrey S. Moorad Sports Law Journal, 20,* 35–67.

Masters, R. (2016, August 24). Australian Olympic shake-up proposes federal take-over of state sports institutes. *The Sydney Morning Herald*. Retrieved from http://www.smh.com.au/sport

Nwoke, S. (2016, October 16). Sports development: Revert to old ways, Okorodudu, Nwamuda tell sports authorities. *Vanguard*. Retrieved from http://www.vanguardngr.com/2016/10/sports-development-revert-old-ways-okorodudu-nwamuda-tell-sports-authorities/

Reardon, D. (2016, February 24). Sports commission better for Hawaii than politics. *Honolulu Star Advertiser*. Retrieved from Honolulu Star Advertiser. (Accession Number: 2W61731445068).

Rishe, P. (2011, October 5). Educating sports commissions and CVBs about the economic impact of sports. *Forbes*. Retrieved from http://www.forbes.com/sites/prishe/2011/10/05/educating-sports-commissions-and-cvbs-about-the-economic-impact-of-sports/#348cec29670b

Roach, E. (2012, September 2). Palm Beach County Sports Commission scores with hometown leader. *Palm Beach Post*. Retrieved from: Newspaper Source Plus. (Accession number: 2W6887037254).

Salinero, M. (2015, December 2). Bucs, sports authority agree on $100 million deal for stadium upgrades. *Tampa Bay Times*. Retrieved from http://www.tbo.com/news/politics/hillsborough-looks-to-carve-a-niche-in-competitive-amateur-sports-market-20141207/

Salinero, M. (2014, December 7). Hillsborough looks to carve a niche in competitive amateur sports market. *Tampa Bay Times*. Retrieved from http://www.tbo.com/news/politics/deal-would-give-rayjay-100m-in-renovations-20151202/

Schmitt, W. (2016, December 9). Political campaigns raked in millions after Missourians voted for contribution limits. *Springfield News-Leader*. Retrieved from http://www.news-leader.com/story/news/politics/2016/12/09/political-campaigns-raked-millions-after-most-missourians-voted-contribution-limits/95010100/

Shank, M. D., & Lyberger, M. R. (2015). *Sports Marketing: A Strategic Perspective* (5th Ed). New York, NY: Routledge.

Silva, C. (2010, January 13). Under new deal, Al Lang Field could be home to baseball again. *St. Petersburg Times*. Retrieved from http://www.tampabay.com/news/localgovernment/under-new-deal-al-lang-field-could-be-home-to-baseball-again/1064876

Towner, N. (2016). Community participation and emerging surfing tourism destination: A case study of the Mentawai Islands. *Journal of Sport Tourism, 20*(1), 1–19.

Usher, L. E., & Gomez, E. (2016). Surf localism in Costa Rica: Exploring territoriality among Costa Rica and foreign resident surfers. *Journal of Sport Tourism, 20*(23-4), 195–216.

Vos, S., Vandermeerschen, H., & Scheerder, J. (2016). Balancing between coordination, cooperation and competition? A mixed-method approach for assessing the role of ambiguity of local sports authorities. *International Journal of Sport Policy and Politics, 8*(3), 403–419.

Wade, C. M. (2009, March 17). Sports authority chief resigns. *Tampa Tribune*. Retrieved from Newspaper Source Plus.

Waller, S., Trendafilova, S., & Daniell, R. (2014). Did the 2012 World Series positively impact the image of Detroit?: Sport as a transformative agent in changing images of tourism destinations. *Journal of Sport Tourism, 19*(1), 79–100.

REFERENCES

Bradish, C. L. (2003). *An examination of the relationship between regional sport commissions and organizational structure.* (Doctoral dissertation). Retrieved from Proquest Dissertations and Theses Global. (Order No. 3137410).

Burden, W., & Li, M. (2009). Minor League Baseball: Exploring the growing interest in outsourced sport marketing. *Sport Marketing Quarterly, 18*(3), 139–149.

Contorno, S. (2016, April 11). Yankees, Tampa Sports Authority agree to $40 million renovation of Steinbrenner Field. *Tampa Bay Times*. Retrieved from http://www.tampabay.com/blogs/baybuzz/yankees-tampa-sports-authority-agree-to-40-million-renovation-of/2272730

Foster, S. B., & McPhee, J. (2017). *A review of risk management literature in sport: Developing a model for student understanding.* Manuscript in preparation.

Gibson, H., & Fairley, S. (2011). Sport tourism. In Pederson, P., Parks, J., Quarterman, J., & Thibault, L. (Eds.), *Contemporary Sport Management* (4th Ed) (pp. 226–243). Champaign, IL: Human Kinetics.

Hinch, T., & Higham, J. (2011). *Sport Tourism Development* (2nd Ed.). Buffalo, NY: Channel View Publications.

Logistics. (n.d.). *In Dictionary.com Unabridged.* Retrieved from http://www.dictionary.com/browse/logistics

Luschen, B. (2009, May 11). Oklahoma City grows into a big league city. *NewsOK*, p. 1.

Moore, T. (2013). Catalyst for democracy? Outcomes and processes in community-university interaction. *Journal of Community Engagement and Scholarship, 6*(1), 70–80, 145.

Ratten, V., & Ratten, H. (2011). International sport marketing: Practical and future research implications. *Journal of Business & Industrial Marketing, 26*(9), 614–620.

Tecău, A. S. (2016). The role of international internships conducted during academic studies in development of entrepreneurial skills. *Bulletin of the Transilvania University of Braşov Series V: Economic Sciences, 9*(58) 1, 169–176.

Varela, A. A. (2016, August 16). Mexican winner in Rio despite sports authorities. *The Baja Post*. Retrieved from http://thebajapost.com/2016/08/16/mexican-winner-in-rio-despite-sports-authorities/

CHAPTER
6

Sport Business Industry Overview: Teaching Sport Management

"During college, my professors emphasized giving back and helping others. They made the greatest impact on my life. I realized, at that time, I was going to become a college professor so I could help and give back to others."
—Dr. Donna Pastore, Professor, Ohio State University, Columbus, OH

THE WARM UP

The workplace of today has changed quite drastically from that of 1995. At that time, a student graduating with an undergraduate degree from an accredited four-year institution was fairly assured of employment opportunities based upon completion of the college degree. College graduates were recruited and provided exciting career opportunities in their respective fields. A college graduate could expect to earn, on average, $43,000 a year across a 30-year career, as opposed to a high school graduate with no college experience earning $19,500 a year in the same career span (Lacey & Crosby, 2005). The United States Department of Labor (2015) reported in 2003, workers with a college degree earned, on average, 62% more wages than workers with only a high school education. Additionally, between 2002 and 2012, 14 million plus job openings were projected to be filled by entry-level workers who have earned a college diploma. In the time span since 1995, enough students have passed through graduation doors from accredited university undergraduate programs to glut the job market. In order to create a job market edge in the competition for employment, one must now supersede the undergraduate degree; in many sport business professions, one must have a master's degree.

Thus, many employees are returning to graduate school in search of the next boost up their personal career ladder, both financially and status-wise. This movement has been accelerated by the demand for advanced training for promotion-worthy employees. Essentially, one must get ahead to stay ahead. The master's degree has been a very successful vehicle for the faster track. Touted as the highest applied degree, the master's degree is based upon a successful undergraduate degree from an accredited education institution, a minimum overall GPA for all undergraduate coursework, successful application to the respective graduate program, and an acceptable performance score on any one of several standardized post-graduate examinations such as the Graduate Record Exam (GRE). Upon successful completion of this graduate degree, the graduate student should have a litany of new, cutting-edge academic skills to apply to the respective job setting. As a result, the career ladder continues with leadership opportunities and advanced financial status, all in response to the degree.

In the field of sport management, the graduate student can pursue the master's degree in sport management (MA or MS), choose the business route and seek the master's of business administration (MBA) degree, or seek an education related degree (MEd) if, perhaps, they wish to move into college coaching or institutional administration. All three of these graduate degrees can provide successful educational support for advanced training and career advancement in the broad scope of employment in sport and sport organizations. So, how does one go about getting into the right graduate program for their a specific career goal?

WHEN IS A MASTER'S DEGREE REQUIRED?

The three areas of sport management where one should strongly consider heading straight to graduate school after completing an undergraduate degree are college athletic administration, college coaching, and campus recreational sport. Since you would be working in a collegiate setting, often the master's degree is the minimum degree expected in order to join faculty and some staff ranks. The easiest way to enter into any one of these three industry segments is through the graduate assistantship defined in Chapter 1, briefly discussed in Chapter 4, and explored later in this chapter.

If you are aspiring to enter into professional sport management (Chapter 3) or entry-level positions with Olympic and amateur sports (Chapter 4), many industry professionals would recommend getting full-time experience before heading to graduate school. In some cases, at least two years are recommended. In fact, some organizations will pay for you to attend graduate school after you have been with the company for a predetermined length of time.

Graduate School: Now What?

If you have decided to enter a master's degree program, much of the information in the previous five chapters is applicable to you. Those of you graduating with an undergraduate degree in sport management probably already have experience. However, many probably did not select sport management as an undergraduate field of study. Begin getting experience right away. Your professional network is probably weak if you have not served an internship with a sport organization. Hopefully, the graduate program selected expects or recommends everyone to get involved. With the number of online graduate programs in sport management increasing, the face-to-face contact with well-connected faculty is seriously diminished. If this is your situation, get to know your online professors and ask them to help you establish network contacts. If they do not have any, you will need to embark on your own network-building project and make the contacts on your own. This book was designed to help you do exactly that. Most master's degree curriculums are comprised of approximately 33–36 hours of coursework (nine to 10 classes), culminating with a major research paper (three credit hours) and/or an internship (three or more credit hours) as capstone courses to the degree. Some programs require more than 36 hours once the capstone courses are included, which are usually completed during the last semester of the graduate degree. Once finished, the graduate student should have a clear indication of the career path they wish to pursue. Occasionally, one may decide to remain in school; the doctoral degree will be discussed later in this chapter.

In Chapter 2, we mentioned that some academic programs may have specialty areas. The following examples will help to illustrate program specialties in more depth. The University of North Carolina offers a specialty program to graduate students with a specialization in sport administration. Claimed to be the first in the United States, this two-year curriculum focuses on preparing graduate students for professional careers in collegiate athletic administration. However, students pursuing this curriculum also obtain teaching experience in their first year which complements our discussion in Chapter 4 about the dual responsibilities of college coaches.

Texas A&M University's sport management program offers a specialty program that addresses intercollegiate athletics. The Laboratory for the Study of Intercollegiate Athletics has a primary mission to advance and enhance how intercollegiate athletics is managed through conducting scientific research.

The University of Southern Mississippi provides students with the opportunity to participate in the National Center for Spectator Sports Safety and Security, promoted through their master's degree in sport management, with an emphasis in sport event security management. This program is the first of its kind in the

Sport event security management is an important skill learned in many sport management programs. (Courtesy of iStockphoto)

United States. The design of this 36-credit hour program is to provide special event managers with specialization skills and knowledge needed to meet risk management capabilities and challenges associated with homeland defense and security in sports environments.

There are many other such opportunities available to the inquiring prospective student. A quick means to access those graduate programs with sport management curricula and, perhaps, additional specialty opportunities would be to access the North American Society for Sport Management (NASSM) website. Choose your preferred graduate school and embark on a graduate program search.

HAVE YOU CONSIDERED TEACHING SPORT MANAGEMENT?

In consideration of career opportunities after graduate school, most sport management textbooks do not include nor discuss the position of sport management instructor/professor as a career field. McNiff (2013) researched the early career experiences of graduates of sport management programs. Included in the study were individuals who possessed bachelor's, master's, or doctoral degrees. Three of 32 individuals studied were teaching sport management at the college level, and one was teaching high school, although the teaching field was not specified. In this study, age was reported to be a factor for some of the individuals and, thus, could be a determining factor regarding the decision to enter the teaching profession. While instructors and professors are not working directly with or for a sport organization, many courses taught in the graduate program encircle sport. Thus, we decided to discuss this very rewarding career segment in this stand-alone chapter. There are many career paths that may lead to one making the decision to teach sport management where obtaining the terminal degree is the ultimate goal for many. In the ensuing paragraphs, we discuss several rewarding teaching paths, two of which do not include obtaining a doctorate.

Before discussing the doctoral degree, it's important to describe the pursuit of this career field in a little more depth. In route to the doctorate, some individuals pursue a master's with an emphasis in sport management while others may obtain a master's of business administration (MBA) since the majority of sport management courses include the application of business to sport. While obtaining a business-related degree is not necessary, a business degree may carry more influence when pursuing a position, especially within a college or school of business at a post-secondary institution. Understandably, this depends on the particular academic institution. Many professors in sport management do not possess a business degree because the preponderance of sport management degree granting programs early on, at any academic level, were not housed in business departments. However, there has been an observable shift of the positioning of some programs in this direction. In order to staff the programs moving in this direction, business departments are recognizing excellent teaching professors with equally impressive research agendas can very capably fill positions within schools of business without possessing a business degree. This is primarily due to the reality that professors with a sport management background possess the qualifications to teach the application of business to sport because many have held positions within the sport industry at some point in their careers. Students respect the ability of their professors to relate real-world industry experience in the classroom. In fact, this type of background makes the classroom come alive for many students. The classroom and program experiential learning examples at the end of each chapter in this textbook are strong testimonials to the business-related assignments provided in sport management programs. In fact, an examination of many sport management faculty positions will ask applicants to have sport industry experience and may not require a business degree.

Please be aware schools, colleges, or departments of sport business possess accreditation by one of three business accrediting bodies. The Association to Advance Collegiate Schools of Business (AACSB) is considered the Cadillac of accreditations for business schools to possess. Most larger universities and some smaller ones pursue this accreditation and accreditation requirements can impact the credentials faculty members possess. Thus, many position announcements will indicate applicants must have taught in an AACSB-accredited university or, at the very least, must possess at least one business-related degree. Therefore, this can impact where one chooses to obtain a master's or doctoral degree. Additionally, these institutions most likely will be looking for an individual with a desire to conduct research or already have an established research agenda with published refereed articles in top-tier professional journals. Other business accrediting bodies are not as stringent in terms of faculty selected. Often, this is because their institution may put a greater emphasis on teaching than research.

There is also a specialized accreditation process for sport management/business programs administered by the Commission on Sport Management Accreditation (COSMA). Institutions that have gone through this accreditation process has had their entire sport management program reviewed by experts in the field. While COSMA is not a required accreditation, their process does provide the student additional confidence that the faculty and program requirements have undergone additional scrutiny based on quality benchmarks. More information about COSMA was discussed in Chapter 2.

PURSUING A DOCTORATE IN SPORT MANAGEMENT

Some master's graduates will choose to remain in school and pursue yet another graduate degree. Referred to as a terminal degree, or the highest attainable degree in the academic field, this degree is formally called a doctorate, with those earning it are referred to as Doctor. Many faculty teaching in colleges across the country have earned this degree, and most institutions recognize either a PhD, an EdD, or DBA. The PhD degree is a doctor of philosophy degree and is granted to anyone matriculating from the institution, having completed all degree requirements (approximately 72 hours above the master's degree), including a dissertation. The dissertation usually takes a minimum of one academic year to complete; for some, much longer, especially if the degree is being pursued on a part-time basis. Some may consider this to be a seriously long term paper, but it is a major research undertaken with guidance by at least three established professors. One alternative to the PhD degree, the EdD, is considered to be a doctorate in education. When sport management programs are housed in an education department, this is often the degree granted. In most graduate program settings, the pursuit of either doctorate can be identical. However, at some institutions offering both degrees, sometimes the PhD is touted as the research doctorate while the EdD is considered the teaching doctorate, but this is rare. The DBA stands for doctorate of business administration. This degree is similar to a PhD in its requirements. Other universities offer specialized doctoral degrees that use different designations, but these are also rare. One such doctorate is the ReD, a doctorate in recreation offered by the University of Indiana.

Teaching sport management in graduate school, or in an undergraduate program, is a career with advancing salaries. Six-figure salaries are possible; of course, one would not start at that level of pay. Different career paths are conceivable. Some professors desire to build their careers around a very productive research agenda, and, often, this is dictated by the type of post-secondary institution at which the professor is employed. However, there are many institutions where professors are encouraged to focus on teaching. Regardless of the path chosen, most institutions require all professors to perform in three to four core academic elements, teaching, research/professional development, service, and academic advising. As an example, Dr. Christopher Atwater's (Time Out Interview 6.1) job focuses primarily on teaching, but he explains his involvement in other areas.

Progression for Faculty

The doctoral degrees previously mentioned above are attainable for any aspiring graduate student who is willing to work and study hard for the additional three to four years. Before moving forward and discussing more about teaching sport management, a clear understanding of academic tenure and the promotion process must be explained. Tenure is typically defined as the process by which a professor is rewarded with a place of employment for as long as they wish. However, there are caveats to this situation. Becoming involved in an illegal or inappropriate activity are scenarios that can result in termination. An example of this would be sexual harassment of a student, but dissolution of an academic program can also result in a professor's release. Institutions do everything they can to honor the tenure contract, but difficult economic times, refocusing of institutional direction, low enrollment, or closure of an institution altogether are other reasons a tenured faculty member could be released from employment.

Most collegiate institutions use the same titles and progression for faculty. An individual at the lecturer or instructor level generally has not completed a doctoral degree or may not be under a tenure track contract; rather, they would be under an annual contract. The title of assistant professor is usually granted to a beginning professor who has completed a doctoral program. Usually, an assistant professor must complete five years of work (dependent upon the institutional rules) before applying for tenure (undergoing tenure review) during the sixth year. How well one teaches, how much research or professional development with which one becomes involved, the quality of work, and amount of service (e.g., committee involvement, special assignments) in which one becomes engaged usually determines the granting of tenure. Academic advising of students may be included in the teaching component or may be an entirely separate requirement also considered in the granting of tenure.

Time Out Interview 6.1 with Christopher Atwater
COLLEGE TEACHING

Position	Assistant Professor – 5 Years
Employer	George Mason University
B.A. Degree	History—Skidmore College
M.S. Degree	Recreation, Parks and Sport Leadership—Virginia Commonwealth University
Ph.D. Degree	Education, Urban Services Leadership—Virginia Commonwealth University
Career Path	• Intern, Ego Trip Magazine – 1 year • Copy Editor/Photo Editor, The New York Times – 1 year • Assistant to the President, National Research Council – 1 year • Bike Courier, Zoom Delivery – 1 year • Resident Advisor, Covenant House – 2 years • Mortgage Banker, Mortgage Network – 2 years • Mortgage Assistant, Prosperity Mortgage – 1 year • Full-Time Graduate Student, Virginia Commonwealth University – 5 years • Graduate Teaching Assistant, Virginia Commonwealth University – 3 years • Adjunct Professor, George Mason University – 1 year

Employment Recommendation

"I am mostly known for being a teaching workhorse. I am a term faculty member with a 4:4 course load but have also taught every summer since beginning at the school. I generally teach 10-11 courses per year. In addition to teaching, I develop courses, serve on multiple governance committees, author book chapters and articles, and serve as a chair or member for students completing dissertations and theses."

In many institutions, one cannot apply early for tenure, but this policy is based on institutional choice. Some institutions allow an assistant professor to apply for promotion to the next level, associate professor, at the same time as tenure review. Faculty applying for tenure or promotion are initially judged by a committee of their peers based on institutional guidelines. The committee then forwards any recommendation to the appropriate administrators who then provide their recommendations. Granting tenure at a nonprofit institution is usually the ultimate decision of an institution's board of trustees. A board generally does not overturn any tenure or promotion decisions, especially if a faculty member has received positive recommendations at all levels. If tenure is not granted, the individual is usually given a seventh year of employment after which the university does not renew a contract. If tenure is granted, many institutions provide an increase in pay with the promotion, but it is less common to receive an incremental pay raise for gaining tenure. The pay increase generally comes with the promotion, not always attached to the tenure processes. However, each institution, particularly private ones, can design their own tenure promotion system or elect not to have tenure; in this case, the institution may elect to have continuing contracts.

In general, there is no limit to the length of time one can stay at the level of associate professor. However, if pay increments are granted, many individuals seek an eventual promotion. The requirements for a promotion to the highest rank of full professor vary greatly. However, this is a time when many professors seek the publication of a textbook or continue to develop and firmly establish a specific research agenda. A promotion to the rank of full professor elicits the highest of faculty salaries, which can reach six figures and not just at the largest of institutions. Field of employment, geographic region, and presence of a faculty bargaining unit can all have an impact on salary. Those professors teaching in a medical field, business, engineering, law, or architecture often elicit the highest salaries. There are sport business professors who fall into this category.

Dr. Sharianne Walker (Time Out Interview 6.2) holds the rank of full professor in her college of business and also serves as the sport management department chair. However, she began her teaching career as a GA, followed by four years as an adjunct professor, before being hired at her current institution. Her career path is a varied one which displays how some individuals decide later in life to pursue the advanced degrees leading to a full-time teaching career.

Ironically, one does not have to have a teaching certificate/license in order to instruct at the college level, but having completed courses in education, teaching methodologies, and classroom management can certainly be beneficial. Many institutions make quality in teaching a requirement for obtaining tenure or to be offered contracts of continuation. The majority of sport management professors in the 1970s and 1980s initiated their careers in a physical education teaching program. When sport management majors began to gain popularity in the 1990s, the vast majority were still housed in physical education departments, but some programs allowed students to choose between student teaching or serving an internship centered around sport.

Professional Development

To be successful as a professor in the field of sport management, one must devote his or her career to professional development. Continuous attendance at professional conferences is typical of the work, and, in this industry, there are plenty of them. The premier organization for most professors in sport management is the North American Society for Sport Management (NASSM).

Time Out Interview 6.2 with Dr. Sharianne Walker
COLLEGE TEACHING

Position	Chair and Professor of Sport Management – 9 years
Employer	College of Business—Western New England University
B.A. Degree	English—Smith College
M.S. Degree	Sport Management—University of Massachusetts/Amherst
Ph.D. Degree	Sport Management—University of Massachusetts/Amherst
Career Path	• Director of Special Events – Northampton Recreation Department – 2 years
	• Public Relations Assistant, Boston Celtics
	• Director of Public Relations and Marketing – Commonwealth Sports Properties – 2 years
	• Director of Public Relations – Clarke Schools – 4 years
	• Assistant V.P. for Development – Clarke Schools – 6 years
	• Graduate Teaching Assistant, Sport Management – University of Massachusetts/Amherst – 4 years
	• Adjunct Professor, Sport Management – University of Connecticut/Storrs – 4 years
	• Asst., Assoc., & Full Professor, Sport Management – College of Business, Western New England University – 18 years

Employment Recommendation

"Often times, there is a misconception that professors just show up and teach class. There is a great deal of preparation that goes into developing course materials, refining assessment materials, and creating meaningful feedback that will facilitate student learning. Successful professors are detail oriented, understand student learning models, and are excellent communicators. They are organized and thorough. They also must be excellent at managing both their time and multiple tasks. Faculty must be mindful of tenure requirements and publication and service expectations, and need to be able to manage all these things as well as course delivery. I think it's also important to note that faculty members need to commit to staying current in their area as well as being able to integrate technology into their pedagogy."

However, one's teaching specialty can determine the appropriate conferences to attend, especially if school reimbursement funds are scarce. For example, if one chooses to specialize in the teaching of facility and event management, organizations such as the Stadium Manager's Association (SMA), the International Association of Venue Managers (IAVM), the Florida Facility Manager's Association (FFMA), and the National Intramural-Recreational Sports Association (NIRSA) have conferences that focus all or part of their conference agenda to the design and management of facilities and the operation of events. To become tenured, most professors must develop and present their research projects at these professional conferences.

Service is usually the third component of the tenure-earning contract. Service can take many different forms, but usually involves committee participation and leadership at the institution. Service to the local community, as well as active involvement within professional organizations, is also accepted. If academic advising is considered for earning tenure, this segment is usually based on an advising model that extends beyond assisting students with registering for classes. A quality academic advisor treats this role just as important as any of the others. Assisting a student in finding their career path and being available when they seek solutions to other encountered hurdles can be part of a professor's role in advising. At the graduate level, guiding students through master's theses and doctoral dissertations is also a major part of an academic advisor's role. In research institutions, it would not be uncommon for a professor to be advising several graduate advisees at the same time they are pursuing their own research projects. The research professor must have a working knowledge of a variety of research methodologies and statistical tools to manage their work and that of his/her graduate students. This responsibility, however, is often reserved for faculty that have achieved the rank of associate or full professor.

For this chapter, we interviewed individuals with a variety of backgrounds in order to emphasize there is no one clear path to becoming a professor. A common recommendation from these interviewees was to obtain practical experience before accepting a full-time position as a professor. Ironically, all of the individuals who have provided information for this chapter have some practical experience but very different backgrounds. As you read the rest of the Time Out Interviews, compare the different degree fields of each interviewee.

Not one of our Time Out Interviewees, but an associate professor and Department Chair at Flagler College in St. Augustine, Florida, Calvin Hunter, possesses a great deal of practical experience. This experience was augmented by the practical knowledge he gained as a YMCA youth sports director and two event management positions, including one as an event coordinator in equestrian and mountain biking for the 1996 Olympics. According to Dr. Hunter, in addition to a graduate teaching assistantship, all of these experiences, "provided me a framework and a reference point for things I want my students to learn and I think they enhance my lectures" (personal communication, January 10, 2010). Dr. Hunter's background also includes two master's degrees—one in sport management and the second is an MBA with a concentration in Sport Business.

THE LAW DEGREE

The law degree, the Juris Doctorate (JD), is not considered a sport management degree, and some academic departments do not consider it a terminal degree. However, since most sport management curricula include one or more sport law classes, some institutions will hire an individual with a law degree to teach these and other courses. A law degree is certainly not required to teach risk management or legal issues, even though some institutions prefer an individual with this credential.

Some students graduating from undergraduate sport management programs become interested in pursuing a law degree after being exposed to one or more legal issues courses. Many law schools offer at least one course in sport law. Two law schools, in particular, have developed specialty tracks related to sport. The Marquette Law School in Madison, Wisconsin, has a sports law program and offers a wide array of sports law courses and complimenting internships with sport organizations. The university has also created a certificate in sports law earned as part of the JD degree ("Certificate in Sports Law," n.d.), and every fall, they hold the National Sports Law Institute. This institute recruits many of the top sport lawyers as speakers to present and discuss American and international sports issues ("National Sports Law Institute," n.d.).

Another law school offering with attention given to sport law is Florida Coastal School of Law and their Summer Sports Law Practice Institute, located in Jacksonville, FL. This institute is available to anyone pursuing or holding a law degree. Experiential learning opportunities are offered to the students via field trips to local sport organization sites and networking with top sport law practitioners ("Summer Sports Law," n.d.).

After graduating from law school, one does not have to pursue the life of a practicing attorney. Some individuals pursue the law degree for prestige, for the knowledge learned, and to obtain a wider array of career options. Thus, applying for sport management teaching positions after obtaining the law degree is an option. Professor Paul Batista (Time Out Interview 6.3) had a distinguished career as an attorney and as a contract advisor for professional football players before embarking on a teaching career. Thus, one could see how his background lends a great deal of credibility to the classroom environment.

Time Out Interview 6.3 with Paul J. Batista
COLLEGE TEACHING WITH A LAW DEGREE

Position	Associate Professor of Sport Management – 10 years
Employer	Texas A&M University
B.S. Degree	Business Administration—Trinity University
J.D. Degree	Baylor University
Ph.D. Degree	Sport Management—University of Massachusetts/Amherst
Career Path	• Hollon & Martion, Attorneys at Law – 5 years • Law Office of Paul J. Batista, Attorney at Law – 20 years • Certified Contract Advisor – NFLPA, 12 years • County Judge – Burleson County, Texas – 4 years • Lecturer, Department of Construction Science – Texas A&M University – 3 years • Assistant Professor, Department of Health & Kinesiology – Texas A&M University – 7 years • Associate Department Head, Health & Kinesiology; Chair, Division of Sport Management – Texas A&M University – 4 years • Associate Professor, Sport Management Division, Department of Health & Kinesiology – Texas A&M University – 10 years • Faculty Athletic Representative – Texas A&M University – 1 year

Employment Recommendation

"Learn as much as you can about all practice areas in Sport Management regardless of your degree field. Obviously, there are more opportunities with a PhD than a law degree, and a PhD has become almost a necessity to move into the upper echelons of the field. For someone with a law degree, it might be problematic to gain tenure at a research intensive institution. When I was hired into a tenure track position, I was able to negotiate expectations for where I would publish, which, in some instances, was in legal journals rather than peer-reviewed journals. Some academicians do not value publications such as law review articles, so be sure you and the administration have a clear understanding of the value given to outlets where lawyers publish."

TEACHING WITH A MASTER'S DEGREE

Individuals with a master's degree can successfully teach in undergraduate sport management programs. Competition will come from applicants with completed doctorates if the position is advertised nationally. However, many smaller programs only advertise locally, so contacting educational institutions in a chosen geographical area with an established sport management program is one path to pursue. It also would not hurt to contact local institutions, including community colleges, and make an appointment with their chief academic officer. Find out if they have plans to begin a sport management program, or perhaps they plan to offer sport management classes. Some two-year colleges are transforming into four-year colleges, and your timing could be perfect. Consider that some may be in the process of entering into articulation agreements with a four-year college and, thus, the addition of sport management teaching positions may be on the horizon. In this case, an articulation agreement would be an agreement where a two- year school may begin offering classes for their students to make transferring to a four-year school easier with less loss of credits. For example, a two-year school may partner with a four-year school locally, or somewhere else in the state, that has an established sport management program. The two-year school may develop an introduction to sport management class or other classes that are generally offered by the four-year school at the freshman or sophomore level (100 or 200 level courses). Examples might be sociology of sport, event management, or facility management. If the students take those courses at the two-year school, the agreement stipulates that those courses will transfer equally to the four-year school. Thus, articulation agreements could create teaching opportunities. In most cases, there is a requirement to coordinate agreeable course content with the four-year school in order to satisfy transfer credits to the four-year institution.

As an example, Matt Seyfried (Time Out Interview 6.4), possesses the title of lecturer, which exists at many collegiate institutions. Notice that he has a specialized background and two degrees related to media and public relations. This type of background could qualify an individual to teach a sport and public relations course.

Patrick Gordon (Time Out Interview 6.5) has two degrees from a sport management related curriculum and serves as the director of experiential learning and outreach for St. John's Fisher College in New York. This is a prime example of how an individual with a master's degree could fill an institutional role in addition to being qualified to teach sport management.

Time Out Interview 6.4 with Matt Seyfried
COLLEGE TEACHING

Position	Lecturer IV – 10 years
Employer	State University of New York at Cortland
B.A. Degree	Radio and Television Communications—SUNY Cortland
M.A. Degree	Broadcast Journalism—Newhouse School of Public Communications, Syracuse University
Career Path	• Broadcast Intern, KOAM-CBS – 3 months
	• Television Sports Reporter, WINK-CBS – 3 years
	• Weekend Sports Anchor/Reporter, KDUH-ABC – 3 years
	• Sports Director/Sports Anchor, WETM-NBC – 4 years
	• Visiting Assistant Professor, SUNY Cortland – 3 years

Employment Recommendation

"My suggestion would be to get as much professional industry experience as possible, before coming back to the classroom. The students benefit from professors who can teach based on their own "real world" experience. My student evaluations often mention how much the students appreciate learning from someone who has done what they are teaching."

Teaching Online

Many sport management programs, particularly at the master's level, are increasingly turning to the internet. This methodology involving a variety of different electronic devices and learning management systems has opened up many opportunities for online teaching. Institutions may hire part-time adjuncts to fill these positions. This offers a great deal of flexibility to the instructor because, most of the time, they do not have to relocate in order to teach. These adjuncts can teach and provide instruction from remote geographic locations, and students need not convene in a single classroom. It may not be the best situation for the institution from a consistency in teaching standpoint nor from a face-to-face advising perspective, but many institutions have found online programs bring in a great deal of revenue. There are existing concerns among faculty and administrators, regarding this decentralized instructional format. Some professors believe degree quality is an issue in an online format, especially for sport management where concurrent course discussion and group projects are often difficult to require. Another concern deals with academic dishonesty and having someone other than the registered student

Time Out Interview 6.5 with Patrick Gordon
EXPERIENTIAL LEARNING ADMINISTRATION

Position	Director of Experiential Learning and Outreach – 1 year
Employer	St. John Fisher College
B.S. Degree	Sport Management—St. John Fisher College
M.Ed. Degree	Athletic Administration—Endicott College
Career Path	• Sports Information Graduate Assistant, Endicott College – 1 year
	• Assistant Director of Athletics, Lakeland Community College – 4 years

Employment Recommendation

"Get involved in college athletics or student services on campus. Our roles will always be student-centered, so a background working with these individuals will prove to be valuable when applying for positions. Look to join a committee on campus, many of which allow for student representation. If you are still an undergraduate, you can parlay those experiences into a graduate assistant position to help pay for the cost of a master's degree, which is a necessity for someone hoping to work in higher education today.

completing and submitting assignments. However, if quality instructors with sound academic and experiential backgrounds are hired or university faculty are properly trained through in-service and professional development programs, the online format for instruction is a win-win situation for students and the host university.

If a quality online methodology for delivery (e.g., Moodle, e-College, Blackboard, Desire 2 Learn) and a mandate for consistent content are part of the formula, quality online classes are possible. However, most professors of sport management will agree an online format will never replace the hands-on team projects, field trips, or face-to-face discussions in the classroom environment where critical discourse can be bantered back and forth—particularly if the online courses are offered using asynchronous delivery methodology (students participating on their own time schedules).

Sport Education at the High School Level

Education has also changed at the high school level. Some high schools have initiated academies where students stipulate the desire to enter a specific course of study that is pre-approved by the state government or the private school. Steinbrenner High School opened in 2009, in the town of Lutz, Florida, and boasts preparation of students in sport, recreation and entertainment marketing, and sports medicine (Hillsborough County Public Schools, 2017).

Sport management courses at the high school level have existed many years. Palm Bay High School in Melbourne, FL, offered a sport management careers course in 1980. Fairfax County, VA, offered a sport marketing course in 1989 (Swanson, 2009). Pickle (2009) reported experiential learning opportunities for Arkansas high school students through an online course in sports marketing and entertainment. Currently, the state of Virginia lists standards for offering courses in sports and entertainment marketing, advanced sports and entertainment marketing, and social media marketing ("Marketing," n.d.). In the fall of 2010, New York City opened a Business of Sports School with a inaugural enrollment of 120 students (Swanson, 2009).

Undoubtedly, other states have similar course and internship offerings related to sport or they may be in the curriculum development stage. If the trend continues to allow schools to be flexible and allow specialized curriculum while also maintaining high standards for teaching basic educational core courses, it is probable that more teaching positions related to sport may be available in the high school setting. This is a good thing for sport management majors, particularly those who are required to take basic education courses as part of their degree program. Many sport management students desire to go back to their high school alma maters and work as a coach, but many coaching positions these days are not full-time. Possessing the credentials or background knowledge to accept a teaching position in a sport management/marketing-related curriculum opens more opportunities for individuals wishing to become high school coaches and educators. Obtaining a state teacher's license or certification may be required. Pursuing a minor in education would be a great idea if this is a route one chooses to pursue. Contact the education department faculty at your institution or your state's Department of Education for more information.

Graduate Assistantships: Teaching, Administration, or Research

In Chapter 1, we defined an assistantship as a graduate level form of experiential learning and expounded a little about assistantships in Chapters 2 and 4. Here, we will discuss the purpose of graduate assistantships (GAs) and their relationship to graduate study.

Financial aid in support of students pursuing an advanced degree is often available in the form of bank or federal student loans and possible specialized scholarships. GAs are offered by most institutions but are often very limited in number, Thus, competition for GA positions at some colleges is quite competitive. A grade point average (GPA) of 3.0 or higher on a 4.0 scale is often expected. Funding of these assistantships can differ particularly at a private institution. At public institutions, a graduate program office may designate a pool of federal funds in support of graduate students. Graduate students apply to graduate school, get accepted, and then can apply for a graduate assistant position. If selected, the student receives a semester stipend, usually presented in a monthly payout over the course of a semester or academic year. In exchange for the pay, the graduate student commits to a 20-hour workweek completed in the host department for the assistantship. For example, a graduate school may provide a $12,000 stipend for the nine-month semester. Students would get paid $1,100 per month. The amount of tuition covered can depend on state laws and may stipulate whether in-state and out-of-state tuition is waived. However, it is not uncommon for all tuition expenses to be waived for the graduate assistant. At larger schools, graduate student housing is often available, but usually not part of the GA stipend. This can substantially lower living costs or can be offered as an additional benefit at no cost to the student. Some states/institutions will even provide full medical coverage as a benefit for graduate assistants. Thus, it can be financially affordable to pursue a graduate degree full-time without holding other employment.

Graduate assistant positions in academics are usually categorized as teaching, administrative, or research and assigned to a designated faculty member or department administrator. In sport management, graduate professors teaching undergraduate courses may allow a GA to develop and/or deliver lectures to a class of students. This is an excellent training ground to learn the art of teaching, especially if the supervising faculty member is an excellent professor of instruction. While serving as a teaching assistant, the student may also provide assistance with taking attendance, tutoring, grading papers, and monitoring or overseeing undergraduate students taking exams. As an administrative assistant, the GA may be assigned duties and responsibilities important to the daily routine of the department. They may assist with department or school projects, grant writing, screening of applications for student admissions in either a master's or doctoral program for an upcoming academic year, or contributing to any project in which their supervising professor or another professor in the department may be involved.

Research assistantships may also be titled fellowships, which are mostly offered to doctoral students or individuals completing additional research after completing the doctorate. For students, this is an excellent training ground for learning how to conduct literature reviews or learning about statistical or legal research methodologies prior to embarking on their own dissertation research. Dr. Shaina Dabbs (Time Out Interview 6.6), now an assistant professor, attended Ohio State University on a GA position for her doctoral degree. From this experience, she offers sage advice for GAs and explains the role she held as a GA.

Eligibility for graduate assistantships will vary, and policies generally stipulate who can and cannot qualify for assistantship positions. Policies will also exist for keeping any assistantship position, and maintaining a minimum grade point average (3.0) is part of most policies. Deadlines for applying for graduate school and assistantships are usually early with many schools establishing a January or early February deadline for the submission of all application materials and admission test scores for a fall semester entry. Some institutions only accept new graduate students in the fall term and conduct rigorous screening of all applicants.

Time Out Interview 6.6 with Shaina M. Dabbs
COLLEGE TEACHING

Position	Assistant Professor of Sport and Event Management – 3 years
Employer	Elon University
B.S. Degree	Parks, Recreation, and Tourism Management—North Carolina State University
M.S. Degree	Sport Administration—Georgia State University
Ph.D. Degree	Sport Management—The Ohio State University
Career Path	• Assistant Softball Coach – University of North Carolina-Greensboro – 1 year • Assistant Softball Coach – University of Tennessee at Chattanooga – 2 years • Assistant Softball Coach – Georgia Institute of Technology – 2 years • Graduate Teaching Assistant – The Ohio State University – 2 years

Employment Recommendation

"If a student is a Graduate Assistant, take any opportunity to be a leader, work with diverse groups of people, and become familiar with the industry segment. Also, undertake research. Do not be intimidated by research as it is the foundation for our teaching. The most important thing students can be doing while in a master's program is getting involved in the industry (volunteer work, internships, GAs, part-time jobs, etc). I actually had a full-time coaching job while obtaining my master's degree allowing me to work closely with athletes, organize travel, maintain a budget, and more. I realized coaching was a stepping-stone towards teaching.

As a graduate teaching assistant, I was a teacher of record which allowed me to create the class and syllabus, teach the content, grade and mentor students. I also had the opportunity to create an online class and teach that course. This experience prepared me for my current position and proved to me it was a profession I wanted to pursue.

Graduate School Admission Test Scores. Many sport management graduate programs require prospective students to submit admissions test scores. If the program is housed in an education or sport-studies-related department, the required admissions exam is usually the GRE (mentioned earlier in this chapter). This exam is the most widely accepted test worldwide and was significantly overhauled in August, 2011. There are computerized and paper versions of the test that measure analytical writing and verbal and quantitative reasoning. There is also an experimental or research section on which a score is reported but does not count towards the overall GRE score. The results of the overhaul is an exam that is adaptive on a section-by-section basis, so the performance on the first verbal and math sections determine the difficulty of the second sections presented. Overall, the test retained the sections and many of the question types from its predecessor, but the scoring scale was changed to a 130 to 170 scale (down from a 200 to 800 scale) A composite score of 280–285 (verbal plus quantitative) is generally the absolute minimum a student could score to be admitted into most graduate programs.

If one is pursuing a degree housed in a school of business, the Graduate Management Admissions Test (GMAT) is often the preferred exam. The maximum scores on the GMAT is 800, and some business schools expect a score of at least 520. The test measures verbal, quantitative, integrated reasoning, and analytical writing assessments. For the analytical writing assessment, the test taker must analyze an argument essay. If taking this test, plan well in advance of any deadlines for graduate school admission. Your full score is not available for at least 20 calendar days.

Some graduate business programs require much higher achievement than listed above. However, because some students just do not test well, some institutions will make exceptions. If a student has been identified by a professor for a graduate assistantship, admission can be granted in this instance as well. Some schools have eliminated required test scores or may grant a waiver, especially if the individual has many years of experience prior to applying to the graduate school.

INTERNING AS A DOCTORAL STUDENT

Some individuals in graduate school, or contemplating the submission of an application to graduate school, inquire about internships as a doctoral student. This opportunity depends on the individual. Consideration of the information below is warranted.

Internships can never be wasted. Even if the experience results in a poor experience, one has learned that not all organizations have quality internship programs or well-designed internship positions. Still, information about the organization has been learned from the inside. The intern has possibly learned what not to do and how they may wish to design internships for their future employer. Most internships at the doctoral level turn out to be a positive learning experience. If a doctoral student is contemplating a career as a professor, an internship in the sport business industry provides the practical experience recommended by all of our interviewees. Assuredly, great contacts will be made and the personal experiences can be relayed to their future students in the classroom environment if the teaching route is pursued.

Most doctoral programs in sport management do not require an internship. The graduate assistantship is a qualified substitute. After all, being a graduate assistant for three or four years is an experiential learning opportunity unto itself. If one is pursuing a doctorate and does not have a GA position, sometimes the individual is also working a full-time job outside of sport. This can be detrimental to obtaining much needed on-campus networking and social experiences within higher education. Students should participate in sport and campus opportunities afforded through athletics, recreational sports, public relations departments, and committee assignments; these opportunities should be pursued, whenever possible, both formally and informally.

Not all doctoral students plan to teach at a university or college upon graduation. In the previous sections, we discussed the pursuit of a doctorate for purposes other than teaching. Internships should definitely be an integral part of the educational plan for those particular graduate students.

FINDING A MENTOR

We discuss mentoring in Chapter 10 for the benefit of an intern or new employee. As a graduate assistant or a new professor, it is equally important to have a good mentor. We like to have a go-to person to test our ideas, to give us the "been there, done that" input, so that we, hopefully, do not repeat their mistakes. As a graduate student begins work on a degree in a sport management program, they should look for a professor who is willing to develop a rapport with students, serve as a faculty advisor to their curriculum, and then guide them through the academic processes of doing the work, growing, and developing academically until it is time for the professor to gently push them out of the graduate nest and into life. Some student-mentor relationships last a lifetime. Many GAs will pursue a particular research topic or a subject matter for the rest of their lives, because it was passed down from an outstanding mentor. Good mentors can influence and persuade performances one would never believe possible. In the exalted realms of higher education, no greater compliment can be extended than that of a great and gentle mentor. If one does not have a mentor, you could possibly be missing out on great advice on issues important for maximum development of the graduate student. Seeking a mentor is a very positive move.

THE FINAL BUZZER

Teaching or conducting research in the college setting can be a very rewarding career path. Talking to current professors or graduate teaching assistants can provide a great deal of insight into this profession. However, as pointed out in the chapter, it is important to first find out where your passion lies and then embark on a search for the right graduate program that fits your needs and, perhaps, your wallet. Graduate assistantships are the best course to pursue if looking to attend graduate school on a full-time basis. Whether in pursuit of a master's or a doctoral degree, the resourceful use of the graduate assistantship can lead to rewarding and enlightened learning experiences. The dedicated GA can also find a willing mentor to provide advice and guidance along the way. Though the master's degree may only last for three or four semesters, the student-mentor relationship may well continue for a lifetime.

Some determined graduates will pursue the doctorate degree. Having read this chapter, it is hopeful the aspiring graduate student will have realized there is a tremendous amount of effort and study necessary for a doctoral program. In order to survive, indeed to thrive in such a program, a good mentor is of paramount importance. Proceeding through the curriculum and sharing teaching and learning symbiosis with a mentor, one can blossom into a well-educated and insightful assistant professor, ready for your first class and mentee. Graduate school and being a graduate assistant can be very rewarding. The whole reward for the process will not be for the pay, but for the payback to those you will teach and mentor during your career.

EXPERIENTIAL LEARNING OPPORTUNITIES

Classroom Experiential Learning Example: Encouraging Doctoral Study

If a master's student is thinking about doctoral study or is undecided, we recommend taking one of our doctoral seminars as an elective in the master's program. We also encourage them to talk with one or more of our current doctoral students. This gives the student opportunities to see what to expect in the program.

Submitted by Dr. Brian Turner, Associate Professor and Program Coordinator
Ohio State University, Columbus, OH

Program Experiential Learning: Sport Marketing Research Institute (SMRI)

The Sport Marketing Research Institute (SMRI) aims to enrich the learning experience of sport administration graduate students by conducting field research for sport enterprises. SMRI provides high quality research opportunities for both graduate students preparing for careers in sport management and organizations in need of management assistance.

The University of Northern Colorado expects their Ph.D. students, and encourages M.S. students, to be active in the SMRI.

1. Students work with the SMRI Director to submit research proposals and budgets to potential clients.
2. Students work closely with the client to provide research expertise in a number of areas (marketing plans, market analysis, economic impact studies, customer satisfaction studies, etc.).
3. Students oversee the execution of the research projects (data collection, data analysis, and results along with implications/recommendations).
4. Students are responsible for providing the client with a final written report, which includes all of the data and analysis, along with recommendations.
5. Students organize, strategically plan, and manage the SMRI. This allows them to conduct research with other students in the program and interact with industry professionals from across the country in developing connections through applied research.

Submitted by Dr. Alan L. Morse, Associate Professor, Program Coordinator for
Sport Administration, and Director of Sport Marketing Research Institute
University of Northern Colorado, Greeley, CO

REFERENCES

Certificate in sports law. (n.d.). *Marquette University Law School.* Retrieved from http://law.marquette.edu/

Hillsborough County Public Schools. (2017). *2017-2018 Steinbrenner High School Course Catalogue.* Retrieved from http://steinbrenner.mysdhc.org/Resources/Guidance/Guidance_Documents/Course%20Catalog%2017-18.pdf

Lacey, J., & Crosby O. (2005). Job outlook for college graduates. *Occupational Outlook Quarterly, 48*(4), 15–27.

Marketing - high school. (n.d.). *Fairfax County Public Schools.* Retrieved from https://www.fcps.edu/academics/high-school-academics-9-12/career-and-technical-education-cte/marketing

McNiff, J. L. (2013). *An examination of the early career experiences among graduates of sport management degree programs* (Doctoral dissertation). Retrieved from Dissertations and Theses Global. (Order No. 3575275)

National sports law institute. (n.d.). *Marquette University Law School.* Retrieved from https://law.marquette.edu/national-sports-law-institute/welcome

Pickle, S. K. (2009, September/October). Close connections set Arkansas distance learning program apart. *Learning and Leading with Technology,* 14–15.

Summer sports law practice institute. (n.d.). *Florida Coastal School of Law.* Retrieved from http://www.fcsl.edu/academics-summer-sports-law-practice-institute.html

Swanson, E. (2009). High schools reach teens via sports business. *Sports Business Journal, 12*(17), 11A.

United States Department of Labor Bureau of Statistics. (2015). Employment projections. *U.S. Bureau of Labor Statistics.* Retrieved from https://www.bls.gov/emp/ep_chart_001.htm

CHAPTER
7

Preparing for the Internship

"An internship is a very vital step in the sport management preparation process as it serves essentially as a doorstep for you, the student, to enter the sport industry and affords you the opportunity to get to "feel" the real world. In that process, you will gain the necessary perception, acquire supervised experience, develop or refine requisite skills, and build up necessary social capital (relationships and networks) for future success."
—Dr. Ming Li, Professor and Dean of the College of Education and Human Development,
   Western Michigan University, Kalamazoo, MI

THE WARM UP

Preparing to find a career position with any organization can be a full-time job. It is no different than any internship. Organization, planning, preparation, and more can make the difference between being a top candidate and securing the position or just being another résumé in the stack.

This chapter builds on the previous ones by assisting you in planning for the internship search, and the information learned can be applied to any job search. Attitude and approach can make the difference, as well. However, it is recommended that any internship—paid or unpaid, for academic credit or no credit—be approached with a positive attitude and a desire to treat each opportunity as a true learning experience regardless of the responsibilities assigned. Bandy (2009) states that self-knowledge and choosing the right career path based on personal skills and abilities is crucial to finding a work environment that best suits an individual. Ross and Beggs (2007) found similar beliefs in a study where recreational sport management students and practitioners agreed that selection of an internship should be based on career aspirations.

Von Mizener and Williams (2009) state that "students are more on task when permitted to make choices about academic work" (p. 110). By using the Foster Five-Step Model explained in Chapter 1 and applying the six Ps in this chapter, a student can devise an outstanding personal strategic plan for finding a quality internship and gaining employment in the sport business industry. The personal strategic plan can parallel institutional requirements for experiential learning.

MORE THAN THE 4 Ps

In 1990, four sport management students preparing for their own careers co-authored an article titled "Marketing Yourself for the Profession: More than Just the Four Ps" (Rose, Denny, Burleson, & Clark, 1990). The article utilized the traditional four Ps of marketing—product, price, place, and promotion—as a foundation, but actually presented six Ps, as described below, to form a strategic approach to any job search. The six Ps explain an in-depth comprehensive approach that takes careful planning and attention to detail. They are presented in the order we believe makes the most sense for those beginning the journey to securing a top culminating academic internship and a first full-time position in the industry.

Product

You, the candidate for a position, are the product. An application for any position is actually an attempt to sell yourself and your skills to an organization. Hence, developing a strategic plan and the self-confidence to get you there is of utmost importance. Knowledge and experience raises self-confidence. Thus, coursework, volunteering, and other early experiential learning opportunities will help narrow your focus to a specific industry segment. The earlier the process is begun, the earlier a prospective intern is able to answer career questions on their own. While professors and others can discuss particular careers, the student has to pave the road. Everyone's background is different and that background forms a personal paradigm upon which only you can build. Nobody knows your background or life experiences better than you. Sell it! Sell yourself! The next three Ps focus on an examination of conscience and where you really want to go in your career.

Planning

The first step in establishing a strategic plan for finding a true career path requires setting personal goals and objectives. The literature has established that setting goals and writing them down allows one to be more focused and more likely to reach those goals (see Suggested Readings for this chapter) and, according to Goldsmith (2003), that likelihood can rise by as much as 300%. Set personal goals high enough so you have to reach beyond your comfort zone. Goals should be measurable so you have a benchmark for reaching the goal. Setting a goal and taking steps to reach that goal can be viewed as a series of steps on a ladder. View the sample personal strategic plan below and envision your career goal at the top of the ladder. Objective 1, then, is the beginning of the ladder.

Goal: To have a full-time position in professional sport on graduation day.

1. Get involved with the Sport Business Association (or the respective major's association) in my freshman year and participate in a minimum of two volunteer opportunities each semester.

2. Find a summer position as early in my academic career as possible working as an usher, ticket-taker, or concession stand employee, and use it as a required apprenticeship or summer job.

3. Nominate myself, or accept a nomination from another individual, to serve as an officer in the Sport Business Association. Follow through to establish myself as a trusted leader and a proactive association member.

4. Explore available internship opportunities found on at least 10 different sport-related websites in one or more employment areas within professional sport (ticket sales, event management, public relations, etc.). Analyze position requirements.

5. After analyzing internship opportunities, obtain additional skills that might be needed in the area of employment I have chosen by searching for additional related volunteer opportunities, on-campus positions, or summer jobs.

6. During my last academic year, apply for at least five internship positions in professional sport for which I have obtained some skills and background knowledge.

7. Accept a full-time culminating internship in professional sport.

The above step-by-step plan is just one example of a personal strategic plan, but it illustrates well that a goal is obtainable through a series of measurable steps. We have heard many students incorrectly state their belief that they have to work several jobs in other industry segments in order to obtain their first job in professional sport. This is an unfounded belief! Please understand there is no guarantee you will be offered a full-time position on or before graduation day. The economy and your geographic location certainly can impact the availability of positions. However, paying careful attention to goal setting and focusing on reaching those goals has proven to be a successful formula for becoming the individual that does have full-time employment upon graduation.

Preparation

Preparation is where you begin to implement your personal strategic plan. According to Rose et al. (1990), most processes are made up of certain steps that facilitate a finished product, but the successful path involves a great deal of preparation. In preparing for your career in sport, preparation can begin by paying close attention in classes and doing your best work throughout your degree program. Gaining skills and knowledge about specific employment roles, attending conferences and guest speaker lectures (even if outside course requirements), and joining professional organizations and student associations are all ways for you to prepare to be the number one candidate for any internship you desire. Of course, the volunteer positions pursued in order to learn about sport and event and facility management will be of utmost importance. Caution is warranted, however. Some individuals will latch onto one organization and want to stay with the organization in the same position for the duration of their education. Although this shows loyalty, if this position is not tied to career aspirations or if the organization does not allow continuous growth by permitting constant exposure to new tasks and responsibilities, then other opportunities should be explored. While attending classes, learn as much as possible about the different industry segments and positions. This is a very important step in order to thoroughly discover all the sport industry has to offer. We constantly direct their students to this approach; it is amazing how even the most dedicated student who has worked with only one organization can find there is much more to be learned by experiencing how other organizations are structured and carry out business.

Networking is also extremely important in this phase. Chapter 1 informally introduced the concept of networking when discussing the concept of who knows you. Chapter 9 explores this topic in great depth. Please read these two chapters, learn about the art of networking, and practice it often.

Price

Price focuses on what an individual can afford in terms of compensation. Can you accept an unpaid internship? Can you afford to accept a small stipend or only be reimbursed for expenses? If some organizations do not offer any compensation up front when the internship paperwork is signed, some will reward an intern for outstanding performance and decide to begin paying some form of compensation during the internship or upon completion. Finally, if the reality of the financial situation dictates a paid internship is the only option a student can afford, there are a lot of paid opportunities. Some students take a semester off to work any available fulltime position and save the income in order to pursue a desirable unpaid internship. Understanding your particular price-fit early will assist you in defining other parameters of your search. Chapter 8 delves into the cost of an internship in more depth. This also leads into the next P. What price do you have to pay to work with the best mentor or to get your foot into the door of the best organization (the place) leading you to your chosen career path?

Place

Do you need to move away from family? Do you need to forego a summer job in the family business in order to take a position related to your future goals? Where are you willing to go? Based on the internship goals you have set for yourself, place can be the desire to go beyond your current geographic location in order to target a specific organization or a related organization in a specific industry segment. This is more fully discussed in Chapter 8.

Promotion

Promotion is one of the most important of the six Ps. Under promotion, you will find positioning and networking. As we mentioned throughout this book, promoting your skills to a potential organization or recruiter might be one's toughest sales job. On many occasions, positioning yourself to be in the right place at the right time is where prior preparation will prove to be extremely beneficial. If done correctly, previous networking, as recommended by many of your mentors/professors, will also prove itself very useful in reaping the fruits of your labor. Continuous networking and self-promotion during this phase is important and will be discussed in great detail in Chapter 8.

UNDERGRADUATE VERSUS GRADUATE INTERNSHIPS

Some disagreement among both practitioners and professors has been observed over the years regarding undergraduate and graduate interns. Certainly, some positions in the field might be more capably filled by a graduate or law student specifically trained in sport marketing, sport law, or another specialized field. However, there are plenty of positions where undergraduate interns can perform as capably as a graduate student. In fact, many organizations prefer a student, undergraduate or graduate, who commits themselves full-time to an entire semester, season, or academic year rather than one who only wishes to work on a part-time basis. Full-time versus part-time internships are discussed in greater depth in the next section.

Full-Time Versus Part-Time Experiences

Dedication and loyalty from an intern can leave a great impression on an organization. Beginning an internship by telling a site supervisor when you can and cannot work does not sit well with some organizations. Gardner (2013) conducted a recruiting trends survey for the Collegiate Employment Research Institute (CERI) involving the perspective of employers. Employers reported hiring an intern was their best recruiting practice for a return on their investment (ROI). Additionally, this study asked employers to define the amount of experience they expected a student to have upon completion of a degree. Of the employers in the study, 45% wanted students to have six to 12 months of full-time experience, while only 35% stated they would accept an employee with less than five months of experience. This study did include employers from a variety of specialty fields and indicated more experience was expected from students completing a graduate degree. Within this study, general business and communication employers and media employers tended to agree with the overall results: 46% and 44% of these employers, respectively, want six to 12 months of full-time experience, and 34% and 29% would accept five months or less. Finance, marketing, and human resource employers reported expecting 41% (six to 12 months full-time) and 29% (five months or less). Of importance to note, this study does not reflect the expectations of sport management practitioners specifically, but it does provide a glimpse into an employer's mindset when hiring entry-level employees. Further results indicated smaller companies often expected more full-time experience than larger companies. However, this could change based on the industry segment. Regardless, full-time internships spanning the length of a season or an academic year support the higher expectations of full-time employment reported in the study.

Another significant result reported in the CERI study discussed above was the number of experiences expected. While 34% indicated one experience would be sufficient, 55% of the employers stated they would like to see experience in at least two different experiential learning opportunities (Gardner, 2013).

Many organizations tell you they will work around exams or class schedules and some do this extremely well. However, when working as a part-time intern, it is very difficult to out-perform a full-time intern that is doing an exceptional job if you come in to work only when your schedule permits. Make every effort to select a full-time internship where you have no outside interruptions. At the very least, work your personal schedule around that of the organization. Accommodating your supervisor's schedule is just as important.

It is recommended by many organizations, practitioners, and professors that a student complete a full-time internship. In fact, the first academic standards for undergraduates in sport management programs defined an internship as a 40-hour per week, 10-week experience and defined the minimum graduate requirement as a 20-hour per week engagement (Sport Management Program Review Council, 2000). The more recent accreditation principles required by the Council on Sport Management Accreditation (COSMA) mandates integrative experiences as a common professional component (CPC). Internships are a great way for institutions to meet this requirement (Council on Sport Management Accreditation, 2016). The shorter the experience, the less time the intern has to establish themselves as a strong contributor to the organization as they are just starting to get to know the organization, their site supervisor, and others in the organization and the internship is over. Many organizations, especially college athletic departments and professional sport teams, ask an intern to commit to a seasonal internship as previously described in Chapter 3.

To support the premise that internships are important, a 2009 study by Petersen and Pierce reported that MLB, NFL, and NBA human resource professionals rated practicums and internships as the most important of 10 curricular areas. Lee and Han (2011) reported 94.4% of internship site supervisors in the four major professional sport leagues in the United States (including the NHL) indicated internships were essential in a sport management curriculum with the majority expressing a desire for more than 500 required hours (or 12.5 weeks). This is a great testimony to the importance some professional sport managers place on internships and a great way for the student to demonstrate commitment to an organization and a desire to enter the industry. By way of a longer, more intense experience, one can experience and observe the inner workings of that organization and better understand the industry segment. This is also the best way for a student to determine if the organization is a good employment fit. Research supporting this was found when Sauder (2014) surveyed 139 students from 13 different institutions that had completed a sport management capstone internship. The interns reported moderate and significant increases in personal and career development even when the students had varying amounts of prior experiential learning.

To highlight what can happen in a full-time internship, it is worthwhile to report the experience of a student who committed to a minor league baseball team for an entire season (January through September). The intern concluded he could not work in baseball in a position where he could not see the game. Thus, he set his goals and embarked on a career in broadcasting. His internship had encompassed sales, clubhouse operations, and a little bit of media work. Had he selected a short-term internship in just one of these areas, he may not have stumbled on his love for broadcasting. A season-long commitment often allows an intern a much broader perspective of the organization, especially if working in the minor leagues where all staff often pitch in to help each other during the course of a day's work. Finding similar passions for a specific segment of the industry through early experiential learning opportunities can result in finding the right career path for an individual.

Seasonal Availability

We discussed the seasonal nature of the sport business industry at the beginning of Chapter 3. However, a few additional comments are warranted when preparing for the internship. Seasonal availability of an internship can be problematic. Careful planning of a student's progress toward an internship and graduation should begin no later than the college sophomore year for an undergraduate and at the very beginning of a graduate student's program. For example, if a student truly wants to work in baseball, a spring or summer semester internship is paramount and a January start date is when many teams want an intern to begin.

Internships on the business or sales side of many sports, including baseball, may be available year round.
(Courtesy of Dreamstime)

A different example of seasonality would involve an internship with the United States Olympic Committee (USOC). The USOC has internships throughout the year. However, if an individual wanted to work in the year of the Olympic or Paralympic Games, the spring or summer semesters would provide that experience, but would occur only once every two years. Needless to say, most individuals would not delay their graduation to wait on an one of these internships. Plus, competition for these internships is fierce, and it is not recommended a student hold out for this type of experience. Nevertheless, if an individual knows the Olympics/Paralympics will fall during their chosen internship semester, we encourage applications to be submitted, especially if one desires to work in event or facility management or within a specific sport. However, if one obtains an internship during these Games, there is no guarantee the intern will get to work at the Games. The Games usually last two to three weeks, and an intern may be asked to stay at the home office and take care of necessary business while full-time employees are working on-site. This also might be required because applications for credentials to work a major sporting event must clear security months before the actual event. An intern beginning the second week of January may not be able to obtain the necessary credentials or clear background checks in time for a Winter Olympic or Paralympic start date. One final consideration when looking for internships during these or other major events is these opportunities may be longer than the academic semester and the application process just might begin much earlier than most internships.

PLANNING FOR THE APPLICATION PROCESS

Saving Money for an Internship

It is very difficult to save money when pursuing an academic degree. Students often live from pay check to pay check or that monthly bank deposit from the parents. From the moment a student begins work on the academic degree, consider putting away $10 a week and do not touch it—ever. In four years, one would have $2,080 plus interest accrued. In two years, $1,040. While it does not sound like a lot of money, any amount saved can prevent one from limiting their decision and finding the best possible internship. The $2,000+ can help pay for many of the costs listed in Chapter 8. While we do not endorse any particular savings plan in this book, we suggest looking into savings ideas such as UPromise.

UPromise is a plan endorsed and supported by businesses nationwide, but requires one to open a 529 account (an educational savings plan). All states have these savings plans available. Businesses supporting UPromise donate a percentage of every transaction you or a family member makes via registered credit cards. Thus, any family member can register their credit card with your 529 plan. It does not cost anything. Every time they shop or eat at a restaurant that supports UPromise, money goes into this account without it costing them any money. Some grocery store chains participate and everyone has to eat! UPromise has specific credit cards that maximize savings even more. Visit their website (www.upromise.com) or a financial planner could assist in establishing a 529 account. Leave the money in and when your internship semester begins, the money can be withdrawn for costs you incur. Four years of a family's contributions, even if pennies at a time, will cover some costs of the internship. It is worth investigating. So, your $10 per month and a UPromise account could possibly pay for living, food, and other necessary expenses during the internship semester.

If time has not been spent to investigate scholarships and there are still a few semesters before the internship, now might be the time. Scholarships today do not always have the meaning they had many years ago when one had to be at the top of the class to qualify. Many private organizations have scholarships tied to ethnicity, religious preference, geographical location, parental employment, and more. Some have very few applicants because they are not widely advertised. Googling the word scholarships tied to some of the categories previously mentioned may reveal available financial sources if one applies.

The Florida State League (minor league baseball) has scholarships available. Each team in the league can recommend one intern a year for the scholarship. An individual can qualify as an undergraduate or graduate student. If you are one of those who has accepted an internship as a summer job to gain experience before the culminating senior internship or if you are considering graduate school, these scholarships can be applied to next year's tuition. Other programs like this may also exist. Check with financial aid or scholarship offices on your campus.

Yes, an internship can be costly. Planning for those expenses in advance is important. Regardless, the overall amount of money the student will spend during the internship, above tuition and semester fees, should and will be outweighed by the value of the experience if properly selected. Koo, Diacin, Khojasteh, and Dixon (2016) reported that students who were satisfied with their internship were more committed to entering the sport management field. Additionally, Hergert (2009) found that business students perceive the value of internship as very high if it leads to employment and if it is tied to career goals. Other research has shown that students who have interned have a better chance of landing a full-time job over those who have not (Gault, Redington, & Schlager, 2000). Future employment and a rewarding career in the industry can start with a carefully selected internship. Yes, the internship can be that important! There is a strong reason why internships are a requirement in many sport management curricula. Take the time to plan in advance, save some money, look for scholarship funds, and carefully select the capstone internship even if it may cost you some money.

Time Management

Time management skills are crucial. Can you meet deadlines? Can you get work done early in order to handle any unexpected circumstances, or are you a procrastinator waiting until the last minute to finish a project? Procrastination can kill a career or a chance for a promotion without even a realization of its impact. Individuals are not always aware of the perceptions of others regarding work habits within the company.

Entire books have been written on time management. We will not go into this subject in too great of depth. However, we do offer some critical information on time management as it applies to the internship or job search. Time, once lost, can never be regained. Missed deadlines or rushing at the last minute to meet a deadline are examples of poor time management skills. Is there a deadline for finding an internship within your academic program? Are you applying for several different internships? In order to prevent last minute problems such as spelling errors in cover letters or incomplete applications, start as early as possible and develop a notebook with dividers for the internship search process. Organize the dividers of the notebook in a manner that makes sense to you (i.e., pro sport organizations in alphabetical order, etc.). Make a copy of any internship or job announcements and place them in the notebook. Write down answers to common questions and keep a copy in the notebook. Often, an organizational employee will call without notice, and ask some questions. However informal the situation, this is an interview! If you are not prepared mentally for the phone call or the questions, having this information in front of you will assist you in answering the questions with confidence and ease. We will discuss the elevator pitch later in Chapter 8, and having a copy of this in front of you will be of great value. If you call an organization, try to get the name of the individual to whom you spoke and write down the date. Highlight any information on closing deadlines. Print a calendar or use a reliable phone app. The calendar should have room on which to write or record all information regarding closing dates for position applications. Just realize phones get misplaced or broken. We highly recommend printing the calendar and keeping it in the notebook. It is much easier to see an entire month printed with closing dates and deadlines if you are applying for multiple positions.

The best recommendation we can give here is to apply for positions before the closing deadline; do not wait until the last minute. Sometimes interviewers will receive great résumés early in the selection process at a time when they are not yet receiving application materials from others, and they will have more time to read information submitted. Thus, your particular skills might stand out in the mind of the interviewer. If exceptional, your skills might be used to judge other applicant qualifications. On the other hand, do not apply so fast when you first see a job announcement that you make errors in your cover letter. In summary, take the time to submit a complete and fully correct application, cover letter, and résumé. Re-read position announcements on occasion. When applying for numerous positions, it is difficult to remember precise information about the responsibilities of a specific internship. Keep the notebook in a handy location, perhaps your backpack, where it can be easily accessed if an organization calls. If you receive a phone call, quickly pull out the notebook and have the position description in front of you.

Every Sunday night, review your calendar and make a mental note of upcoming deadlines for that week. Perhaps re-read a position announcement from a company whose deadline is approaching to refresh your memory in the event a company official calls. This is a great time management skill for any individual and a great way of keeping track of important deadlines. If

Maintaining a weekly, monthly, and annual calendar is an important time management practice when applying for multiple internship positions. (Courtesy of Unsplash)

contacted by the company, make a note of the date and who contacted you. If offered an interview, record the accurate date, time, and location on your calendar or on a notetaking app. Once you interview, find out before leaving when the organization hopes to make a final decision. Write this information on your calendar and on the position description.

Having all of this information in one place creates incredible organization, cuts down the time spent on the internship search, and prevents scrambling for information when a company calls. The whole process constitutes a great time management practice in which certain aspects can be transferred to other projects. Yes, all of the above information could be kept on a computer, smart phone, or other tablet. If one does not keep the computer turned on at all times and others possibly share the computer, your access may be limited. As mentioned earlier, smaller electronic devices can be misplaced or broken; when possessing multiple electronic devices, one might not remember where they placed a particular company's document. What you do not want is inaccessibility to the information when that all important phone call happens.

Classroom Experiences

In all of our chapters, the Time Out Interviews contain a great deal of information from industry professionals. A continuing recommendation from these individuals is to take advantage of time in school. Most everybody working in the sport business industry has at least one college degree. In other words, we have all been there. We understand fraternities and sororities, intramural sports, and the need to have time to just relax. However, if your résumé does not reflect good use of your time to volunteer, hold leadership positions, and maintain a solid grade point average (GPA), some internship and entry-level positions will be out of reach; getting your foot in the door may take much longer. Many individuals believe a GPA has little or nothing to do with job success. While some industry professionals will tell you stories about their early years as a college student that may not all be flattering, at some point they woke up and realized spending more time studying than partying was, most definitely, the best path to pursue. Starting off with a low GPA and trying to bring it up in the immediate semesters prior to graduation is often a very difficult task.

GPA is important as some sport management programs require a minimum GPA in order to be eligible to intern. If the minimum GPA is not met, a student may be required to take additional courses in place of the internship. Some students believe this is an easy substitute in place of the tedious process of finding, applying, interviewing, and securing the internship. But, you want to intern! It is your ticket inside this fabulous industry! Taking courses as a substitute does nothing to increase your professional network unless your classmates are already working in the sport industry. Although extremely beneficial, the classroom is not the actual operation of a sport organization; class projects can show experiential learning on a résumé, but it does not assist one in growing their list of individuals willing to serve as references. You have worked too hard in your academic program to take the easy way out and elect not to intern, if opting out is an option within your program.

Some sport organizations seriously consider the GPA as a measure of persistence, intelligence, leadership, and excellence in work and, thus, require a minimum GPA to be eligible to apply for any posted positions. An overall GPA of 2.8 or higher is not uncommon for many prestigious internships. Many graduate schools request a minimum of a 3.0 to be considered for admission. Even if an individual believes they will never go to graduate school, time and circumstances can alter future plans. A future employer may even require a master's degree for advancement within their organization.

Some individuals also believe their general education, usually the first two years of coursework in a four-year undergraduate degree program, has little to do with a career in sport. Nothing could be further from the truth. A course in psychology, for example, can expose a student to a better understanding of the behavior and actions of individuals including consumers. This is a critical business skill. A course in philosophy can establish critical thinking skills and strongly support those planning to attend graduate or law school and future decision-makers. Even if you find these types of courses tough, seeking them out may pay long-term dividends when dealing with the largest component of the sport business industry—people. Math, as well, plays a critical role in future business decision making. While not critical for every position in sport, the ability to understand essential business components involving math is very important. Comprehending and applying analytics and research and their place in a growing number of organizations may land you a position or get you a critical promotion. If there are business research or analytics courses at your institution that may help in a future career but is not required for your degree program, take at least one. Many sport management programs are adding analytics courses to their curriculum. A minor or an Associate of Arts (AA) or Associates of Science (AS) degree in another field may also be beneficial. Investigate these opportunities early.

We will not prolong the discussion in this area. Other chapters have and will refer to your college education. The main point we wish to make is that any project and any class can impact your background conceptual knowledge and experience. The Foster Five-Step Model, explained in Chapter 1, includes classroom learning and projects as a separate step in experiential learning. It is advised that one not underestimate the importance of any homework assignment and be sure to give it full effort. Furthermore, keep an electronic copy of all written projects on a flash drive and keep back-up copies as well. One never knows when these projects will come in handy for an interview or an assigned task at work. During the interview, those wishing to enter a position within the media are often asked for an example of a press release they have written. A facility design project may be a great one to brush up and present in a portfolio during an interview for a facility management position. This is especially important if the projects were awarded a high grade and you completed this project on your own.

Establishing an Internship Timeline

This is another section where we do not intend to use a lot of print space. However, it is important to reemphasize one should start early—as early as possible on thinking about the culminating internship and by establishing a personal timeline with the setting of goals. Utilizing the six Ps presented earlier in this chapter is a great way to organize one's time in school; use every experiential learning opportunity afforded, and you will find securing the internship much easier. Not just any internship, but the right one for you that has the best opportunity to provide a great learning experience with the right mentor. Finding an experiential learning position (culminating internship) with an organization where you will have a great chance of being offered full-time employment upon graduation is icing on the cake. A student can never predict if this will be the final outcome, but spending quality time on this component and focusing early on the right industry segment can result in long-term dividends.

Summer Jobs

We mentioned in Chapter 1 that finding a summer job in sport and using it as an apprenticeship within the experiential learning model is a great idea. Why not do this each summer while pursuing an academic degree? A student could actually have three summers of different experiences with different organizations or progressive experience with the same organization. This is often just what employers want to see.

Sometimes, students indicate they cannot afford to take an hourly job in the sport industry while foregoing a higher paying job with the family business or with a hometown organization. Reality often dictates that summer jobs are a way of paying for part of next year's tuition and other bills. Nonetheless, if one truly wants to get into the industry, taking a summer position unrelated to your career goals is not always the best decision. Actively searching in the sport industry for a job that will pay some of the bills is a proactive way to approach this important step toward the future. Looking early, perhaps during Christmas or spring break before others across the country begin their search, is a good strategy. Late searches may not produce as many available opportunities because positions have already been filled.

If one is from a small town without any large sport organizations, it still may be possible to find a position during the summer that will help build background skills. Any small facility may have scheduled events where one could learn the beginning steps of event management. If this type of position is available but will not pay enough, then taking that family job and volunteering to work events may be another strategy to pursue. Constantly building the résumé and learning more about a specific industry segment should be a strategic goal.

Volunteering

Volunteer, volunteer, volunteer! This is step one of the five-step model in Chapter 1. Take advantage of every possible opportunity to learn about your career early and often. For example, if event management is where you think your future lies, find local events. If you are fortunate enough to live close to an area where a professional golf tournament is hosted, volunteer every year in a different role. Bring your significant other to volunteer as well. With major golf tournaments, there are many roles such as marshals, walking scorekeepers, security, social hosts, roles affiliated with transportation, standard bearers, maintenance crews, driving range or parking attendants, media support, and more. It is one of the best sport opportunities to learn a great deal about how a tournament or other large special event is organized and operated. Find out who the volunteer coordinator is and ask if you can help in the months leading up to a tournament. As mentioned earlier in Chapter 3, most professional golf tournaments are not organized by the PGA, LPGA, or other professional tour staff, although these associations will send individuals in advance to a tournament. Instead, they will have a small staff of local organizers that prepare nearly year round. Volunteering often so the staff gets to know you might land you an internship or professional position.

Volunteering for a variety of positions, events, and organizations is the best way to discover one's true calling and to narrow down the industry segments prior to a culminating internship. Less time may be spent down the road jumping from organization to organization in search of your passion. This jumping around once you have graduated from college is often viewed as an inability to stay employed and can raise a red flag for individuals reading your credentials. Once you enter the professional world, you want to show persistence and continuance with an organization for at least a few years. So volunteering early and often helps one become secure later on in knowing they have found their true employment path.

JOB VERSUS CAREER

Job versus career is an important concept to understand. Certainly, any paid position can be considered a job. However, from a professional standpoint, there is a critical difference. Approaching these two terms from this perspective, a job can be defined as an hourly paid position, with or without company benefits, where one simply fulfills the requirements assigned that day and takes no work home with them related to that position. Flipping hamburgers at a restaurant could be considered a job. A career can be defined as a life calling whereby a series of paid positions are related to the same industry and where each new position builds in advancement and responsibility. Webster's Dictionary (1997) distinguishes between the two by calling a job "a post of employment" (p. 441) and a career as "an occupation or profession followed as one's lifework" (p. 122). One could further distinguish the two by having a need for the job and a passion for a career.

Gone are the days when most working adults were hired by one company and stayed with that company until retirement. Careers in sport, today, are no different. This is especially true when teams change ownership, new head coaches are hired, and loyalties change. Heritage (2001) defines a career as an "evolving sequence of a person's work experience over time" (p. 16). Heritage also explains that a career can now take on different appearances. Traditionally, one could climb the ladder and stay with one organization. However, the employment landscape of today's sport organizations embraces consultants, individuals taking on several different part-time positions linked to one industry, independent contractors, the self-employed (labeled as a portfolio career by Heritage), and multiple lateral or vertical moves with several different organizations in order to rise to top levels of management.

Russ Simons, a managing partner with Venue Solutions Group, LLC—an operational consulting firm specializing in the public assembly facility industry, rose through the ranks of facility management after starting as an intern. He once explained his definition of career versus job in a presentation at a sport management conference in 1995, "Don't send me a résumé if you are looking for a job. I hire for jobs locally. I look far and wide for people who want a career. I look for content of character and a commitment necessary to join a winning team. Someone in a career focuses on something a little bigger than the job description." Are you ready for a career in the sport business industry?

THE FINAL BUZZER

This chapter focused on preparation and planning for achieving the best internship and entry-level position offers. Getting hired in sport for many is a career goal. Taking the time to carefully plan early, once started in a degree program, can assist you in realizing your dream and forego spending months or years in search of a life goal. The six Ps, in addition to the Foster Five-Step Model from Chapter 1, laid the groundwork for preparation and planning. In the next chapter, much more will be discussed for the actual application process. Coursework alone, regardless of the degree program, will not gain most individuals a position within the sport business industry. If the hints, ideas, and assignments provided in this book thus far are combined with the next chapter, obtaining quality position offerings should not be a problem.

EXPERIENTIAL LEARNING OPPORTUNITIES

Classroom Experiential Learning Exercise: Role Playing

Students are assigned one team to manage the National Women's Soccer League (NWSL). Each group pitches their franchise to a potential sponsor. While one group represents the NWSL franchise, the others act as the potential sponsor's marketing team. The NWSL teams need to prove their fan base matches the target market of the sponsor company, whose marketing team will accept or deny the proposed relationship. Students take turns role playing as NWSL franchise and company executives

Submitted by Dr. Dina Gentile, Professor

Endicott College, Beverly, MA

Program Experiential Learning Example: Required Student Involvement

We require all of our students in our on-campus iteration to be involved in an industry-related position (internship or full-time employment) from the day they set foot on campus. We assist in finding the work, but it is ultimately their responsibility. We feel it is important to introduce the experiential piece early on during the student's graduate academic career. As a result, many of our students have secured permanent, full-time positions prior to graduation day, and a very good number of the aforementioned group were employed by their internship organizations.

Submitted by Dr. Jim Riordan, Director of the MBA in Sport Management Program

Florida Atlantic University, Boca Raton, FL

SUGGESTED READINGS

Collins, K. (2012). Strategies for using pop culture in sport psychology and coaching education. *Journal of Physical Education, Recreation & Dance, 83*(8), 20–22, 31.

Drake-Knight, N. (2012). Creating a consistent and sustainable customer experience in retail networks. *Training & Management Development Methods, 26*(1), 301–316.

McIntosh, C. R. (2008, November). Yes, you can! *Essence, 39*(7), 140–143.

Tracy, B. (2008, June). Success is no accident. *T + D, 62*(6), 76.

Turkay, S. (2014). Setting goals: Who, why, how? *Harvard Office of the Vice Provost for Advances in Learning.* Retrieved from http://vpal.harvard.edu/publications/setting-goals-who-why-how

Zonar, S. (2007, November). Five steps to a life that works! *Coach and Athletic Director, 77*(4), 70–71.

REFERENCES

Bandy, K. (2009, March). Launch your career with self-assessment tools. *Student Lawyer, 37*(7), 16–19.

Career. (1997). In *Webster's University College Dictionary* (1st ed., p. 122). New York, NY: Random House Publishing.

Council on Sport Management Accreditation. (2016, May). Accreditation Principles & Guidelines for Self-Study. Retrieved from http://www.cosmaweb.org/accreditation-manuals.html

Gardner, P. (2013). Framing internships from an employers' perspective: Length, number, and relevancy. *Collegiate Employment Research Institute,* Research Brief 6. Retrieved from http://www.ceri.msu.edu/wp-content/uploads/2010/01/internshipCERI-Research-Brief-XX.pdf

Gault, J., Redington, J., & Schlager, T. (2000). Undergraduate business internships and career success: Are they related? *Journal of Marketing Education, 22*(1), 45–53.

Goldsmith, B. (2003, November). The outrageous power of self-evaluation. *Cost Engineering, 45*(11), 30.

Hergert, M. (2009). Student perceptions of the value of internships in business education. *American Journal of Business Education, 2*(8), 9–13.

Heritage, A. (2001, March). Career management: From ladders to wings. *Training Journal,* 16–20.

Job. (1997). In *Webster's University College Dictionary* (1st ed., p. 441). New York, NY: Random House Publishing.

Koo, G., Diacin, M. J., Khojasteh, J., & Dixon, A. W. (2016). Effects of internship satisfaction on the pursuit of employment in sport management. *Sport Management Education Journal, 10*(1), 29–42.

Lee, S., & Han, J. (2011). Practitioners' perceptions of student-intern skills necessary to be prepared for an internship experience in major professional sport organizations. *Sport Management Education Journal, 5*(1), 32–43.

Petersen, J., & Pierce, D. (2009). Professional sport league assessment of sport management curriculum. Sport Management Education Journal, 3(1), 110–121.

Rose, T., Denny, D., Burleson, C., & Clark, C. (1990, Spring). Marketing oneself for the profession: More than just the four P's. *NIRSA Journal, 14*(3), 24–26, 51.

Ross, C. M., & Beggs, B. A. (2007). Campus recreational sports internships: A comparison of students and employer perspectives. *Recreational Sports Journal, 31*(1), 3–13.

Sauder, M. H. (2014). *Early Experiential Learning and Perceived Outcomes from Capstone Sport Management Internships* (Doctoral dissertation). Retrieved from ProQuest Dissertations & Theses Global. (Order No. 3581759)

Simons, R. (1995, February). Presentation at the Georgia Southern University Sport Management Conference, Statesboro, GA.

Von Mizener, B. H., & Williams, R. L. (2009). The effects of student choices on academic performance. *Journal of Positive Behavior and Interventions, 11*(2), 110–128.

CHAPTER
8

Selecting and Applying for the Appropriate Internship

"I cannot stress enough the importance of an outstanding cover letter, one that does not read like a generic form submission."
— *Kerryann Cook, Co-Founder, MK Sports & Entertainment Group, New York, NY*

THE WARM UP

Internships have become quite an essential component of educational preparation in a variety of academic curricula, especially in sport management programs (see Suggested Readings). This was even true when Abernethy reported consensus within the literature in 1996. The selection process of your internship may well be one of the most important parts of your curriculum. Through a careful and well-planned process, the student intern can select the most appropriate organization with which to intern, and when combined with a determined and enthusiastic effort, the specific experiential learning process may lead to employment with the same organization. The respective curriculum program should have prepared the student intern in a variety of academic areas, any one of which may serve as the basis for an internship experience. As indicated earlier in this book, the global sport markets of today are unlimited in career opportunities, and the proper internship can prepare sport management students for a very exciting and rewarding career in many corners of the world.

The wide world of sport we have come to know today may appear to run the gamut from glamorous and glitzy (celebrity-hosted events such as golf and boxing), to treacherous and daring (the Eco-Challenge cross-country races and motor cross), to adventurous and ex-hilarating (America's Cup and balloon racing). As explained in Chapter 1, according to the research found, the size of the sport industry in the United States grew from $225 billion ("Academic Degrees," 2008) to $472 billion in 2015 ("Sports Industry," 2016). Traditionally, we have flocked to facilities or seen on television the intercollegiate and professional sport arenas in which our favorite athletes perform. In order for these sport segments to be so eco-nomically successful, each has to provide effective and enthusiastic employees willing to serve the customer base. As sport business is becoming more sophisticated and competitive, young, highly-skilled, and educated entry-level employees are needed to ensure forward growth and success. It all begins with an internship! The desires and dreams of student-interns are unlimited. If a student wants to work in a specific field of the sport industry, a successful internship can launch a career.

THE INTERNSHIP SELECTION PROCESS

In earlier chapters of this book, the Foster Five-Step Model and the six Ps for planning and preparation were presented. Thus, you already have learned the planning process for a successful internship begins as early as possible in the academic program of study. When starting a major in sport management, most individuals do not know exactly what industry segment or entry-level niche to pursue, although many believe they do. Others will have a strong sense of direction. This is true for both the graduate and undergraduate student. Several important things have to occur for such an outcome. Students should first be introduced to all of the industry segments as we presented in Chapters 3–6. This introduction usually occurs through a foundations course in sport management offered through an approved curriculum.

Looking for an internship or a full-time position is a full-time job itself. So, do not expect to start looking a week before your internship selection deadline occurs. Once again, we are building upon the theme of starting as early as possible, but certainly by the very beginning of your capstone pre-internship course or the semester prior to your internship semester.

Finding Your Niche

Hopefully, you have already started your experiential learning by using step one in the Foster Five-Step Model, volunteering. You also did not wait around for formal experiential opportunities and created volunteer experiences for yourself. You have progressed through step three or four and have already served an apprenticeship/practicum, perhaps, to gain experience through observation or at an event. The point being made here is this: there is a wide variety of athletic venues existing in collegiate sport programs, and many events desperately need volunteers, certainly from within the university and sometimes from the local community. A prime place for the athletic department to recruit is from the sport management program at an institution. Previous chapters discussed planning and preparation in-depth, including summer jobs; therefore, we will not belabor the discussion here. By now, you have experience on your résumé and are ready to begin the internship search process. At this juncture, the level of observation, background knowledge, and the number of experiential learning opportunities you completed will now determine qualifications for an internship. The process you implemented assisted you in eliminating areas in which you may have no desire to work. It is just as important to know and understand the career you do not want as much as the career you do want (Kelley, 2004; Verner, 2004). The more you understand about the sport industry prior to your selection of an internship, the better the fit may be for your specific skills. Odio, Sagas, and Kerwin (2014) reported the amount or levels of learning opportunities can influence internship satisfaction and, subsequently, career outcomes. Therefore, the more preparation you have for your eventual career in the sport industry can seriously impact the quality of that career. The above study, reporting on the pre- and post-internship reflections of a small group of undergraduate sport management interns, brought to light the students' vague plans for career progress (goal achievement) following their capstone internship. Of importance to note, the research did not report the amount of experiential learning prior to the internship or whether the students had participated in a pre-internship course. This concept is discussed in the next section.

While the glitz and glamour of working with professional team sport organizations or college athletic departments can be exciting, finding the right internship for you should be the primary concern. (Courtesy of Dreamstime)

Capstone Courses

After a student has progressed through the first four steps of the five-step learning model, it is time for the student to formally apply for the culminating internship at a full-time sport organization falling under one of the broad categories in the Sport Employment Model explained in Chapter 1. Some post-secondary institutions will have what is often called a capstone course or pre-internship class. In many instances, this capstone course is organized to assist students in the internship selection process, to prepare them for all facets of the internship including required assignments, and to finalize the selection and required paperwork. Even though most students will already have prepared a résumé, especially if they followed the five-step learning model, a main topic in this type of course will be résumé writing or perfecting the résumé format (Pontow, 1999). Other typical topics include how to write proper business correspondence including cover letters and emails; the interview process complete with a list of possible questions and appropriate responses (Porot & Haynes, 1999; Yates, 2004); analyzing job descriptions to determine whether one is qualified; professionalism and professional organizations; the importance of punctuality and time management; strategic planning; organizational structure and how to utilize organizational charts to better understand reporting structures and position responsibilities; management and leadership styles and how to effectively deal with each type; topics such as sexual harassment, gender bias, work place and dining etiquette, and the avoidance of "office politics"; and management roles and skills.

Some capstone courses are structured as a senior seminar/management course where students create strategic plans, study the importance of SWOT (strengths, weaknesses, opportunities, and threats) analyses, participate in role playing exercises, examine human resource management, and more in order to immerse the student in a complete understanding of the organizational environment. Why is this a good component? The intern is getting ready to work a full-time position and learn how management truly works on a day-to-day basis. What drives the organization? How do they live out their mission and vision? How do they evaluate if they met their established goals? What can they do better? If this is part of the capstone course, it sets up the internship as a strong academic course worthy of typical course grades vs. a pass/fail evaluation. An organizational analysis paper during the internship can be the final senior paper including content learned in the capstone and from other courses (Young & Baker, 2004). When there is a culminating internship, we recommend a capstone course approach.

Often guest speakers are invited to speak to students in the capstone course. This is a great advantage if the individuals are actually looking for interns. But not all capstone courses include the guest speaker facet because many programs invite speakers to other courses within the sport management curriculum. Some believe the students should already have selected a specific industry segment to pursue when the student is nearing the end of academic coursework. On the other hand, some students may not have found an area for which they have a passion, particularly if the student did not select sport management as their major until their junior year or transferred from another institution. If you are one of those who are unsure, we recommend two approaches. First, participate in some intense self-analysis quickly that will include how you feel your skills may fit within a specific industry segment. Engage the assistance of a career counselor at your institution. Sometimes personality tests can help identify particular strengths, weaknesses or skills. Second, begin to interview people. These can be classmates who have identified their career focus, sport management faculty who generally have intense background knowledge, other students who are currently working or volunteering for a sport organization, alumni, or actual practitioners in the field.

TeamWork Online sponsors networking events around the United States where one can meet mid- to upper-level management. This is an excellent opportunity to meet practitioners and expand your personal network. If time is not on your side, you can still select and apply for any internship position that interests you. During the internship, you can then identify or eliminate a particular segment or position that is not a good fit. We do not recommend this approach because it could lead to the acceptance of numerous internships after graduation just to find what does interest the student. We often call this process post-graduation meandering. The goal is to avoid this meandering, because we have found students lose interest, need financial support, and end up looking for just any job, and thus may never become employed in the industry for which they spent two or more years preparing. Ideally, by the time you get to this point, you are already focused and the internship you accept will lead to a confirmation of your choice and a full-time position (see Tooley, 1997, in Suggested Readings for more information).

Researching Sport Organizations

We are going to assume an industry niche has been identified if you have progressed to the culminating internship. Begin by looking for organizations and announced positions tied to this selected industry segment.

As the saying goes in sports, the best defense is a good offense. Being proactive in the search for the best internship is a lot like having the best offense. The internship fairy will not drop by in your sleep and place an internship under your pillow. Many of the best internships are the ones a student recruited or pursued relentlessly for themselves. In other words, the student should recruit the internship, rather than the internship recruiting the student. In the case of the former, the student intern and the pursued agency have a win-win situation, because the student may be genuinely interested in the agency and the respective role it has in the industry. In the case of the latter, the internship sites may accept anybody, because just anybody will suffice.

Employment Websites

Applying for positions today is easy. With computers and technology, one can apply within minutes via the internet because any position an organization wishes to publicize for external applications are posted on their website and perhaps on other employment websites. To find positions within an organization, most websites will have a button or a link to current job opportunities on their homepage. Sometimes, one has to search for the link and often it is in small print at the bottom. This is the first place to look if you wish to work for a specific organization.

When looking for internships or jobs anywhere in the industry, the next place to look is on the websites that allow one to search for openings and post a résumé without paying a fee. A great place to start is TeamWork Online. TeamWork Online is not the only place to find positions. Several others exist. As mentioned previously in Chapter 4, the NCAA Market website is an excellent place to look for internships, graduate assistantships and other positions within college athletics. Bluefishjob.com posts positions from internships to top level director positions in recreational sport management. Work In Sports, Women Sports Jobs, and Sports Careers Institute (positions in college athletics) are good places to search as well. Appendix A displays a long list of websites that post sport business industry positions.

Organizations often pay for the opportunity to post their positions. If an organization is paying a website to do this, this generally means they truly are interested in the individuals who apply through that website. Of more interest to some employers is when the applicants have to pay to apply; this can exhibit true interest in a particular position by the applicant.

Print Media

Print media provides another possible location for position announcements although it is not used as widely as it once was. The *Chronicle of Higher Education* provides an outlook for locating positions on college campuses including those in athletic training, college athletic administration, coaching, and teaching positions in sport management. The *Sports Business Journal* occasionally has a few position announcements placed by sport organizations. Your local newspaper may also announce positions, particularly if you live in an area with professional sport teams or postsecondary institutions. Small or unknown sport marketing firms or other sport organizations may also advertise in this manner. Once again, this outlet is not widely used, but if the organization is looking to hire quickly or hopes to find local applicants, it is very likely they will utilize this media outlet. Finally, do not forget to look in membership newsletters published by sport-related professional associations. While many of these no longer occur in print, most will appear in an online format.

Your sport management program or library may have directories that list a multitude of sport organizations and their contact information. Conducting an internet search for sport organizations and their contact information and then saving this information in a spreadsheet is a great way to maintain your own informational listing. Figure 8.1 provides a sample spreadsheet one could easily construct to list websites and sport organization information that have internships or entry-level positions for which you intend to apply. (Constructing the spreadsheet in a landscape format provides the best space allowance).

Site Name	Contact Person	Phone	Email	Cover Letter	Résumé	Response Y or N	Comments

Figure 8.1. Sample Internship/Entry-Level Position Documentation Spreadsheet.

Finding Non-Advertised Positions or Creating an Internship Position

Some sport career specialists indicate that sport organizations do not need to advertise position openings. While this can be true, most advertise some openings, especially internships and entry-level positions. Another strategy for learning about non-advertised positions might be to find out who receives applications for internships or position openings. Some organizations do not have formal internship programs or, believe it or not, have never considered hiring an intern. An assertive individual might be able to create an internship position for themselves by finding the right person to contact and then sending a cover letter and résumé to that person. Caution is warranted, though. It is not recommended to apply to every organization in this manner. It can be an incredible waste of time. Be selective when using this strategy. Smaller organizations and ones not known very well are more likely to accept and read materials received in this manner.

Preferred Agency Listing

Some academic programs maintain a list of preferred internship sites. Certainly, this can make the internship search much easier for the student. Through this contact list, the university program can allow the student to choose or can assign a student to an approved internship site. Such a listing can be of benefit in some instances and extremely restrictive to the student intern in others. Of benefit, the school program may control the experience, provide guarded accessibility for the student, or have an established reciprocal agreement with another school program for shared supervision.

However, through the use of a preferred agency listing, the student may be missing out on a crucial learning method by not being allowed to practice the actual job application process. Furthermore, the institution may be restricting the ability of the student intern to earn a position through hard work. If a university sends students to the same sites every term, the agency is less likely to hire students into full-time positions because of the revolving door of interns. The student may also be denied the best opportunity to select an internship site that best fits their desired employment niche when restricted to an approved list of internship placement sites. When institutions place student interns in certain designated areas of these programs, this may be a good practice if the internship provides an outstanding experience and the site supervisor is a dynamic leader. However, it is not a good situation if the organization never hires an intern into a full-time position, as mentioned earlier, or if the student has already worked in the position in an earlier experience and relatively few new skills are learned.

Students should be encouraged to expand their network and experience the job selection process when looking for an internship. Many students do seek a dynamic and challenging experience away from their institution. This is especially important, in our opinion, when dealing with college athletic departments. When a student remains on campus, they are still often perceived as a student and not as a working professional. They may not be invited to full-time staff meetings or other professional events due to their student status. When a student intern is removed from a student environment and is treated as a professional, the student often experiences a tremendously different environment. As a maturing adult about to enter the professional world, do you want to stay home and fly kites or would you rather take off in a hot air balloon and be set free?

ANALYZING POSITION ANNOUNCEMENTS FOR INFORMATION AND QUALIFICATIONS

Chelladurai and Kerwin (2017) presented information on analyzing job announcements in their book *Human Resource Management in Sport and Recreation*. They state, "the purpose of job anal-ysis involves collecting information about the job's operations, responsibilities, working condi-tions, and other such critical elements" (p. 191). Snell & Bohlander define it as, "the systematic process of collecting information about the parameters of a job—its basic responsibilities, the behaviors, skills, and the physical and mental requirements of the people who do it" (2013, p. 144). If one truly analyzes an organization and job announcement before applying, the applicant can gain clues about the operations, job skills required, and what it may be like working in that organization. One very frustrating element of recruiting is receiving application materials from an individual who does not even meet the basic minimum requirements of a particular position. It truly is a waste of the applicant's and organization's time. By law, an organization must hire an individual meeting the stated minimum requirements. However, if the organization uses the terminology preferred requirements, studying the organization and the announcement with an enhanced critical eye may reveal to an applicant their qualifications actually meet the preferred criteria.

MARKETING YOURSELF: THE PROFESSIONAL LOOK

Promotion, as one of the six Ps, was presented in Chapter 6, but this section will spend a little time on how to professionally promote, present, and position yourself for hiring. Networking can be done incorrectly as will be discussed in Chapter 9; so, too, can self-promotion.

Professional Dress

This is a key area in which to begin. Different individuals possess different perceptions on what constitutes professional dress. Let us begin with the basics. At the very least, when attending most conferences, meetings, or becoming involved in any opportunity where you might meet individuals who can assist in your career search, your clothes should be neatly pressed. What you wear should be dictated by the situation. A career fair or professional conference (especially the first day) most often demands a shirt and tie, dress slacks, and sport coat, at the very minimum, for males. A suit is appropriate for many positions dependent upon the job description. If in doubt, wear the suit. If you plan on interviewing or introducing yourself to a speaker, wear the suit. Some pre-internship seminars will address this issue with a guest speaker from a local haberdashery and may demonstrate proper dress with the use of mannequins.

For women, a professional suit should be part of your wardrobe. It can include a skirt or dress slacks. Navy, black, gray, brown, or tan is your best color choice. Never wear red. In all situations, never wear anything provocative such as low cut or very tight blouses. Tight slacks or very short skirts or dresses are out as well. It is tough to wear your best high heels and then take a tour of a stadium walking up and down stairs and on the playing turf during an interview. Wear comfortable shoes that still fit with the style of dress you choose. Some individuals recommend one should never wear open toed shoes in a professional situation. Closed toed shoes are considered professional. Again, geographic location will often dictate the wardrobe including the shoes to be worn.

When interviewing at the organization's offices, the situation may dictate appropriate dress other than described above. However, do not assume anything and do not ask what to wear. The interviewer may assume you are looking for an opportunity not to wear your business best. As with other situations, err on the side of caution. There is rarely a situation where you can be overdressed. Nonetheless, here is an example. Interviewing with a recreation department or a professional baseball team can be tricky. In either situation, often the staff wears dress or khaki-style slacks and a professional looking golf shirt. In the professional baseball offices during the off-season, an individual may never leave their office because they are working on sales calls or marketing projects. In a recreation department, the staff may be constantly running out of the building to check on an event at a facility or may be checking on a youth sport league tournament in progress. In these situations, a business suit may be deemed inappropriate. Geographic location may also dictate dress as those working in warmer climates may never wear a suit while those working in an office during the blistery cold days of winter may always wear a suit for warmth. Never wear a hat indoors or at any time during an interview.

In any situation, do not be afraid to be overdressed. It is possible the interviewer may give a male interviewee permission to remove a coat and tie for comfort. We recommend you do not get too laid-back. The staff working for a minor league organization might wear more comfortable dress than their major league counterparts. Again, pay attention to the environment and use your best judgment. There is a lot of truth to the saying "Dress for success!"

One would think hygiene would not be a topic we would need to cover. However, a few comments are warranted. In our experience, the most violated rule here is the failure to clean under the fingernails, and this is especially true for males. Interviewers are going to notice. A private organization can ask males not to wear earrings and can request that you not have facial hair. For an interview or any time one is meeting with an industry professional, it is better to err on the side of caution and leave the earrings at home. A good haircut and a clean shaven look is our best recommendation. While the law may not be able to prohibit a public organization from enforcing a dress code, the interviewer may have a personal bias.

The Position Application

Portraying yourself as a professional can also be demonstrated when you submit an organization's job application often required in addition to a résumé or cover letter. Most organizations will send an online application via e-mail. Hopefully, it will be sent in a word processing format so you can type information directly on the application. Some will ask you to print the application and sign it before sending it in the mail. Type it before printing it if possible, even if the formatting makes it difficult to do so. Sometimes, applications in a PDF format will not allow the applicant to type the necessary information. If you have to print it out or receive a printed application in the mail from an organization, print the information in a very neat handwriting so it can be easily read. You would not want illegible information to keep you from being considered for a position. This is another example of paying attention to detail.

Cover Letters and Résumés

Cory Miller has seen many résumés. In fact, pardon the language, but his book *I Want to Hire You, But Your Résumé Sucks: 30+ Tips to Help You Get a Job* (2012) is a very poignant critique of what he has seen in his career. Cover letters and résumés are definitely the professional presentation of oneself, and Cory believes most résumés are bad because "people haven't done all the right things to make themselves truly stand out effectively" (p. 1). His book is truly about the "ingredients employers want to see" (p. 1), which leads to the presentation of your background to make you unique. While we discuss the content of your documents later in this chapter, presenting them to an employer in an appropriate manner is of utmost importance. It is often the first opportunity to introduce yourself and your skills. It is the most important time to pay attention to detail. No spelling errors! Proper punctuation and grammar should be exercised. Spelling the name of the contact individual correctly and ensuring their proper title is used are key.

While one rarely mails application materials anymore, an individual may decide to mail a portfolio to visually present a compilation of their work. One may wish to follow-up an online application with a mailed one if the contact was through email. Emails get lost in junk and spam folders, and one can never be sure the application was received. Just be aware, sometimes an organization will only accept application materials via online or a job website. Read the position announcement very carefully. However, if one is mailing documents, the envelope is the first element observed. A sloppily addressed envelope is not a good professional presentation. A typed mailing label with a typed return address label must be used. We no longer recommend folding the résumé; instead, mail your documents flat in a large brown or white envelope. In this case, it is okay when the résumé paper does not match the envelope.

Answering Machines and Email Addresses

After you have begun sending application materials, consider changing any answering machine or cell phone messages to reflect a very professional image. Eliminate music or any other material that may not be received in a positive manner by an employee attempting to call to set up an interview. Notify family members or roommates of your position applications and request they answer the phone in a very positive and polite manner. The same is true for email addresses. Make sure email addresses do not include questionable identifiers such as lazyeddy@aol.com or bourbonbetty@gmail.com.

Social Media Sites

If you intend to use social media spaces created for the purpose of marketing your professional skills, these also need to present only professional information. LinkedIn is a popular social media site used by professionals for networking, posting open positions, and connecting with individuals in organizations. Some personal information can be viewed by everyone, but an individual determines what information can be seen. Thus, if being used to assist in a position search, most would allow access to vital career information. Twitter and Facebook are also popular sites to market skills. Use them wisely. Remove or hide content or pictures taken at a party where alcohol remnants or questionable activity may be observable. Employers check social media sites!

DEVELOPING A QUALITY COVER LETTER AND RÉSUMÉ

When applying for positions, never proceed without a polished cover letter and résumé. Yes, some online application processes do not ask for a cover letter. If emailing your application materials, the cover letter can constitute the body of the message for the email or can be attached to the email. If mailing a résumé, always submit a cover letter, even if one is not requested.

The Cover Letter

Learning to write a great cover letter is a key skill. Each time you apply for a position, the cover letter should be changed to fit the position description and to address how your individual skills fit that particular position. It is a crucial error to write a generic cover letter and just change the name and address at the top for each position. This practice does not position your skills in the best possible way. See Figure 8.2 for a sample cover letter.

Please note in paragraph one of that document, the applicant makes very clear the position for which she is applying. Sometimes, an organization will have several positions available at the same time. Dorothy also indicates where she found the announcement. This simply provides advertising info the employer sometimes likes to see. If needing space for your one-page cover letter, this information can be deleted.

In paragraph two, Dorothy brings attention to several skills she possesses and her perceived strengths. These were prerequisite skills mentioned in the position announcement. This is where you need to make yourself unique. It is the most important section of your résumé. Explain very clearly why you are the ideal candidate. Many applicants like to state they have been a life-long

Dorothy T. Brown
8473 Edgemont Place
Wichita, KS 67208

July 29, 2017

Ms. Faith M. Files, Director
Event Operations
SBC Golf Tournament
6422 Corporate Way
Land O'Lakes, FL 12345

Position is identified.

Dear Ms. Files:

This is a letter of application for your available position as the Assistant Event Director for the SBC Golf Tournament. I found this position on womenssportsjobs.com.

How skills are tied to the job announcement are presented.

My passion is using my creativity and great planning skills in Sport Event Management. My satisfaction is seeing the fruits of my labors when an event is completed with very few problems encountered. This is how I believe my skills can assist your company if I am chosen for this position. I am a team player and pay extreme attention to detail!

My résumé is attached. I also have a LinkedIn profile (dorothytbrown@linkedin) and three individuals have posted recommendations for me. I can be reached via e-mail or my cell phone at any time. Please do not hesitate to contact me. I will call you within two weeks to see if my application materials were received. I look forward to meeting you and having the chance to interview for this position.

Attention is brought to on-line profile and how one can be contacted.

Sincerely,

Dorothy T. Brown

Dorothy T. Brown

Letter is brief and not wordy.

Figure 8.2. Sample cover letter

fan of a particular team for which they may wish to be applying. Wrong approach! While we mention this in our interviewing section below, it is equally important to mention it here. An employer wants to know you understand you will be working during the event and not watching the event. Thus, it is our recommendation to never include your fandom or affinity for a particular player. Keep your content about how you fit the job and how your team player approach to work will fit their organization. Of importance to note, the wording you select might be picked up in the software being used by the employing organization. Fair or not, this is how some companies screen out applicants if certain words for which they might be looking does not match their position description.

Finally, in paragraph three, the applicant brings attention to her résumé and is creating a networking opportunity by indicating she will contact the organization. She also has a professional profile on LinkedIn and has invited the interviewer to review. These two items may urge the interviewer to read her materials, but there is no guarantee. She also has not limited her availability for contact; this sends a message of flexibility in scheduling. One final note: if you indicate you will be contacting the organization, do so within the time frame promised. This confirms reliability and supports the applicant's claim about paying attention to detail. If the position announcement specifically indicates no phone calls, do not call and do not put this statement in your letter.

The Résumé

Putting forth a complete and accurate portrayal of individual successes and achievements continues with the résumé. Your written presentation of personal credentials must be well ordered and concise but also attractive enough to the reviewer's eye to pique interest and command the all-important interview. Information in the résumé should be organized under section headings preceded by the interviewee's name and complete contact information. Suggested headings can include:

- **Education Information.** This should include degrees held or pursuing, graduation dates, name, and location of the degree granting institution.
- **Sport Management Experience.** Collectively placing all experience gained from the sport business industry on the first page highlights one's skills tied to sport.
- **Other Work Experience.** Exhibiting additional positions and skills outside the industry displays responsibilities that may apply to any position and demonstrates the ability to hold a job.
- **Honors and Awards.** It is not the time to be shy! Displaying accolades bestowed in jobs or in education sends a strong message to any interviewer that you take pride in your work.
- **Volunteer Work and Extracurricular Activities.** Activities outside work and education exhibits the propensity to be a well-rounded individual. These activities may also be a common interest of one of the interviewers—an immediate conversation starter. Organizations also like to see displayed interest in the local community.
- **References.** This is a must and is discussed in the question and answer section that follows.

Every job seeker has résumé questions about format and content. The information presented below addresses frequent concerns about résumé format.

Resume length and presentation. In our experience, some organizations want no more than one page and often believe an undergraduate has not done enough to warrant more than one page. Others want to see all experience and often it will not fit onto one page. The best answer is to find out the type of résumé the interviewer prefers. Sometimes, this can be done through a secretary or receptionist at the organization or network contacts. However, this information is often quite difficult to obtain. Consequently, the best answer is to formulate a résumé that best presents you and your skills. You want to tailor the résumé to each and every different position to which you apply. Often a functional résumé is the best way to do this. A functional résumé highlights skill sets and does not list experience in chronological order. This type of résumé is often better for those who have been in the industry a while who want to encapsulate their skill sets. This format can also be beneficial to entry-level applicants that have built their résumé through many experiential learning opportunities but have not had a full-time position. A great deal of experience in specific areas can be sold under one large section such as "Event Management Experience" instead of displaying a series of one-week events, one day volunteer opportunities, or a series of internships.

Chronological format is the most common type of résumé used, especially by entry-level applicants and interns. As its title indicates, sections showing education and experience include entries by dates in reverse chronological order. Employers generally want to see the most recent information first. See our first example of this type of résumé in Appendix C. The last template exhibited in the same appendix is a combined chronological and functional provided by a MLB vice-president. He felt this was the best format he had ever seen. However, the font is quite small and increasing the font might be recommended.

High school information. Generally, high school information is not included. If you must submit a résumé when applying for an apprenticeship or summer position and you are only a freshman or sophomore, yes, some high school information may be very valuable. This is particularly important if you have not yet gained new experiences in college.

Consider the specific situations that may warrant the inclusion of high school information. Your high school location can often be a conversation starter in an interview or can create an immediate tie to an individual if you know the interviewer attended the same school or was from the same area. If you were a play-by-play announcer for your high school athletic department, had the opportunity to participate in internet broadcasting, or wrote for the school newspaper, and are applying for a job in a media sector, this information may be extremely relevant. If a coaching position is the intended employment target, but you did not play college sports or gain any collegiate related experience, summarizing any sports played and awards won may be helpful.

However, if you are nearing the end of a college degree and have actively applied the Foster Five-Step Model, you have a great deal of experience to include. Beyond the examples mentioned above, omitting high school information and allowing additional space for more recent skills and positions held is our best recommendation. If you are completing a graduate degree, no high school information is needed. However, any college experience or positions held since completing an undergraduate degree, where you can exhibit related experience, should be included.

Paper Considerations. As discussed earlier, rarely does anyone send hard copies of a cover letter or résumé in the mail. However, one may hand one to someone at a career fair or during an informational interview. The safest answer for color and type is white and a minimum of 28 pounds (the weight of the paper). Copy paper (20 pounds) should never be used when submitting a résumé. It is generally okay to use an off-white or light colored paper (cream, light gray, or light blue), but some people will recommend white. A colleague who was in charge of screening résumés for an athletic director's position once told us four of the top five candidates submitted a résumé on non-white paper. While these are not the results of a well-designed research study, it is food for thought! Color of paper will not matter if your skills are top notch. Conversely, never use dark colored paper; it does not copy well. Résumés are often photocopied so all members of a search committee can have a copy.

Presentation of employment information. Always use bullet points instead of paragraph format. It is much easier and faster to read phrases presented in a bulleted format. Most interviewers are too busy to read a narrative and simply want to scan information. Bullets often save space as well.

Résumé templates. When we speak of a template, we are referring to the ones with pre-established formatting prohibiting you to move things around and set up your personal look. Often, these are the type you find online or within word processing programs. For that reason, we do not like them. However, a template that exhibits a clean and organized setup with little section formatting, such as the ones we have provided in Appendix C are good templates to use to get you started. They exhibit categories and recommendations on where to place dates. Another great resourced for résumé information is the book *What Color is Your Parachute* (Bolles, 2017). This book is updated annually.

References. This is one of the most common questions. Many campus career advisors or business personnel will tell you to simply place a statement such as references available upon request. Our recommendation is this: when applying for an internship or employment position within a sport organization, always include references. There are two main reasons. Sport organizations, especially those well known, advertising a position on a popular employment website will often receive hundreds of résumés for one position. Think about the time involvement of going through all of the submitted documents. One way your materials may stand out is if they recognize the name or personally know one or more of your references. Do not be surprised if this happens to you even if you live in a remote section of the country. Remember, individuals in sport network very well and are very connected. This is even truer in today's market with all of the opportunities to connect through online social media opportunities. As we mentioned earlier, LinkedIn is a popular networking sight for professionals. There are many sub-groups of networking individuals interested in sport, and this does not count the private ones universities have started for their alumni to stay connected. On this site, individuals can post recommendations attesting to skills and work ethic. Make sure your posted information is prepared in an extremely professional manner. You never know who might be looking for someone with your skills.

Because of the volume of résumés received, the person or persons charged with sorting through each one often look for ways to cut their time committed to this project. If you have included reference names and contact information, this is one less step for them. They do not have to find you to first find your references. If references are not listed, it is very likely you may lose out simply because six other individuals with very similar skills to yours supplied their references in advance. As an example, Joe, a college junior was working the 2016 National Championship football game. He met an ESPN employee who does hire employees and interns. They clearly explained if a résumé was submitted without any references, it was tossed in the circular file (the trash) (J. Carlino, personal communication, January 11, 2017).

Creative Online Résumés. Technology has changed the job application process. Individuals are now posting very creative résumé formats on the internet. From pages that turn to video insertions, the ability to link a creative webpage to a social media site or an online application could result in immense dividends. Eric Krupa (Time Out Interview 8.1) indicates one can set up their own URL and post an online portfolio and additional information one cannot fit on their résumé (personal communication, September 13, 2016). Résumé links with quality information and these bells and whistles can make a plain paper résumé seem pale in comparison. Please remember, though, some résumé information should be treated as private information and handled accordingly.

Eric Krupa has worked in professional baseball for over 20 years and has seen many résumés. Throughout this chapter, he provides many helpful hints on résumé writing and more. We recommend paying close attention to the sport industry experts who have provided food for thought within this chapter.

APPLYING FOR POSITIONS

We hope by now, especially after reading Chapters 1 and 3–6, it is clear that a plethora of career opportunities are available to the sport management student in the United States and abroad. One of the most difficult decisions to be made is narrowing down the fields of opportunity if the entire realm of employment possibilities has been thoroughly examined. These factors are discussed below.

Time Out Interview 8.1 with Eric Krupa
RÉSUMÉ WRITING

Position	President – 9 Years
Employer	South Atlantic League
B.A. Degree	Mathematics & Economics—Lafayette College
M.S.A. Degree	Sports Administration & Facility Management—Ohio University
Career Path	• Intern & Visiting Clubhouse Manager – Reading Phillies – 6 months
	• Intern – Disney's (ESPN's) Wide World of Sports – 6 months
	• Director of Business & Finance – Minor League Baseball (NAPBL) – 10 years

Employment Recommendation

A paper résumé represents the applicant, so it should be flawless in order to present the best impression of the applicant. Flaws in the résumé will often be inferred to mean there are flaws in the applicant. It is, therefore, paramount careful attention be paid to all aspects of a this document.

In addition to the actual information that comprises the résumé, attention should be paid to how the information is presented. The layout can also have an impact (sometimes a subconscious impact), so applicants should invest the time to learn more about design principles and how they can be applied.

I also believe we are in a period of change when it comes to résumés and what is valued. These changes will benefit those who are willing to put in the extra work to differentiate themselves. It is important for applicants to share what they have done. Even students or recent college graduates can share what they have created. Declaring proficiency in particular software programs is not nearly as powerful as providing examples of what you have created. Whether it is spreadsheets or websites you have created, logos or landing pages you have designed, or blogs or sales copy you have written, real examples of your abilities not only demonstrate your capabilities but also provide some excellent opportunities for discussion topics during an interview.

Geography

Geography impacts many decisions. In previous chapters, we briefly mentioned some considerations relating to the location of an academic program or internship. When planning the internship, proximity of the internship to the program of origin may be one factor. Potential internships located within the city where the curriculum program is offered may be conducive to travel and accessibility, as well as the personal dynamics of living arrangements and finance.

Internship sites where the climate is important to the performance of the activity, but may be remote from the curriculum program need careful consideration. For instance, if the student wants to intern at a ski resort, then travel and relocation logistics play an important role in leaving major urban areas in the south for the internship. With the unique access and implementation of the worldwide web and the internet, many academic institutions can manage the progress of the internship through email and electronically-submitted correspondence (e.g., Blackboard, D2L, or e-College). Other transportation considerations are discussed in the following section.

For the culminating internship, we strongly recommend the student not limit themselves to a specific geographical location or only positions allowing them to live at home or to remain with an organization where they already know everyone, the organization, and their procedures. All of these situations prevent the intern from expanding their network, learning how other organizations work, and allowing them to enter a truly professional situation away from parents or a residence hall and the typical life of an on-campus student. Change your geography, especially if you have never lived away from home or in another state. Learn how others live and work! Of course, one positive contradiction to this would be if a full-time position has already been promised in a current location.

Economics of the Decision

In Chapter 7, we briefly discussed paid versus unpaid internships and some financial considerations to examine when preparing for an experiential learning opportunity early in your academic career. In the present chapter, we are providing additional information to consider regarding other economic decisions that must be explored. A major consideration for the prospective intern is the cost of doing the internship.

Can you afford the actual costs of participating in an internship? How does one prepare for the cost of the internship? What values does one weigh and/or sacrifice for the sake of a good internship experience? The actual cost of an internship experience may be difficult to determine. Many items must be weighed when selecting an internship. These items are explored below. A good faculty mentor should be able to direct the student intern to resources and information necessary to answer most of these inquiries.

Tuition Costs. The student intern must pay the tuition and fees associated with the credit hours to the respective institution for academic credit applied to the internship. Some institutions require students to pay added fees (e.g., $250–$400) during the semester of the internship to help the university defray the costs of faculty to travel and visit internship sites during the semester. Some programs require at least two visits from the university supervisor and the added fees help programs afford these visits. Many students are shocked when they learn of this added cost since, most often, they will not be living on campus. Faculty members are supervising the internship, sometimes traveling to the internship site, spending time discussing an intern's progress with the site supervisor, and grading papers and projects. Internship assignments many not be considered as part of a faculty members regular teaching load and supervision may create an overload. This is particularly true during the summer term. Thus, the faculty member must be compensated for their time and travel expenses.

College costs are an ever-looming burden to most students. The internship cost depends on the number of credit hours associated with the particular internship. A graduate internship is usually three to six hours. The undergraduate full-time intern will usually pay for six to 12 credit hours. Graduate and undergraduate programs have a minimum hourly requirement to be considered full-time students. Maintaining full-time status is important in order to qualify for scholarship monies or federal financial aid. Some graduate programs offer assistantships (see Chapters 1 and 6) to students that may cover the cost of tuition and additional incurred fees while interning. Some institutions will require a student to be full-time if living in university housing. An additional consideration is that governmental financial aid requires full-time student status and is not generally available during the summer. The chosen industry segment and completion of courses often determine the semester of the internship. If a student's chosen industry segment does not dictate a seasonality consideration, investigating and comparing the cost of an internship during the fall and spring versus the summer is warranted. Some institutions lower tuition costs during the summer to attract students to enroll in a summer term. Even if any form of financial aid is not available, the cost of tuition during a fall or spring term may be more than in the summer. This decision will depend upon the availability of any savings the intern may have accumulated (see Chapter 7), a low cost bank loan for the summer, personal savings, or family contributions versus college tuition loans funneled through the schools.

Transportation Costs. The intern must consider the cost of travel and room and board for the duration of the internship. When the internship is in close proximity to the host institution or the student's home, an internship site will appear more conducive to the economic need, rather than recognizing the benefit of a new and different learning opportunity for the student. In either case, the cost of transportation must be included in any internship selection consideration.

In cases where the internship site must be visited by a supervising faculty member or designated program official and school budgets have been restricted, the intern may have to sacrifice a distant preference for a more local or travel-friendly site. This is becoming less of a factor, as more and more internships can be effectively monitored with internet connections, online learning platforms, and email.

We realize often a student's family simply cannot provide the financial support for a separate automobile for a student nor the expenses involved in providing insurance and upkeep. If a student knows this early-on, a quality internship in a location with mass transportation that will still provide a great opportunity should be researched well in advance. Cities such as Atlanta, Chicago, and Washington, DC, have subways and trains, but these are just a few examples.

Smaller cities with less notable names where minor league teams or great sport marketing agencies are located may have great bus transportation systems or other means for local transport. The important thing, if at all possible, is to select an internship for the quality of the experience and not to limit yourself to a specific geographic area simply because you do not have a car. Again, caution is warranted. Safety is an important consideration for anyone who would have to walk to and from a transportation stop to get to the internship site, especially when working a game that may not be completed until early the next morning.

It is not recommended a student attempt to live on campus or at home, and commute an hour or more for an internship. Since the work schedule of an intern can be unpredictable, late hours on competition dates are a common occurrence. The position may require the intern to be back at the office by 9:00 a.m. or earlier, and the cost savings is often not worth the gasoline, wear and tear on a vehicle, tolls, and insurance. Insurance companies charge more when commuting long distances to and from work. Plus, the lack of sleep is not conducive to a healthy lifestyle when working a full-time position.

During the course of some internships, a student may be required to use their personal vehicle. Inquire about this in advance. Travel costs incurred while performing business on behalf of the internship agency are usually covered or reimbursed by the agency. The student intern should confirm this, have it written into the internship agreement, and have it signed by the appropriate parties. Otherwise, these transportation costs must be included in the financial summation of internship expenses.

Housing. Some internship sites may provide housing to the student intern. This is the case of internships with the USOC because on-site housing has been provided in the past. This is a huge benefit and, sometimes, is better than receiving minimum wage or a monthly stipend. Do the math! Explore the costs of local housing if one needs to rent an apartment as compared to the selection of an internship where housing is provided. Four- to six-month leases may be difficult to obtain; the cost of utility connections and moving must also be considered. As mentioned in the previous section, long commuting times nor the acceptance of a less-than-preferred internship is not how an internship selection decision should be made, even if you have a rent-free place to stay during the internship opportunity. Perhaps, another student is interning in the same area; sharing an apartment may be a good alternative.

Dress. As mentioned in an earlier chapter, most internship sites will have an office dress code in place for student interns. The student intern should inquire about any dress code that might be in effect, so as not to be in violation of that code on the first day. Remember what they say about first impressions; you only get one chance. The intern might have to incur a cost for purchasing business clothing where weekly dry cleaning or laundry costs ($50–$200 range) would need to be added to the budget.

Mailings/Correspondence. This cost should be minimal because your college will probably allow electronic submission of internship assignments. However, it requires mentioning. If you must mail anything to your supervising faculty members (e.g., end-of-semester assignment portfolio), students should expect to pay for their own postage. Some programs may be collecting hard copies for an upcoming accreditation site-visit. These are not considered agency products or part of the internship organization's daily business. One should not expect the internship site to incur this expense. Mailing documents early can save you money; last-minute mailings (e.g., overnight) to meet an assignment deadline can be extremely costly.

Certifications and Insurance. Of benefit to some interns is the availability of personal certifications and in-service training that may be offered through or by the internship agency. Some agencies will require the prospective interns to be CPR (cardiopulmonary resuscitation) or First Aid certified. Some training may be for security sensitive information and documentation by the human resources (HR) department, while others may require in-house training to obtain keys and building access. In cases where the intern is dealing with equipment and player locker room/ facilities, Occupational and Health Safety Administration (OSHA) guidelines and certifications may be required, for which the agency may be willing to reimburse or pay for in advance. For international internships or international travel, the intern will be required to bring up-to-date shot and booster inoculations charts. Incurring the personal cost for such items must be calculated and included in the overall cost of the internship. Some internships, such as fitness or event management or college coaching, may require an intern to purchase liability insurance. This is often available through the academic institution at a nominal cost and may also be available through a parent's insurance policy. Student teachers often have to purchase a similar insurance package, effective for the semester of the internship or student teaching experience. Even if not required by the organization or your institution, it is worth investigating. A 3 million dollar liability policy can often be purchased by a student for less than $20 and provide coverage for 12 months. It is better to be covered with a policy and not need it than to need the insurance and not be covered.

Job Search Costs. While searching for a full-time job should not really be considered as a cost for completing an internship, one can often tell early in an internship if the sponsoring organization may not be hiring for full-time positions once the internship is complete. Thus, including the cost of a job search during the internship is not a bad idea.

If a student maximizes their efforts in seeking an appropriate internship, costs will be incurred during this search process. It is no different when searching for a full-time position. One will need to set aside some money for this process. While some organizations allow an individual to apply online, thus reducing mailing costs, not all individuals are hired in this manner. As recommended earlier for the internship search, purchasing memberships to websites that require a fee is a great idea. Often, competition for the job is lessened because not everyone is willing or cannot afford to purchase a membership. But if fewer people are applying to positions found on these websites, it is well worth the cost. Most often you can purchase a two to three week membership, three months, or more. We recommend nothing less than a three-month membership because this is generally a better value. Annual memberships are also available, but, hopefully, one will find a full-time position in less than three months. Be aware: a downturn in the economy can make the job search much longer.

One very good way the student intern can hedge on the cost of a job search, during the internship experience, is to make your talents become very valuable to the agency. Many individuals interviewed for this book have mentioned this: a strong work ethic and the personal determination to do a good job on any assignment the agency requests may lead to a full-time position. If the intern spent a great deal of time in choosing the right internship and maximized the opportunities to impress the staff at the agency, then, hopefully, the agency will not let the competition hire the graduating intern. Many first jobs have been earned through a well- performed student internship.

This section has focused on the costs involved in the completion of an internship. Some internship programs provide the student intern with a budget worksheet to help in the planning of the financial arrangements for the duration of the internship. If the student intern already has established a personal budget, subsequent estimated projections will allow for a much easier comprehension of the cost to live while interning. An example of a personal budget worksheet is provided in Figure 8.3. One can insert or eliminate items; obviously, fixed and variable costs will fluctuate depending on one's individual situation. Amounts will vary based upon the geographic location of the internship site.

Use of the worksheet will assist in making financial decisions about the internship. If a student has financially planned for the internship from the beginning, the opportunity to select the best possible placement, regardless of location, will maximize this career-making experiential learning opportunity.

The dollar amounts involved in an internship are often viewed as a negative. However, you or your family can recoup some of the costs via the Internal Revenue Service. Educational and job search costs can be deducted from your taxes. Save all of your receipts and documentation for any cost incurred. Maintain actual mileage incurred or print a Mapquest log for each interview trip, job fair attended, or any other trip tied closely to the job pursuit. Mileage to and from work during the internship cannot be counted.

Applying Over the Internet

Applying for jobs over the internet can be convenient but tricky. We all take the time to format our résumé perfectly, but not all word documents transfer easily into online résumé submission programs. Saving your documents in a PDF format preserves your document in the format you

Budget Worksheet				
FIXED COSTS		**VARIABLE COSTS**		
	Amount			Amount
Rent/Insurance		Water/Electric/Other Utilities		
Car Payment		TV/Cable/Internet		
Phone Service		Entertainment		
Liability Insurance (If required)		1. Foods		
Credit Card Payments		2. Other (Movie, Club, etc)		
1.		Dry Cleaning		
2.		Non-Auto Travel		
Student Loans (If not deferred)		Clothing/Uniforms		
Laundry		Gifts (Xmas, B-days, weddings)		
Savings (min. $25/month)		Gasoline/Tolls		
Other		Groceries		
		Miscellaneous		
		1.		
		2.		
TOTAL F		TOTAL V		
* Total F + Total V = Ts	Ts x 12 months=	Amount you will spend in 1 year		
**To spend $2500 a month for 12 months		One needs to earn an absolute minimum of $35,000/year		

**The 2016 federal income tax was between 10 and 15% for individuals earning what could be considered a student income. Tax bracket varies based on income, marital, and filing status.

Figure 8.3. Sample Internship Budget Worksheet

want an employer to see. It is recommended that you learn how to create your résumé in plain text, email, and scannable formats in addition to the word processed format ("How to," n.d.). For more information on applying by email or online, visit the Ontario Council of Agencies Serving Immigrants website ("How do I apply," 2016).

Contacting the Organizations after Applying

Two common questions from students are if I have not heard from an organization, how long do I wait before contacting them and how often and how should I contact them? First, review the position announcement. Make sure calls are accepted about the position. Calling individuals or organizations when there are specific directions not to call can be disastrous. We mentioned earlier paying attention to detail is important, and this is one situation where making an error can take you out of the running for a position. Make sure you read job announcements and follow the information in them explicitly.

In Figure 8.2, paragraph three indicated the applicant would contact the organization within two weeks. This is a good length of time to first contact an organization after applying. This inquiry is primarily to ensure your materials were received, but it may not hurt to ask when top candidates may be contacted or when interviews may be conducted.

INTERVIEWING

Advance Planning

Interviewing for any job can be a nerve-racking experience. Advance planning, though, can decrease or even eliminate the feelings of anxiety. The key to creating a successful experience allowing the interviewee to control a great deal of the environment is preparation. You have already done some of the work by developing a notebook with all of the position announcements as recommended earlier in this chapter. Now you have been contacted for an interview.

Do your homework! Your first step is to review the position announcement and refresh your memory. Second, go to the organization's website and study it intensely. Learn as much as you can about the organization. Of particular importance is studying the organizational chart if one is available. At the very least, find a staff directory and try to learn as many names and position titles as possible. Definitely, concentrate on finding the individual(s) who might be meeting you at the airport, with whom you may be sharing a meal, and any individuals who you will most likely meet during the interview process.

Another place to find information about the organization would be online from the *Sports Business Journal/Daily, Athletic Business, NCAA News,* or any other trade journal/publication linked to the particular position for which you are interviewing. Besides official publications, many professional associations have newsletters that highlight news, awards, and other information about organizations and individuals. Newsletters often require a professional membership to access. Finding information about an individual might be found by conducting a name search, but LinkedIn can be an extremely helpful resource. Googling an individual also may raise information about personal news items or accolades. Perhaps they have their own website. Try to find out about impending facility projects, spectator attendance, an organization's bottom line, and more. Regardless, your goal is to find as much information as possible about the organization and its employees, and arm yourself with critical information that may be asked in an interview.

The Interview Week Has Arrived

What you do during the week, and especially the two to three days before the interview, can also make or break your chances of being hired. We already discussed some elements of professional dress and hygiene earlier in the chapter. Now is the time to make sure your clothes are neatly pressed and you have everything you need. Depending on the position for which you are interviewing, you may want to have a portfolio neatly prepared with work you have completed. These can be sample press releases, a risk management project you completed, or at least portions thereof, and anything else that represents the type of work of which you are capable.

Mock Interviews. If you have not already participated in a mock interview, now would be a great time to initiate a practice interview with family members or professionals on campus. A campus career office can probably assist. Individuals who have been employed and have experience in interviewing can provide you with a realistic situation and professional feedback on your performance. Supply anyone assisting you with a copy of the job description and your résumé in advance. Websites exist that present a set of commonly asked questions in a job interview. Type mock interview questions into an internet search engine to find some websites. Most provide you with solid answers for specific questions, but some of these internet sites have questions related to a sport business. Appendix D presents extensive lists of interview questions categorized by industry segment to assist in interview preparation.

Preparing Questions for the Interview. Prepare intelligent questions to ask during the interview. Most interviewers will make sure the interviewee has time to ask questions. Some interviewers do this on purpose to see what type of planning the applicant has done in advance. The quality of the question is extremely important. This is a tough situation because it is possible the interviewers will have answered every prepared question during the interview. Questions dealing

Practicing for an interview with your academic mentor, campus career counselor, or other professionals on campus will help you be prepared and confident at your interview. (Courtesy of Dreamstime)

with the organization's strategic plan including mission, vision, and goals are often very good topical areas particularly if these have not been addressed in the interview. Top managers love discussing their organization's mission and vision. Just make sure your questions are honest and sincere and you can intelligently respond if they follow up with questions for you. The questions in Appendix D can also prompt one's thinking when developing questions more applicable to the specific organization with which you will interview.

Some questions you may not want to ask. Information about company benefits may be readily available on a company website. Asking questions about a topic that can be found on their website may send a message one is not adequately prepared. A question about benefits is best addressed when you have been offered the position. Asking about vacation time and sick days does not display an approach that focuses on work ethic but rather how much time off you get from the organization.

Another approach to developing solid questions is to exhibit that you did your homework in preparing for the interview. For example, mention that you noticed on their website the organization recently secured a sponsorship with Nike and ask if the person being hired for the position will have a chance to work with and learn from the individual responsible for monitoring the satisfaction levels of the client. Besides showing preparation for the interview and knowledge about the organization, it also shows you are anxious to work with, assist, and learn from individuals tied to this project. It does not show arrogance that you will want to come in and take over the project. Obviously, here, the position for which the applicant applied would be tied to marketing or sponsorship sales.

There are two more points we need to convey that are applicable to the sport industry, whether writing a cover letter or résumé or during an interview. First, never tell an organization you are a fan of their team. This is a turnoff for many managers because, when working for an organization, you may have very little time to actually watch an event. This raises a red flag and may eliminate you from consideration. Reconciling tickets, taking care of facility problems, or handling other situations not near the actual event, are typical responsibilities.

Second, be careful of how much you praise the organization in an interview or a cover letter. Some refer to this as fluff. Praising a particular aspect of the organization in an interview on one occasion, depending on the topic, is usually appropriate. Continuous accolades might be considered overkill and may be received as insincere in hopes of simply getting the job.

The Interview Location. Make sure you know the exact date, time, and location down to the room number if interviewing in a large building home to many businesses. If the interview is local and you have never been to the facility, take the time the day before the interview to scope out traffic and directions, find the building and locate the room or general area without being too conspicuous. This preparation will prevent you from having to concentrate on one more thing or risk being late when you should be thinking about the interview itself. On the day of the interview, plan to arrive at least 10 to 15 minutes early to the parking lot and arrive at least five minutes early to the actual interview location at the reception desk or designated interview area.

If the interview is not local and you will be renting a car, arrive the day before in plenty of time to prepare as recommended in the previous paragraph. It is even more crucial if you have never been to the city. Having maps and directions, a portable global positioning system (GPS), or the mobile app Waze will ease this task, but do not rely on these tools being absolutely correct. Often a GPS system will only take you a general organization address and not to a specific building. Therefore, arrive in plenty of time the day of the interview in order to find the interview exact location.

Always carry with you the phone number or numbers of individuals who you will be meeting. Just in case something unexpected happens over which you had no control, you will be able to call the individual and alert them to the situation (e.g., closed down interstate due to an accident). Make sure it was something under which you had no control. Just being late because traffic was too thick or you got lost are not acceptable excuses in this situation. You want to send a message to the interviewers that you are calm and well prepared. On-time arrival sends this type of message. Remember, on time means at least five minutes early!

One of the toughest questions for a prospective intern or entry-level applicant to ask when the interview offer is extended is whether the host organization will reimburse the applicant for interview expenses, especially if a plane fare and hotel expenses are involved. It is definitely okay to ask the question if presented in a very tactful manner. For example: "Will I be reimbursed for my expenses?" Dependent upon the answer, the interviewee can accept or decline the interview, but if this is a position you really want, we recommend finding a way to finance the trip if the organization does not plan on paying expenses.

Listening and Answering Questions. During the actual interview, listen very well to the interview question being asked. Let the interviewer finish the question before you start your answer. It is okay to pause a few seconds and gather your thoughts to completely and confidently answer the question. If you do not understand a question, ask the interviewer to rephrase or explain some aspect of the question. However, you do not want to do this for numerous questions. With advance preparation, most questions can be answered with ease, but do not monopolize the interviewer's time by doing most of the talking.

The Phone or Video Chat Interview. It is now more common for organizations to use or require live interviews as an initial assessment process for top candidates. This is especially used for screening interns. One should prepare for this type of interview in the same manner as you would for an on-site experience. If the interview will be via video chat using Skype or ooVoo, professional dress is required. It is even recommended to dress up for phone interview because it is as important as one taking place face-to-face. If you feel professional, you may perform better.

Many will not go to this length. The key thing to remember is your approach and preparation for this type of interview is no less critical.

Voice intonations are crucial in any type of interview. Record yourself to see how you sound over the phone. Perhaps your capstone class or campus career center will offer to video a mock interview. If you come across as monotone or have very little change in the sound of your voice, you may not be portraying your personality to the interviewer, something you can do more easily in a face-to-face interview. Since the interviewer cannot see facial expressions in a phone interview, it is important to display an upbeat and positive approach through voice tone and even humor when and if appropriate.

THE FINAL BUZZER

Serious consideration must be given to the selection of an appropriate internship experience. In this chapter, we have attempted to provide the student with enough resources and information to present oneself in the utmost professional manner and to assist in making the absolute best decisions for a successful internship experience. The student must pursue the internship with diligence and knowledge and have reasonable expectations for the final outcome. Application for several internships may be necessary due to the competition among the agencies to recruit the very best personnel and the number of individuals pursuing sport business industry internships. The student that has prepared themselves throughout their educational career should have little trouble securing a quality internship provided they adhere to the start early mentality, utilize the six Ps from Chapter 7, and apply the information presented in this chapter.

The internship is likened to a golden egg and, when properly nurtured and hatched, it can grow into the most beautiful and rewarding learning experience leading to a lifetime of career successes. Truly, a dream come true—a career in the management and business of sport!

EXPERIENTIAL LEARNING OPPORTUNITIES

Classroom Experiential Learning Exercise: Interviewing

For the Sport Studies Program, the senior-level students prepare for internships, future job openings, and graduate school by learning about interviewing techniques and skills for which human resource officers are searching. In this class, we practice Skype/online interviews before they bring potential employees in for an actual live face-to-face interview. Cal U uses a program called Hire CalU, which is an online interviewing/hiring program where you can add questions to personalize it for the sport industry. Sport management students are asked 20 general questions and several more related to the sports industry.

After the Skype/online interviews the students will find a job or internship announcement for which they qualify in the sport industry. Students will complete their résumé and cover letter for that job in the sport industry. The students are then assigned to a professor to do a live face-to-face interview using their résumé, cover letter, and job description they found. The same questions they used for the Skype/online interview will be used, but the interview will develop questions based on the student résumé and job description. Finally, the students would go out and do face-to-face professional interviews in business attire with professors, coaches, athletic administrators and career services departments all across thecollege campus. All the interviewers will give feedback to the students to help them improve their interviewing skills for the sport industry.

Submitted by Dr. Charles Crowley, Assistant Professor
California University of Pennsylvania, California, PA

Program Experiential Learning Example: Job Fairs
Every year, Bemidji State University receives announcements from the Minnesota Timberwolves, Lynx, Twins, United, and Wild inviting our sport management students to attend their upcoming job fairs. Students are encouraged to dress their best and carry along their résumés for on-site interviews by numerous sport organization representatives in attendance. Several students have been granted internships with various sport organizations afterwards and are working their dream jobs with these organizations. This experiential learning example is the same for many sport management programs throughout the country and abroad. All students should realize the importance of attending sport-related job fairs.

Submitted by Dr. Eric Forsyth, Sport Management Program and Internship Director
Bemidji State University, Bemidji, MN

SUGGESTED READINGS

Abenethy, Jr., E. H. (1996). *Factors influencing student selection of sport management graduate programs: Marketing implications* (Doctoral dissertation). Retrieved from Proquest Dissertations and Theses Global. (Order No. 9713154)

Adams, S. (2012, July 26). Odds are your internship will get you a job. *Forbes.* Retrieved from forbes.com

Anast-May, L., Buckner, B., & Geer, G. (2011). Redesigning principal internships: Practicing principals' perspectives. *The International Journal of Educational Leadership Preparation, 6*(1), 1–7.

Batty, K. A. (2011). *The role of motivation, perceived constraints, and constraint negotiation strategies in students' internship selection experience* (Doctoral dissertation.) Retrieved from Proquest Dissertations and Theses Global. (Order No. 3576810)

Bull, S. (2014). *Sport management internships:* A multiple case study of practitioner perspectives of communication (Doctoral dissertation). Retrieved from Proquest Dissertations and Theses Global. (Order No. 3617553)

Cuneen, J., & Sidwell, M.J. (1994). *Sport Management Field Experiences.* Morgantown, WV: Fitness Information Technology, Inc.

Figler, H. E. (1999). *The complete job-search handbook: Everything you need to know to get the job you really want.* (3rd ed.). New York, NY: H. Holt Publishers.

Gualt, J., Leach, E., & Duey, M. (2010). Effects of business internships on job marketability: The employers' perspective. *Education + Training, 52*(1), 65–88.

Grabel, D. G. (2014). *Sport management internships: Undergraduate student and practitioner perceptions and expectations* (Doctoral dissertation). Retrieved from Proquest Dissertations and Theses Global. (Order No. 3581800)

Hergert, M. (2009). Student perceptions of the value of internships in business education. *American Journal of Business Education, 2*(8), 9–13.

Hurst, J. L., Thye, A., & Wise, C. L. (2014). Internships: The key to career preparation, professional development, and career advancement. *Journal of Family & Consumer Sciences, 106*(2), 58–62. Retrieved from http://www. ingentaconnect.com/content/aafcs/jfcs/2014/00000106/00000002/art00010

Krannich, R., & Krannich, C. (2001). *Directory of websites for overseas job seekers: A click & easy special report.* Manassas Park, VA: Impact Publications.

Krannich, C., & Krannich, R. (2002). *The directory of websites for international jobs.* Manassas Park, VA: Impact Publications

Odio, M., Sagas, M., & Kerwin, S. (2014). The influence of the internship on students' career decision making. *Sport Management Education Journal, 8*(1), 46–57.

Seagle, E.E., Jr., & Smith, R.W. (2002). *Internships in recreation and leisure: A practical guide for students.* State College, PA: Venture Publishing Inc.

Schambach, T. P., & Dirks, J. (2002, December). Student perceptions of internship experiences. *Proceedings of the International Academy for Information Management (IAIM) Annual Conference: International Conference on Informatics Education Research (ICIER).* Barcelona, Spain. (ED481733)

Tooley, J. (1997, November 17). Working for credit: How to make the most out of a semester-long internship. *U.S. News & World Report, 76*–78.

Verner, E. M. (2004). Internship search, selection and solidification strategies. *Journal of Physical Education, Recreation and Dance, 75*(1), 25–27.

Wanless, D. (2013). *Perspectives from internships and co-ops with industry.* Presentation at the 120th ASEE Annual Conference & Exposition. Atlanta, GA.

REFERENCES

Academic degrees no longer a luxury in the burgeoning business of sport. (2008, June 9–15). *2008 Programs in Sports Business Special Advertising Section,* 29.

Bolles, R. N. (2017). *What Color is Your Parachute.* New York, NY: Ten Speed Press.

Chellaruai, P. & Kerwin, S. (2017). *Human resource management in sport and recreation,* 3rd edition. Champaign, IL: Human Kinetics.

How do I apply for a job by email or online? (2016). *Ontario Council of Agencies Serving Immigrants.* Retrieved from http://settlement.org/ontario/employment/find-a-job/applying-for-a-job/how-do-i-apply-for-a-job-by-email-or-online/

How to job search. (n.d.). *The Riley Guide.* Retrieved from http://www.rileyguide.com/execute.html

Kelley, D. R. (2004). Quality control in the administration of sport management internships. Journal of Physical Education, Recreation and Dance, 75(1), 29–30.

Miller, C. J. (2012). *I want to hire you, but your résumé sucks: 30+ tips to help you get a job.* Retrieved from http://corymiller.com/books/i-want-to-hire-you-but-your-resume-sucks/

Pontow, R. (1999). *Proven résumés: strategies that have increased salaries and changed lives.* Berkeley, CA: Ten Speed Press.

Porot, D., & Haynes, F.B. (1999). *The 101 toughest interview questions: And answers that win the job!.* Berkeley, CA: Ten Speed Press.

Snell, S., & Bohlander, G. (2013). *Managing human resources* (16th ed.). Mason, OH: South-Western Cengage Learning.

Sports industry statistics and market size overview. (2016, June 10). *Plunkett Research, Ltd.* Retrieved from http://www.plunkettresearch.com/statistics/sports-industry/

Yates, M.J. (2004). *Knock 'em dead with great answers to tough interview questions.* Holbrook, MA: Bob Adams, Inc.

Young, D.S., & Baker, R.E. (2004). Linking classroom theory to professional practice: The internship as a practical learning experience, worthy of academic credit. *Journal of Physical Education, Recreation and Dance, 75*(1), 22–24.

CHAPTER
9

Networking: Establishing Internship Relationships

"Networking is the reality that opens doors. In its simplest form, it is a circle of friends that self-promotes those they know. The more people you know and network with, the more they will promote the brand in which you are most interested—you! Sport business is a very popular industry, one that often promotes from within or provides opportunities based on recommendations from others or their network. Your network will provide you opportunities. Your education and skills will land you the job.

—*Scott Glaser, Associate Executive Director of the Alumni Association (Former Associate Athletics Director, University of South Florida, Tampa, FL*

THE WARM UP

In several earlier chapters, we introduced the concept of networking. In this chapter, we will delve deeper into networking as a professional art form. It is crucial in this industry. New employees are hired based on a colleague's recommendation. People know people; they may call colleagues working in another organization or country. It is extremely important students thoroughly understand networking and not simply rely on the contacts of a faculty member or a friend's parents.

NETWORKING DEFINED

Networking is a professional skill utilized to meet industry professionals for a variety of reasons. It is a way to meet individuals with whom you want to do business, but it also provides an avenue for meeting individuals who might be hiring or who work for a particular organization. This is a skill that should be learned early and learned well. While some individuals will make mistakes in their attempts to network with busy professionals, some networking skills take practice. In the following sections, we provide valuable networking information and common pitfalls to avoid.

Networking can take several forms. Telephone, email, blogging, socials, social media sites, guest speakers, mentor relationships, attendance at conferences, informational interviews, job fairs, and chance meetings all provide networking opportunities. Used appropriately, networking can mean an immediate job offer or it can lay the groundwork for future possibilities. Even so, networking must be done properly or it can actually turn individuals away.

Student Role

Just as a student is responsible for beginning their volunteer experiences as soon as they step foot on their college campus, so, too, are they responsible for beginning the development of their network. We realize some students are more outgoing than others. Perfecting one's networking skills decreases the time others must spend assisting with an experiential learning placement opportunity and increases employment possibilities. Though some institutions will provide volunteer opportunities and insist on placing students in apprenticeships or practicums, often a student's contacts can be just as valuable in fulfilling their experiential learning needs.

A faculty member cannot find placements for every single student from a practical standpoint. Students have unique career goals, varied skills, and differing personalities. One organization might be a perfect fit for one student but may not be even a close fit for another. Even faculty members with an extensive network of professionals working in sport business may not know of a placement within a specific industry segment every single academic term. Thus, it is imperative for students to begin early in establishing a network and continue to build it throughout their academic careers. As discussed in earlier chapters, this can be done in a variety of ways found throughout the Foster Five-Step Experiential Learning Model. For a review of this model, please revisit Chapter 1.

From a legal perspective, liability is often transferred to a student when an institutional policy prohibits a faculty member from placing or requiring a student to work with a specific organization. In this situation, the student assumes the risk for accepting a placement with a particular industry. *Nova Southeastern University, Inc. v. Gross* (2000) is one example of this (Foster & Moorman, 2001). Nova Southeastern, a private university, was named in a lawsuit regarding the placement of an intern in what was determined to be an unsafe area of town. Where a policy exists that prohibits institutional control over placement, a faculty member can still provide information about available experiential learning opportunities. It is up to the student to take action and contact the appropriate individuals or apply to intern with the organization through the appropriate channels.

Faculty Role

In sport business, a faculty member has many opportunities through conferences, meetings, field trips, advisory councils, and invited guest speakers to expose and introduce students to industry professionals. Every academic year brings new opportunities to search for individuals in different industry segments and involve them in the academic setting or program. Faculty members can also volunteer to work events to further extend professional networks. A wide network still does not guarantee an internship placement for any student. Organizations go through periods where no interns are needed or may have accepted an intern from another institution. Seasonality, as previously discussed, may vary internship needs at different times of the year.

Students benefit from a faculty members' network early in an academic career. This is especially true when finding volunteer opportunities for first-year students or recommending an organization to a student for a summer position or apprenticeship. When students work on developing their own networks, the pressure is removed from the faculty member to provide a perfect fit for student placements and students begin to establish professional independence.

TAKING ADVANTAGE OF OPPORTUNITY

Cities, counties, and university campuses always have opportunities for a sport business student to build a professional résumé and expand a network. Sport management programs and student associations often search for special events where a student can play a role and gain valuable experience. One can never know who they may meet or what type of responsibility they may be given simply by working a sporting event, regardless of its size or impact. Even if you have built a solid résumé, the very next person one greets at the next event may be the all-important owner or business person who will offer that chance of a lifetime!

Sometimes a particular reporting time such as 6 a.m. may deter a student from accepting an early morning responsibility. A Super Bowl work-day can begin as early as 4:00 a.m. The Super Bowl, a divisional playoff, and a specific professional golf tournament are examples of events that happen once a year and, sometimes, once in a lifetime in a geographic area for the volunteer. Foregoing this fantastic chance to gain experience and meet the professionals working the events

When volunteering to work a sporting event, small or large, introduce yourself to fellow volunteers and ask for business cards from volunteer coordinators and other key individuals to grow your professional network. (Courtesy of iStockPhoto)

or organizations may be a colossal missed opportunity; the sad closure to this example is that the individual who chose the preferred social event will never realize the professional opportunities that may have been squandered, even a link to a life-long career. As some of our colleagues have explained it, you don't know what you don't know. Here is one example shared by Dr. Eric Forsyth from Bemidji State University in Minnesota and verified by Kevin Nevalainen, now the senior director of weekly racing operations for NASCAR.

> Kevin always had a dream of working in the auto racing industry. In my introduction course, I have students interview professionals in the field that hold a position the student would like to pursue one day. To complete this assignment, Kevin called the Michigan International Speedway headquarters. His contact welcomed the idea of providing answers to specific questions Kevin wanted to ask. This contact ended up being the president of the speedway. He shared he had a two-hour layover in Minneapolis, Minnesota on an upcoming trip. Instead of interviewing him over the phone, Kevin drove the four hours to the airport to interview him in person. Kevin ended up interning with NASCAR and still works with them more than 15 years later. (E. Forsyth, personal communication, February 24, 2017; K. Nevalainen, personal communication, February 27, 2017)

How is that for networking? Kevin did not take the easy road, and his story is similar to the one told in Chapter 1 about Kerryann Cook. Kevin took advantage of an opportunity, incurring financial expenses and a great amount of time out of his schedule, to fulfill an assignment resulting in an internship. Kevin states:

> Networking is definitely a big piece of the puzzle when trying to find work, but it continues to be important throughout a career as relationships and networking are what keeps you relative and will help prepare you to get opportunities to advance when they become available. (K. Nevalainen, personal communication, February 27, 2017).

There are many similar stories other faculty members could share. Maybe even one of your professors has a similar assignment. Do they require you to meet face-to-face? Are you allowed to just call someone because you do not have a car? Can a friend provide you with transportation? What about using your local bus station? One of the authors had a student who did just that and took a bus to a neighboring big league town to conduct his interview. Networking is so important and can lead to so many great things if done correctly. People will remember you more in a face-to-face encounter. Cathy Griffin (Time Out Interview 3.7 in Chapter 3) has taken networking to an extreme level. She worked with Pepsi-Cola as an intern and was hired back years later. She now owns her own executive search firm where she turned years of knowledge and networking contacts into a private lucrative business.

Professor Todd Koester's (Time Out Interview 9.1) career exhibits experience as a marketing professional whereby networking is a required skill. In order to sell a company's product, one must be able to network and continuously make new contacts. As you view the career progress of Professor Koester, you will view quite a quick advancement from intern to vice president in positions related to law and corporate marketing. He also points out, the importance of who knows you in his interview; we highlighted this important concept in Chapter 1. This is different and, in our opinion, more important than the typical myth we attempted to dispel in that same chapter. It's who knows you and remembers you and your capabilities instead of it's not what you know, but who you know. Acquaintances may not remember you or be able to vouch for you well enough to provide an exceptional recommendation. Will an interviewee over the phone remember you months or even years later?

Time Out Interview 9.1 with Todd Koesters
NETWORKING

Position	Assistant Professor – 6 years
Employer	University of South Carolina
B.A. Degree	English—The Ohio State University
M.S.A. Degree	Sports Administration—Ohio University
J.D. Degree	Capital Law School
Career Path	• Athletic Compliance Intern – The Ohio State University – 1 year • Intern – Ohio Office of Civil Rights 1 – year • Intern – Agency Won – 6 months • Director, Motorsports – Agency Won – 1 year • Account Director – GMR Marketing – 3 years • Vice President, Account Group – GMR Marketing – 4 years • Vice President, Sports Group – GMR Marketing – 4 years • VP Sales & Marketing – Churchill Downs Entertainment Group – 2 years

Employment Recommendation

"Once a student sees an open position, the first thing they should ask themselves is who knows me, whom will also know someone within that organization? Once they've identified that person, they then need to work with that person to ensure their résumé is read."

Many experiential learning opportunities turn into a full-time internship or entry-level employment. It is not uncommon. However, it often happens to very involved individuals, especially if extra effort was expended. For example, one student served an apprenticeship with a minor league team during the summer between the sophomore and junior year. The apprenticeship required him to work alongside the director of concessions. When it came to serve his senior culminating internship, the student was offered the position as director of concessions and, upon graduation, was employed full-time by the same organization. The student never planned on entering the food services arm of minor league baseball, but the opportunity offered him entry into the sport business industry. Ultimately, he moved into sports media. Yes, an unlikely path, but nevertheless, full-time employment within the industry of his choice upon graduation. This is confirmation of Bernie Mullins's identification of career paths as a unique parameter of the sport business industry discussed earlier in the book.

THE ART OF NETWORKING

We have addressed networking in several different ways in this book. However, we have not provided a step-by-step strategic plan for assisting the novice. Examples below will cultivate ideas and, hopefully, motivate even the most timid individual in starting a professional network.

Getting Started

Networking can be affirmed as an art for meeting people. We mentioned earlier that networking is difficult for some individuals. As with many things, one gets better with practice. We recommend a variety of pathways to establishing one's own professional network. Observing how others network is a great place to start. Once different outward methods of networking have been scrutinized, it is time to embark on the development of a personal networking style. If meeting people for the first time is uncomfortable, begin by writing an introductory letter to a particular professional in the industry. This person might be someone who spoke in a sport foundations course and invited students to follow up and contact them. This letter can simply be an opportunity to introduce yourself and your desire to tour the organization's facility or to conduct an informational interview, as discussed later in this section. The worst that can happen is that you do not hear back, which is a sad display of professionalism, especially if the individual invited students to contact them. However, you are more likely to get a positive response. As we have pointed out in previous sections of this book, an email may get lost in the spam or junk folder of the receiver. We recommend sending them a typed and well-constructed personal letter to their business address.

Perhaps you have a course assignment where you have to research career paths as our time out interviewees have mentioned in several chapters. Construct a very professional letter free of all writing errors and select a certain niche area within the industry, for example, event management. Address a letter to each event manager in a particular league, conference, or state;

personalize the letter for each person using their actual name and specific title; explain your assignment; and craft a set of questions that will satisfy the directions of your assignment. Anyone can go online and find out what others say about certain positions in sport. However, there is no better research method for discovering the necessary information about a certain position than asking those who hold that position. Many professionals will respond to this type of inquiry much faster than to a newspaper interview or survey attempts from a researcher. This is primarily because many individuals working in sport had the same dream you do, completed similar assignments, and performed an internship or two. Because they are living their dream of working in the sport industry, of waking up every day loving their work, they have a strong desire to help students in the same pursuit.

After the letters are sent, sit down and create additional questions you would like to have answered were this individual to call you. Craft answers to questions the individual might ask you. Preparing in advance will allow you to talk to this individual in a professional manner should they pick up the phone and desire to initiate a conversation. Most will not have the time, but being prepared will work in your favor should the unexpected happen. Above all, write a personal thank-you note to anyone who responds, making sure it is free of all writing errors, and put in the mail. Do not send a text message or an email as this can sometimes misconstrue sincerity. As we mentioned in Chapter 7, very few people take the time to complete this step and, most often, it will leave a very favorable impression on the individual to whom it was sent. It might even change someone's mind about using your services. Maybe the very next week a position does open and it is offered to you just because you took the time to send a personal thank you.

If you feel completely comfortable in talking with these professionals, request the opportunity to schedule an informational interview, a facility tour, or perhaps a chance to shadow an individual and assist with the set-up or take-down of an event. Someone you contact will grant these types of requests. It happens more likely with those in the minor leagues or less popular sports, but do not be surprised if an extremely busy individual in a high profile position takes the time to assist in your pursuit of gaining knowledge of and experience in this industry. This was the case of the example we used in Chapter 1 involving Pat Summitt.

An informational interview is not considered an interview for a job but is a great networking tool. It is a professional situation one arranges to learn more about an organization or an individual's job while exploring different career options. Working professionals are busy. Offer to take someone to lunch since, even on the busiest of days, individuals must eat. Be prepared to initiate the discussion with well-thought-out questions. Most individuals will go with the flow in this type of casual atmosphere and the conversation should proceed with ease. Do not ask for a job in an informational interview; however, do bring an updated résumé just in case one is requested. Bring a nice portfolio with paper to take notes and store the résumé where it will not get bent or wrinkled. After the meeting, follow immediately with a thank-you note in the mail. Individuals will appreciate the time taken to express your gratitude.

If a chance meeting results in an invitation to stay in touch, do so, but do not hound the individual. The same recommendation applies: Follow up with a letter that mentions the meeting and thank them for their time. Why a letter? Besides the lost email we mentioned earlier, there is a better chance they will remember you and the conversation if you remind them in a letter sent directly to them at their work location. Yes, they might get a lot of mail as well, but a personal letter might have a better chance of reaching them and getting read than an email sitting in their junk box or with the 100+ other emails they get every day.

Demonstrate creativity! Even a student can develop a business card and use it in networking. Microsoft Word and Publisher are easy software programs to use and business card paper can be purchased at office supply stores. Develop a sharp looking card with correct contact information. Be careful about using logos that may be copyrighted. When in doubt, develop your own logo or do not use one. Invest in a small business card holder so the cards do not get creased or dirty and keep them with you at all times. When meeting individuals, some will be impressed that a student had a card. It is easier for people to maintain a card than hold onto a full résumé. A card may also help them remember you more readily. An exchange of business cards should become a standard part of your professional greetings.

Networking is not without its pitfalls. Errors are made when networking. Here are a few tips to consider. Do not consistently call individuals or email them when given permission to do so. Most often, many individuals in the sport industry are extremely busy and may receive hundreds of résumés in a given week or month. Respect their time. Yes, it is okay to call to follow up on a conversation, to find out if your application materials have been received or to find out the status of a job search if you have not heard from an organization within a predetermined amount of time—generally about two to three weeks. However, we suggest you do not pester anyone at the organization with continuous e-mails or phone calls. Some will reward those who conduct simple follow-ups and perceive these contact attempts as a measure of assertiveness, a trait organizations want in a candidate.

While we mentioned attendance at conferences as a preparation tool in a previous chapter, attending conferences or job fairs, for the main purpose of meeting individuals, is one of the best ways to position oneself to promote your background, professional goals, and skills. Some individuals actually go too far and "stalk" a certain individual in hopes of getting a personal interview. Chance meetings can happen in an elevator or at a drinking establishment; be prepared for those types of situations with what some call a 30-second elevator pitch that includes a brief introduction of yourself, your strengths, and maybe how you believe your skills can assist an organization. However, do not monopolize an individual's time or conversation by prolonging the chance meeting. One can usually tell if that individual wants to prolong the meeting by asking additional questions and showing a true interest. Job fairs and conferences afford job seekers an opportunity to mingle with industry professionals at a social or in a bar. Regardless of the site, these events are not the time to drink a lot of alcohol. Yes, if one is of legal drinking age, it is

Some sport management programs sponsor conferences for students and invite a variety of speakers to enhance student networking.
(Courtesy of Freeimages)

okay to have one or two drinks dependent upon the situation. Erring on the side of caution and not drinking at all is the best recommendation if one is unsure.

If you make any promises during a networking experience, follow through. If a promise to send an e-mail or to make a certain phone call is given, do it by the day or time promised. The individual may be testing you!

Improving Your Networking Skills

You are pursuing step two of the Five-Step Experiential Learning Model, the apprenticeship. You can take the broad approach explained in the previous section where you wrote letters to a variety of individuals hoping one or more will respond, but it is time to practice a more direct approach. Do not wait until one or two weeks before your institutional assigned deadline to approach a specific individual and confirm an apprenticeship offer. Select an organization and an individual in a position for whom you wish to work. Draft an introductory comment before you dial the phone just in case you are able to talk with them on your first call. Know what you want to say and how you want to say it, but do not read it off a sheet of paper. Many can tell when you are doing this. Get a faculty member to help you draft some questions or advise you as to how best to introduce yourself. Make the call. Many times you will be asked to leave a message. It is our recommendation, if this happens, to follow-up your phone call with an email that is very clear regarding the purpose of your call. It is also suggested you not use a cell phone when making these important calls. You may believe your cell has great coverage and messages you leave are not garbled, but one can never be sure. Landline phones are the best option to ensure your message is clear and all information is received. If you do not have access to a landline phone, then test sample messages left with friends from a residence hall or other location you may often take calls.

By starting your pursuit early to fulfill step two, in all probability, you will be able to find an apprenticeship or summer paid position to satisfy your academic requirement and more than satisfy your need for professional growth. When starting late in the process, often a student has to accept just anything that becomes available when, in reality, they know the opportunity offered to them would not have been their first choice. Even if you must accept a less than ideal choice for you, you never know how that decision can change your life and your path for entering the industry. Make sure you make the most of any opportunity afforded you. Approach it with a positive outlook and an open mind that you will learn everything possible and be the best apprentice the organization has ever had. Even if you do not end up liking the position or the responsibilities, your coworkers will not be able to tell and you will come away with great recommendations to utilize for your future internship search. Oh, did we mention, after you leave, follow up with a personal thank-you letter to your site supervisor, boss, or anyone with whom you worked, even those who may not have been 100% in your corner?

Do not be disheartened if the first individual contacted does not respond. Move on to the second person on a list you have created of potential work sites and professionals to contact. Not getting a response most likely has nothing to do with you. Perhaps that individual has moved to another organization or is going to be moving on and cannot yet announce the move. Yes, they might just be displaying poor ethics or professionalism by not responding even if only to tell you they cannot accept your services at this time. Maintain your positive outlook and the confidence you now have in your abilities to network.

One never reaches ultimate perfection in networking. Yes, some individuals are very good at it, but even the most accomplished networker will tell you they can always find a better approach or a more creative way to ask a question. Many will tell you there was that thank-you letter they never wrote. With social media outlets increasing and the opportunity it affords individuals to meet or stay in touch with colleagues they knew 10 or more years ago, this is another avenue where even the most accomplished networker can learn and hone this important skill. Remember to take the time to say thank you to individuals who offer comments or words of encouragement on these social networking sites. This time, it is okay to email them because, chances are, you do not have their mailing address or would not be able to find it without asking them directly.

In closing this segment, we would like to recommend purchasing a great book and its accompanying workbook called *The Power of Who* by Bob Beaudine. Bob is a part owner of the Texas Rangers, a highly sought after speaker and recognized as a top sports/entertainment search executive in the United States, and his book is an easy and very interesting read. His book is all about networking and using your personal contacts identified as your spheres of influence to get your foot in the door and climb the corporate ladder regardless of what stage you are in your career (Beaudine, 2009). He does claim you already know everyone you need to know, but it is our opinion this quote targets individuals already working in the industry. You will probably need to spend a few more years meeting people. However, maybe you have already met enough key individuals.

THE FINAL BUZZER

Hopefully, this chapter will assist anyone, even the most apprehensive individual, in improving personal networking skills. We challenge you to come up with a networking exercise or event not presented elsewhere in this book and introduce it at one of your on-campus sport management association or other group meetings. You will not only be able to get feedback on your networking skills, but you can assist fellow students in honing their networking abilities. Remember that every one of your fellow classmates represents a network connection, as each of you are pursuing your individual paths in the same industry.

Perhaps you have noticed we have constantly reinforced the practice of saying thank you in this chapter. We cannot emphasize enough the importance of this simple practice, a networking exercise in and of itself, and the effect it can have on the individual at the receiving end. Though this practice is, in actuality, an act of paying back the good deeds of another, it can truly end up being a practice of paying it forward, just as demonstrated in the practices established by the young boy in the movie Pay it Forward (McLaglen, Treisman, & Leder, 2000). However, no expectations should accompany the thank you. Send a thank you today to someone that has assisted you. Surprise a current faculty member, a mentor, a family member, a high school teacher, or coach!

Our efforts were to emphasize the importance of learning the art of networking early. If practiced, hopefully, the pursuit of finding the culminating internship, step five in the Experiential Learning Model, results in a less complicated endeavor. Remember, the ultimate goal, presented earlier in this book, is to have a full-time job in the industry on graduation day. Icing on the cake is having the offer extended as a result of the internship, thus eliminating the job search process.

EXPERIENTIAL LEARNING OPPORTUNITIES

Classroom Experiential Learning Exercise: Experiential Learning in Public Relations
Students participate in a semester-long experience in public relations. Necessary components include a Twitter account, an online blog site, photography equipment, and athletic department support. This is recommended for class sizes with no more than 30 students. The course establishes a partnership with the athletics department (AD) in an attempt to increase the publicity of university athletics. Students are required to communicate directly with those individuals responsible for managing the media for athletic events. Students must follow the same requirements as media to obtain press passes for sport events.

Students become sideline reporters and photographers; they attend live events on campus and participate in post-game press conferences. They post their final product of the experience and story, along with images to a live, online blog. In addition, students are provided access to a single class Twitter account to supplement their blog posts where they can share short videos and images of the events they attend. Every student shares in the responsibilities as one editorial team for their blog posts. These posts are not game summaries, but designed to foster relationships with the public. They work together to determine the best images captured at the events and are all required to partake in the photographer experience.

The benefits they receive are the experience of being a sideline reporter, networking with AD managers, working with strict timelines, equipment used in the field, and publishing their stories and experience on the Internet. All are pieces that can be used on future résumés.

Submitted by Chad Witkemper, Assistant Professor of Kinesiology, Recreation, and Sport
Indiana State University, Terre Haute, IN

Program Experiential Learning Example: Comprehensive Networking
At York College of Pennsylvania, students start applying the concept of networking early in their initial semester of college. The first required practicum course provides instruction on the art of networking, focusing on how to prepare effectively before a networking opportunity (e.g., creating an elevator speech, conducting preparatory research), making a positive impression during a networking opportunity (e.g., generating small talk, showing positive nonverbal communication), and growing the relationship after a networking opportunity (e.g., finding meaningful ways to stay in contact). Students engage in common networking scenarios to practice their skills, and then apply them during four required practicums as they complete real-world work in York College's Department of Athletics & Recreation and meet many different people. Students also use these networking skills when they conduct informational interviews with sport professionals or engage in real-world projects during their classes. Further, students receive instruction in the use of social media for networking, and can even work with the college photographer on a professional picture for LinkedIn.

York College also hosts Sport Management Professional Day each semester. Sport professionals in diverse areas of the industry from around the country attend and critique students' cover letters, résumés, and interviewing skills. Roundtable and panel discussions are also held and students can participate in speed networking activities. This event has led to internship/job offers and great relationships. It plays a big role in influencing the career and professional development of the students and is another wonderful opportunity for them to use their networking skills, especially as they approach graduation.

Submitted by Dr. Molly Hayes Sauder, Assistant Professor and Coordinator of
Sport Management Practicum and Work Experience
York College of Pennsylvania, York, PA

REFERENCES

Beaudine, B. (2009). *The Power of Who*. New York, NY: Center Street.

Foster, S. B., & Moorman, A. E. (2001). *Gross v Family Services Agency, Inc.*: The Internship as a special relationship. The Journal of Legal Aspects of Sport, 11, 3, 243-267.

McLaglen, M., & Treisman, J. (Executive Producers), & Leder, M. (Director). (2000). *Pay it Forward* [Motion Picture]. United States of America: Warner Brothers and Bel Air Pictures, LLC.

Nova Southeastern University, Inc. v. Gross. (2000). 758 So. 2d 86.

CHAPTER
10

Ending an Internship and Starting a New Position

"Interns who demonstrate a high level of professionalism take initiative, pay close attention to detail in the work they do, and make great use of their time throughout the duration of their internship create the most favorable impression on their employer and colleagues. Timing is also important. If you've done all of these things and a full-time role opens with the organization during your internship, then you have set yourself up well to be considered for that position."

—Bree Parker, Recruiting and Training Manager, Tampa Bay Buccaneers, Tampa, FL

THE WARM UP

Congratulations! Successfully completing an internship and graduating with any academic degree is an outstanding milestone. How you finish an internship and start a new position is vitally important. These situations lend themselves to important ways for handling both scenarios. The following sections will explain in more detail.

REQUESTING ADDITIONAL RESPONSIBILITY

If you have not already done so, during the last weeks of an internship, ask for additional responsibility. You understand your capabilities; you are comfortable with the work environment, and you want to learn and do more. One of the most prolific efforts put forth by a student intern to enhance the quality of the internship is that of seeking additional responsibilities. Interns have plenty to do some of the time; conversely, there can be down time between projects or assignments. Interns also become very familiar with their work environment and have a keen awareness of where their skills complement an unmet need within the organization. In these situations, ask for additional assignments, propose a plan to fill the unmet need, or go above and beyond on even the smallest of tasks. Perhaps you will be running an errand or delivering a finished product and will be able to further coordinate the movement of the product beyond what is expected. The little bit of extra effort expended to get the item one step above your destination, to upper level management, can make a difference in just being an intern or being an exceptional intern. The following story will illustrate this point.

An undergraduate student was serving an internship with a major league baseball team in one of the southern states. The student intern was working on a group project in early spring and the agency had not completed its hiring for the upcoming season. The project was a major marketing effort requiring coordination between three in-house departments of the agency. The organization had one coordinator on staff, but hiring efforts had not yet filled two additional coordinator positions for the project. The student intern was very proficient and detail-oriented in her work efforts. Before long, she was moving the information and project items between the three separate departments working on the project. The coordinator and the intern were able to get the marketing project completed ahead of time, and it was a huge success for the team. The internship supervisor for the agency called the sponsoring university program coordinator and requested the student intern be hired before the completion of her internship, all based upon her work efforts and commitment to the organization. Yes, the project required overtime on the part of the intern (four 70+ hour weeks), as well as functioning with three supervisors instead of one, but consider the payoff. She started at the agency with a $32,000 salary in a job she basically designed for herself! Needless to say, the agency did not bother to rehire for the two open coordinator positions.

Similar opportunities may not always be available in an internship. In this setting, it was the young lady's diligence and willingness to go the extra mile that made a difference. She did not act out of self-interest; on the contrary, her actions were to make the workload easier for the organization. She simply assumed additional responsibility to make a situation better for all of the workers involved. This was simply maximizing the purpose of the internship experience and providing a win-win result for all involved parties.

COMPLETING AN INTERNSHIP

One of the biggest mistakes we have seen students make is leaving an internship relationship inappropriately or without any intent to continue networking with individuals within an organization. Just because one is not hired full-time does not mean your contributions were not valued and the colleagues do not want to maintain contact. Hopefully, full-time employees extend to you the appropriate gratitude, well-wishes for success, and a desire to maintain communication. However, this does not always happen. We will assume you did a great job in the internship and, if so, several individuals will be willing to write a letter of recommendation and allow you to retain them as a reference on your résumé. Accept these offers graciously. In return, never list an individual as a reference for a position unless you send them a copy of any positions to which you apply along with an updated résumé. If significant time has passed, before you list them as reference, contact them and ask their permission. It can be very frustrating for an individual serving as a reference to get an email or phone call unexpectedly indicating a particular person has listed them as a reference, while not having all of the necessary information in advance. Additionally, it does not allow a reference to give you the best possible recommendation because they are unfamiliar with recent responsibilities. They are unaware of the requirements of the position for which you are applying and cannot attest, in the best possible way, to how your skills meet those requirements. An individual serving as a reference is devoting time from their own very busy work schedule when a letter of recommendation is required; respond with gratitude and provide as much information as possible before they are contacted by the organization.

After you leave an institution or organization, maintain contact with former professors and coworkers. You never know what can become of this continuous networking opportunity.

If, by chance, your internship presented a rocky road or you are not leaving on the best of terms with some of your coworkers, in your last weeks of the internship, do anything possible to show the organization your best work. Make every attempt to smooth any remaining bumps in those relationships. It is immensely important to leave on a positive note. Perhaps you made some mistakes in how you communicated or worked with one particular person. Take time and make the effort before you leave to apologize and show gratitude for their assistance helping you to grow as a professional. Any extensions of appreciation will be observed positively and this is the impression you want to leave with the organization. Ignore the often-heard saying that apologizing is a sign of weakness. This is not true, especially in networking and creating relationships.

The same is true when you are applying for internships or graduating and leaving your university. Depart on great terms with all of your professors and individuals for whom you may have worked. Professors are the first individuals an organization might contact for a recommendation,

On your last day at an internship, shake hands with your supervisors and other employees and thank them for the opportunity, as this will help you leave a positive and professional impression with the organization. (Courtesy of Dreamstime)

especially if they are well-known by one or more employees within that organization. Also, not listing a professor from an institution that is well known may work against an applicant, particularly if the professor has a good track record of recommending outstanding interns and employees.

SALARIES TO EXPECT

Your work as an intern may be limited to an uncompensated internship. Paid internships exist and are growing in number. Those who receive any form of compensation during the internship are very fortunate. Upon completion of the internship, one should graduate to an entry-level working position. In times of a tough economy when organizations may not be hiring full-time employees, accepting another internship might be necessary. However, we would not recommend consenting to another unpaid position. Although this can vary, repayment of student loans generally start within six months after a degree is completed and some income will be important. Likewise, we do not advocate leaving the industry to take a full-time paying position if a career in the industry is truly the goal. When you have lost daily contact with a network of sport professionals, it is much tougher to get back into the industry. If you have no full-time career offers and are in a paid internship, strongly consider staying in that position after you graduate if the opportunity is extended.

Should you remain at the internship site and your position is converted into a paying job, you may have the opportunity to negotiate your initial salary. Some agencies may not have an open position available immediately and will offer to pay an hourly wage to keep you on board. The individual would have to make that decision at the appropriate time and should weigh such factors as the actual wage amount, any benefits associated with employment, and the expected length of time until a salaried opportunity becomes available. Basically, if you optimized your required internship time at the site (often 400–500 hours per semester) and maximized your experiential learning opportunities within the organization, you should qualify as an entry-level employee. After all, you now have several months of on-the-job training with the organization. If the agency has no positions available for you, there are other organizations that would be interested in offering you a career position. Some agencies will not train and teach you their respective secrets and then turn you away to work for the competition. This is the beauty of the internship process; if done well, you can, more than likely, expect an offer for employment if any positions are available.

So how much is one to expect in the form of salary and compensation? Entry-level positions in some segments of the industry are on the low rung of the pay-scale ladder. With your degree in hand, your starting salary can depend on the specific industry segment. Positions typically start anywhere from $23,000–$35,000 a year, plus benefits. Even when entering the field with a master's degree, the salary can be the same. These entry-level rates are especially true in professional team sport organizations. Because there are so many individuals hoping to enter sport business through professional sport, the law of supply and demand is quite applicable. Teams can offer low salaries and, be assured, they will find a qualified applicant who will jump at the chance. Salaries for sales jobs may even be lower, but many offer a commission based on sales for tickets, sponsorships secured, group and suite sales, and more. Sometimes, it is these very same sales jobs that offer the highest salaries. It is the commissions earned that bumps the salary to a very respectful level. For example, if you have the opportunity to sell sponsorships and suites. A 10% commission on a $100,000 sponsorship results in a very good payday! All positions with some organizations offer basic perks. Tickets for your family and friends to games and special events and logo clothing for you are common.

Salaries in other industry segments will vary based on several factors. We mentioned some of these factors in earlier chapters. Private and public sector salaries may differ. Any entrepreneurial business requiring you to earn income for the organization may offer higher income with the expectation the employee will recoup that income through their position. An example would be in sport marketing where the procurement of corporate sponsors is part of the job description. Of course, the higher salary may also come in the form of a commission based on the size of the contract. Five percent of a one million dollar sponsorship deal is a hefty payday! Starting salaries in collegiate recreational sport management often pay more than an entry-level position in professional sport, however, a master's degree is often a prerequisite. According to the National Intramural-Recreational Sports Association (2015), the average salary for an intramural sport employee with less than five years of experience was $41,075.

After you have proven yourself, promotions would gradually increase your salary. Looking for positions with other organizations is a common way to gain promotions and achieve salary increases. Other organizations will have openings. Perhaps your organization is top-heavy where individuals with families feel very comfortable and choose not to move a family or seek a move up the corporate ladder. Be aware, in order to climb the corporate ladder in sport, moving frequently may be required. This is because individuals often love their jobs and have created significant and important relationships in the community they serve. This is not only to enhance their position, but personal friendships for their family members and themselves are often hard to leave. Thus, you may have to make more than one move to ultimately get to the top of the corporate ladder if this is your long-term goal.

As you climb the corporate ladder in sport business, additional perks or benefits may accompany upward mobility in most sport organizations and agencies. Upper management positions may include company phones, a company car, an expense account, and a travel budget. Because you are working with a sport organization, a variety of sport-related perks may be offered. Access to the owner's suite, additional tickets, and signature memorabilia are possible. Trips to championship or special events that may include family are also considerations.

Usually the pay scale is directly proportionate to the length of employment time and the quality of job performance. Few positions, if any, in the sport industry will pay an employee for little or no work. Accepting the realization early that to be successful in the sport industry, or in any industry and remain employed, long hours and producing a profit or added value to the agency is a necessity. It will help immensely if you have a passion for this type of work.

YOUR NEW POSITION IN SPORT BUSINESS

Congratulations! Your hard work has paid off and you have taken the first step into what can be a long and very satisfactory journey—your career in the sport business industry! Welcome to an industry where individuals wake up each day loving their work and are enthused about tackling a new sponsorship proposal or the opportunity to initiate the registration process for a new youth league. A career in sport business, in many instances, is different each day; the uncertainty of the outcome of a game or event where new challenges and rewarding outcomes result are often the ingredients for an exciting career. *Carpé diem!* Seize the day!

We could have ended the book before this chapter, but we would have been remiss in leading you to believe your work is done. A career in sport now becomes a series of experiential learning opportunities leading to promotions, new directions, and new geographical regions of the United States and internationally. Sport is ever expanding and the globalization of sport will continue to reach even the most remote areas of the world. What you do in your first full-time position can define your career. Aiding you in the realization that seizing every opportunity to make those experiences the most rewarding possible is the intent of this chapter.

Political Risk Management

One topic most internship related books, including our first edition of this book, fail to cover is political risk management. Sport business, at any level, is very much a political industry. Knowing how to maneuver the political land mines as well as manage political issues and the power one holds within their position in a positive way is extremely crucial at every level of employment, including internships.

Warren Miller (2002) handles this topic well in his book *Political Risk Management in Sports.* Although the book mostly focuses on the political environment within educational sport (college and high school), much can be learned and applied to all areas of the sport business industry. The student entering an internship and their first entry-level position should be extremely aware of the political environment. Perhaps you learned in a pre-internship class not to participate in office gossip. This is only the beginning! According to Miller, "Politics are the rules and force behind policy, communications, leadership, philosophy, accountability, planning and advancement" (p. 3). Furthermore, Miller reports in surveys and interviews conducted, more than 94% of firings or resignations of coaches and athletic directors are not caused by incompetence. Rather, and not surprisingly, these are caused by the failure of one to handle the political environment in which they are employed, otherwise called a political failure.

Office Etiquette and Rules

Arriving for work and meetings on time, as previously mentioned, is just one element of proper office etiquette. This practice also shows respect for all others in your work environment. However, there are often more rules, manners, and protocol for proper office etiquette.

It is not appropriate to utilize office supplies, letterhead, or company postage for personal uses. Nor is it appropriate to surf the internet, send personal emails, or make personal phone calls, especially long-distance ones, on company time. All of this can allow a supervisor to charge an individual with inappropriate use of company resources that can be grounds for dismissal. If you ask permission from your supervisor and it is granted, then it is probably okay, but having it in writing via an email, memorandum, or in some other format is recommended. Save this correspondence. Nevertheless, the best recommendation is to not use any organizational resources for personal needs.

Participating in office gossip is, first and foremost, a practice in which one should never participate. It is of particular importance for a new hire to refrain from this practice. You are attempting to establish your professionalism and your importance to the organization. Nothing will ruin another's perception of you faster than this type of discussion at the water cooler, over lunch, or in any other environment. Sometimes, you cannot prevent someone from pulling you aside or an inappropriate topic being raised in a lunch time conversation. The best recommendation, if you cannot excuse yourself from the situation, is to simply listen and forget. At no time should you share what you heard with anyone else. Additionally, any information you learn should not cloud your perception of a working relationship with the colleague who was the target of the possible misinformation.

Your First Week

A great way to approach one's first position in this industry is to perceive it as a training ground for your next promotion. During your first week, in most instances, you will be meeting many people. As everyone knows, first impressions are important. Take interest in those introductions and the work of your colleagues. Show an enthusiastic interest in their work responsibilities and learn how your tasks will serve or impact their work as you become an integral part of the organization's team environment.

The faster you learn everyone's first name and their role, the more impressed your colleagues will become. It will also aid you in communicating with colleagues and enhance your productivity and, perhaps, that of your coworkers.

Establishing Positive Work Habits

During the first few months in a new position, the importance of establishing positive work habits cannot be overemphasized. However, nothing we recommend should come across as a surprise as these work habits should already be part of the positive work ethic shown throughout the internship.

Arriving at least five to 10 minutes before the organization's start time for each day is recommended. This means arriving early enough so you are at your work station and beginning work at the designated time. If a meeting is scheduled, you are at the meeting with necessary writing materials and your full attention given to the meeting manager. There is nothing more frustrating to a supervisor than to have a meeting scheduled for an allotted time in the day and then have key individuals arrive late and unprepared. The meeting then becomes abbreviated and rushed in order to maintain the remaining daily agendas. As a result, the productivity of colleagues and the group as a whole is diminished. In fact, late arrival by some often dictates the need for additional meetings—something nobody likes.

As in the internship, you are also not darting out the door at the designated end of the workday. Yes, there will be times where family or outside event interests will create a need to depart quickly on occasion, but professionals ensure that a project the boss needs at the very start of the next workday is completed and ready for delivery before they leave the office. In fact, it is a very good practice to get projects completed and submitted in advance. If by chance, your supervisor wants to change a component or requests additional material, you then will still have plenty of time to complete the additional requests long before the original deadline. Quality work is best completed well in advance, allowing time to proofread, to review the requirements requested, and to add the finishing touches to enhance the project. The finished product will produce evidence of the quality time and effort taken to complete the work, and your supervisor will notice even if nothing is communicated.

Yes, additional work is often assigned to an individual who completes projects in a timely manner with exceptional quality. Sometimes, within your particular work environment, it might appear that more work is coming your way as compared to the amount being sent to your colleagues. While this can be true, it can also mean your supervisor respects your work and, when it comes to that important promotion you are pursuing, it is quite possible you will be at the top of the considered list. If your organization is looking to release workers because of low ticket sales, tough economic times, or a redirection of the organization's mission and vision, a supervisor would be remiss if they dismissed you even if you were the most recent hire. Obviously, there are no guarantees and the seniority of other workers may work against you. Even if you are released for one of the reasons above, your supervisor should be more than willing to provide an outstanding reference for another organization.

Professional Dress and Appearance

We spent quite a bit of time on professional dress in Chapter 7, so we will not belabor the point here. We do want to emphasize the point that private organizations can dictate office dress, facial hair policies, or any other facet applicable to appearance. It is up to you to accept those policies as a new hire. Any policy can change down the road with new management or with a relaxation of current policies.

A public organization has to pay more attention to the rights afforded individuals in state or federal constitutions. Hopefully, this was learned in a legal issues class. For example, an athletic director at a public institution, by law, should not be allowed to dictate hair length simply because of personal taste. However, such rules can be tied to a strong rationale for the establishment of such a rule. An employee can choose to comply or address the situation in another way. If no rationale for the rule can be established, the rule might be a violation of the First Amendment of the United States Constitution, specifically freedom of expression.

It is not our recommendation as a new employee and, perhaps, even at any other time, to challenge such rules. While it would be difficult for an employee to be dismissed based on such a rule, a supervisor can find other reasons to release an individual with no claim or a perception presented that it was tied to the employee's questioning of the rule. Plus, the rule's rationale, even if it would not be accepted by a court, is often to establish a team environment and a sense of camaraderie. When an individual attempts to go against the desires of the majority of individuals in order to promote their own self-interest, the situation rarely has a positive outcome.

During the first few months in a new position, it is especially important to arrive to meetings on time, dressed professionally, and ready to listen and learn. (Courtesy of Dreamstime)

Listening and Observing

As a new hire, listen to others and observe as much as you can. Listening is a skill that will serve you extremely well. You are in a new setting where others probably have more experience, have worked more events, and perhaps have designed a policy or procedure that has been revamped many times over to derive certain results. While you may have worked a few events or experienced similar office or work procedures at another location, it is not in your best interest to come into a new work environment and promote another organization's process just because it worked well elsewhere. Yes, maybe your ideas might be better and may result in better productivity or a simpler process, but it is best to wait and observe until an opportunity arises where you can, very tactfully, present an alternate solution or process. Many individuals are resistant to change, especially those who have been with an organization for a long time and have tried many different ways of accomplishing a task or running an event. Respect their experience. If the solution you present is not accepted, then at least you tried.

Observing how others perform can increase the speed of your learning curve. Learn through these observances. If you show respect for the skills and abilities of coworkers through attentive listening and careful observations, eventually the same respect will be given to your performance. This is especially true when others utilize your recommendations. Coworkers will notice how your work, and possibly theirs, is enhanced or streamlined, resulting in a more timely result.

Being a manager may be part of a new role. Entire textbooks and majors cover human resource (HR) management; this is not the purpose of this section, but a few comments are warranted. The content of the previous paragraph is just as important if you are hired into a supervisory role. Asking, learning, and listening is an exceptional method to being accepted quickly as a new supervisor. Learn about the organization before proposing or making sweeping changes. Make a point to meet with any individuals who will be reporting to you; get to know them and their strengths. Exhibit an honest interest in each employee and trust everyone, unless someone gives you a reason to question their actions. Managing employees can be extremely rewarding, but it can also be very frustrating and time consuming if everyone is not on the same page. Trying to foster a team-oriented environment is a good approach. After all, you are working for a sport organization. Establish an environment where each individual's background and skills are valued. Asking for input before making important decisions always invokes a sign of respect. An environment where everyone does their part to establish collegiality is important. It starts with leadership and setting an example.

Communicating With Clients: Manners and More

While many are very polite and were taught by parents at an early age all about manners, a few tips on communicating with clients are still important. Many entry-level employees deal directly with clients. People expect quality customer service, and poor service over the phone is one setting that can lead to contentious situations. Hopefully, your organization continually conducts training sessions with individuals who will be dealing with customers, such as would be encountered in a ticket sales position. This is not the time to be rude or return an acrimonious comment. If you are unsure of how to handle a frustrated customer, ask for assistance from your supervisor. The same is true if you are in a position where you might need to deal with parents or coaches. This is more likely to be the case if you are working in youth or high school sports. Newspapers and television have increasingly portrayed accounts of parents who address coaches and officials in an unproductive and irate manner. While most of these incidents involve violence against referees, other instances include a fourth grader filing a $10,000 lawsuit against a coach for violence during a game (Findlay, 2002), athletes versus athletes, fans versus athletes or coaches, and parents versus coaches. Furthermore, there are probably cases of violence against league administrators or sport supervisors. The key point here is that an employee can infuse tranquility into situations involving irate individuals by calmly addressing the situation and being educated in advance on how to do so. Therefore, as a new employee of a sport organization, treat a customer, client, or coach involved in any negative or volatile situation with courtesy and respect. Curt responses to comments or conditions can result in the escalation of a situation to an unnecessary stage involving rage and anger.

Using Modern Communication with Colleagues

Where would our society be today without the cell phone? Even when not talking on it, we juggle it, flip it, scroll it, scan it, and text on it incessantly. Modern communication has come a very long way in the last twenty-five years in improving connections with the important people in our lives: family, friends, children, students, bosses, and employees. Answering emails alone consumes a large part of most people's days. We can receive emails, text messages, and videos on our phones; thus, we are available 36/8—at least it seems more than 24/7! Answering a phone or continuing to work with earphones when another individual is talking is a sign of disrespect. When a colleague is attempting to communicate, give your full attention.

Technology allows us to keep notes and running lists, schedule appointments on an interactive calendar, or command a computer from a remote location. Do we need technology to be effective in sport business? Yes, when it allows one to be more productive, decreases work hours, and increases how we effectively contend on a level playing field with the competition. When conducting business, today's technology is indispensable! However, its primary purpose must remain in focus—operating and serving a sport business agency and its clients. We discussed proper use of letterhead and office supplies in a previous section. As an intern or a new employee, the same rules apply in the use of technology. The organization may provide access to the most advanced office equipment and technology and one should follow a polite and sincere code of behavior when using that equipment and technology. The key to this code would be recognition and acknowledgement of the proper rules of use and access and restriction of usage for personal reasons, especially on company time. Many pieces of office equipment, especially in larger organizations, will have a log-on user code assigned to individuals or departments, and abuses of the equipment or sharing a personal log-on code could result in dismissal from the agency. Surfing the internet on company time for reasons unrelated to the business is discouraged. Know your parameters—maintain your boundaries and illicit use of technology in the work place can be avoided.

Respect those who despise technology; yes, some individuals would rather not use a smart phone. However, those that feel very comfortable using the most advanced equipment on the market can be a true asset to the organization, while many non-users simply may not have the time to learn. Offering to show how a computer program or a new app can make one's tasks easier and faster can make you a hero! In fact, Tyrone Brooks (Time Out Interview 3.1 in Chapter 3), the author of this book's foreword, indicated he was retained after the completion of an internship in baseball operations with the Braves because of his technology skills (Personal communication, February 3, 2010). Today, generations are growing up with technology usage, and non-technology users will very soon be a thing of the past. However, there will always be newer and more complicated equipment. The cycle will always continue. Be patient with your colleagues who are not using the latest and greatest. One day, you may be in their shoes and will be asking for assistance from your new employees!

What If You Are Released by the Organization?

It is recommended a generic letter of reference from a site supervisor or colleague be obtained before the last day of an internship or a full-time position. It is common for a supervisor to leave the organization, as well, and sometimes it can be difficult to locate a former boss for a reference. Additionally, any future reference letter from that individual will not be on the respective organization's letterhead. Sometimes this is important to future employers or human resource offices.

Finally, perhaps your supervisor and you are being released because of down-sizing or change of ownership at the organization. Your work habits may be the very thing the supervisor remembers when s/he moves on to another sport organization. Do not be surprised if you are contacted to come and work under a previous supervisor at a different organization. This is a regular happening in sport business.

ORGANIZING YOUR NETWORK

Having a network of individual people upon whom you can call within the sport industry can mean the difference between the success and failure of your organization. Knowing whom to contact with an inquiry or a request for information is paramount in keeping at the forefront of competition with other similar agencies. One of the best ways to stay ahead is to organize your contacts and your method for reaching them as needed. Early in a career, practice gathering necessary information from your contacts in the industry. An imperative resource is the personal business card.

A business card is not a very expensive item if you have to purchase your own. It is a vital exchange item for keeping track of individuals met and introductions made within the sport industry. One could literally gather one hundred or more a year when attending seminars, symposiums, and conferences. Remember, other individuals seeking internships or employment are a valued source of networking contacts, and contact information can be hard to keep organized. One of the best methods for the necessary organization of all of the cards accumulated is to file them alphabetically by name or organization in plastic card-holder sheets with indexing tabs, generally available at a local office supply store. Based upon the number of cards, you may have a one-, two-, or three-inch ring-binder full of business cards with contact information of individuals in all sectors of the sport industry. Either alphabetized by name or agency, one can then access information needed quickly and accurately by retrieving the notebook and accessing the appropriate tab. Update the listing frequently (at least once a year), in order to maintain the most recent contact information. This prevents excessive time spent in finding information in a moment's notice for your, a fellow student's, or another interested party's use. Knowledge is power and this technique puts the necessary knowledge at your fingertips, literally!

Finding a Mentor

Everyone would like an edge to help them be successful in their chosen work endeavors, especially when new to a job setting or location. You would like to find someone you can approach with questions, to help resolve a dilemma in the work setting, or from whom to occasionally seek advice when making difficult decisions. This person to whom you would go in your new work setting is known as a mentor. A mentor is generally an older, wiser, or more experienced individual who has worked in the industry for several years and made such an impact as to have earned an important title or name recognition. This particular person may have several additional people under his or her supervision as understudies—learning and experiencing training from this particular mentor. This person of high esteem usually provides important feedback for decisions, conflict resolutions, or future agency or organizational direction within the job setting. They may or may not have a legal background, but would be able to call upon vast knowledge, information, and experience in order to render a good judgment or decision. As a student, this person may have been a distinguished faculty member or major professor. In the work setting, keen observations of colleagues and the work environment will assist when choosing a mentor. Sometimes, one does not have to choose a mentor. Such a relationship can result simply from a close working relationship with a colleague or supervisor.

Mentors provide advice; weigh that advice and act appropriately in order to be effective and successful in your job. As a young employee, you want a mentor! A good mentor will always go to bat for you whether it is in seeking a promotion, making a phone call to a colleague for an open position in another organization, or serving as a great reference. A mentor is in your corner! As you learn and grow from that mentor's example, one day, you may become a mentor for others to seek and follow.

Hiring a Consultant

A career coach, consultant, or a head hunter can be hired to assist in finding a job. By doing so, one may actually be extending their personal network. Career coaches or consultants may have worked with individuals within sport organizations and have a good track record of recommending quality individuals. It will cost you, but if a full-time position results, it is money well-spent. An average cost to hire a consultant can vary, but most charge $125 an hour or more. Some may give package deals especially for individuals just graduating and starting in the industry. Consultants and career coaches generally do not guarantee a client a full-time position in the sport business industry. These individuals do not control the hiring practices of sport teams or organizations. Their role is to assist in preparing application documents, reviewing cover letters and résumés, making recommendations, providing interviewing tips, and perhaps assisting in locating available positions for which the client may be qualified. Most students looking for internships cannot afford to hire a consultant, but it should definitely be an option, especially in a tough job market. If a student has built a great résumé and they market themselves well, a consultant is not necessary. For those laid off from full-time positions, a career consultant may accelerate a new position search resulting in an earlier return to much needed income. Thus, the money spent may return an earlier dividend.

Head hunters or professional recruiters are usually paid by organizations to actively recruit individuals on their behalf for a position opening. Using a head hunter may cost you, especially if you contact them. However, their fees are usually paid by an organization so if a head hunter has your résumé, it might not cost you anything. Their fees will often depend on how the contract is written with the employing organization. Be aware head hunters are normally only used to find excellent candidates to fill top-level positions. Hiring a career coach or consultant can be a desired route for an entry or mid-level employee if finding a position by oneself has not resulted in a position.

THE FINAL BUZZER

The intent of this chapter was to provide the new employee with information to effectively make the adjustment from completing an internship to starting a new position. Education, concept knowledge, and skills assist one in doing a job well. Manners, etiquette, and establishing positive professional relationships are equally important. The fortunate intern may be the one who has the internship converted into a job with the same agency. There may be advantages and disadvantages to this situation, so weigh all options carefully.

Ending an internship properly can reap many benefits. Maintaining contact with agency colleagues leads to the strengthening of a professional network. Strange things can happen; an unexpected turn of events can result in immediate employment openings when just a few days before no apparent opportunities existed. Having proven oneself in the internship and having shown true gratitude for that internship and the learning opportunities an organization provided may lead company executives to look first to exiting interns for open positions.

When starting a new position, making the right moves at the right time are equally important. No two office environments are the same. Seniority, political positioning, egos, and pursuit of promotions have an interesting way of changing an individual's perspective and motivation. Remaining neutral on many issues, as a new employee, is a positive move. There will be plenty of time to learn how any issue, positive or negative, will impact each individual and the organization.

Individual work habits and skills can enhance opportunities with a hiring agency. Seeking a mentor can help one integrate into a new setting more gracefully and effectively. Remember that mentors provide advice and one must act upon that advice and their own convictions in order to be effective and successful in a new position.

Should you be released from the internship or the new job, exit gratefully and refrain from burning any bridges. One way or another, those who know your work ethic and assets will be looking out for you down the road. Finally, as you live and learn in this new career setting in the industry of sport, know that your own experiences from both successes and failures will contribute to the wealth of knowledge and wisdom that will one day make you a mentor for those to follow you.

EXPERIENTIAL LEARNING OPPORTUNITIES

Classroom Experiential Learning Exercise: Classes Preparing Questions

The Premier Sport and Event Society of Elon University (an organization led by sport management students), organizes an annual visit to the PNC Arena in Raleigh, NC, each fall. Carolina Hurricanes games, North Carolina State University Basketball, concerts and other events are held in this facility. Students from any class can attend; however, the trip is preceded by contemporary sport management students (our intro class) preparing advance questions for the PNC Arena staff upon our arrival. The general manager (GM) and other key staff respond to the questions pertaining to their particular area. The GM loves the fact he receives the questions in advance instead of blank stares while he waits for questions. We meet in a suite or in the seats near the ice while the professionals respond. Students then get a tour of the facility. We purchase advance tickets and stay for a hockey game. Following the Q&A, students have the opportunity to interact with staff members, build relationships and contacts, discuss internship opportunities, or simply ask for career/professional advice. Students then return to class to discuss their involvement while others write reflections to process their experience in subsequent classes.

Submitted by Dr. Hal Walker, Professor of Sport & Event Management
Elon University, Elon, NC

Program Experiential Learning Example: Evaluating Interns

The internship experience is a capstone experience for our students that address some of our direct and indirect student learner outcomes for our COSMA accreditation. Prior to their field experience, students must submit a list of responsibilities and objectives. These are reviewed and approved by their site supervisor and faculty advisor. Throughout their field experience, students' activities are monitored by their faculty advisors through weekly submissions of log sheets addressing the previous week's tasks, what they learned, and how an in-class experience related to those activities. Site supervisors complete an evaluation of the intern at midterm and conclusion of the field experience, and all interns receive either a site visit or conference call with their site supervisor and faculty advisor. Upon completion of the internship, students submit a final reflection paper addressing how they fulfilled their objectives, and relate their experiences to a number of content areas such as diversity, critical and ethical thinking, research, technology, and communication. Additionally, an updated résumé that includes their internship experience is also required as part of the intern's final assessment.

Submitted by Dr. Jeff Noble, Assistant Professor and Undergraduate Coordinator
Wichita State University, Wichita, KS

REFERENCES

Findlay, H. A. (2002, August). Violence in sport: Policy consideration for the amateur sport organization. Paper presented at the Symposium *Sports management: Cutting edge strategies for managing sports as a business,* Toronto. Retrieved from http://www.sportlaw.ca/2002/08/violence-in-sport-policy-considerations-for-the-amateur-sport-organization/

Miller, W. (2002). *Political Risk Management in Sports.* Durham, NC: Carolina Academic Press.

National Intramural-Recreational Sports Association. (2015). *2015 NIRSA Salary Census.* Corvallis, OR: National Intramural-Recreational Sports Association. Retrieved from Nirsa.org

APPENDIX

A

Sport-Related Internship/ Employment Websites

In today's internet society, many organizations post their employment opportunities online. However, many also utilize websites hosted by other organizations. Some of these sites charge a fee while others allow the person looking for a position to look for free. There are so many sites available, there is no way to list all of them. Teams, colleges, and other sport organizations have their own websites, and several of these have been listed in the following section Appendix B.

http://www.athleticlink.com/Employment/Jobseekers.aspx

http://www.bluefishjobs.com/jobs

http://www.canyonranchjobs.com

http://www.careerbuilder.com

http://careers.adidas-group.com/?brand=reebok

http://careers.njcaa.org/

http://www.cbsinteractive.com/careers

http://www.collegegrad.com

http://www.cooljobs.com

http://www.coolworks.com

http://cubs.hirecentric.com/jobs/

http://www.dice.com

http://www.disabledsportsusa.org/get-involved/jobs-internships/

http://www.disneycareers.com

http://equipmentmanagers.org/community/ad-jobs

http://espncareers.com/

http://www.eventsonline.com

http:// www.exercisejobs.com

http://www.fifa.com/about-fifa/home-of-fifa/careers/index.html

http://www.foxcareers.com/

http://www.getcoachingjobs.com/

http://www.golfingcareers.com

http://www.golfsurfin.com

http://www.hcareers.com

http://www.helpwanted.com

http://www.higheredjobs.com

http://www.hospitalityonline.com

http://www.indeed.com/

http://intermatwrestle.com/jobs

http://www.internabroad.com

http://www.internjobs.com

http://www.internships-usa.com

http://www.internweb.com

http://jobcenter.nacda.com/

http://www.jobs.com

http://jobs.nike.com/

http://jobs.nsga.org/

http://www.jobsinsports.com/

http://www.jobvertise.com

http://www.laga.org

http://www.latpro.com

http://www.leisurejobs.com

http://www.malakye.com

http://www.marketingjobs.com

http://migalareport.com/jobs

http://www.milwaukeejobs.com

http://www.naia.org/

http://www.nationjobs.com

http://www.nbcunicareers.com/

http://www.ncaa.org/about/join-our-team

http://ncaamarket.ncaa.org/jobs

http://www.pbeo.com

http://www.pepsicenter.com/kse/company/employment/

http://sites.vans.com/careers?ref=footer

http://www.snagajob.com

https://www.sneakerjobs.com/

http://www.spectraexperiences.com/careers/

http://www.sportbusiness.com/job-listings-2

http://www.sportscareerfinder.com/

http://www.SportsJobBoard.com

http://www.summerjobs.com

http://www.teamworkonline.com

http://www.tennisjobs.com

http://www.timeinc.com/careers/

http://www.timesonline.com/careers/

http://www.tvjobs.com

http://www.ujobbank.com

http://www.usgolfjobs.com

https://wbca.org/about/our-staff/employment

http:// www.womensportsjobs.com

http://www.womenssportscareers.com

http://www.workinsports.com

http://www.workopolis.com

http://www.wsnsports.com

https://pgatourcareers.silkroad.com/

https://usagym.org/pages/aboutus/pages/employment.html

https://wbca.org/connect/career-center

https://wbca.org/about/betty-f-jaynes-internship-program

https://www.ihiresportsandrecreation.com/

https://www.imgacademy.com/careers

https://www.jobscore.com/

https://www.monster.com/jobs/

https://www.rebelmouse.com/MattWeinberger/Sports_Biz_Job_Board/

https://www.womeninsport.org/careers/

APPENDIX
B

Professional Sport Leagues Websites

We have included a comprehensive listing of some of the more notable and not-so notable leagues in North America. We felt compelled to list the lesser known leagues since many of their teams are in smaller towns where universities with sport management programs exist providing additional experiential learning opportunities. We are fully aware, smaller start-up leagues often do not make it and may cease to operate during the publication of this book. Still if you can gain experience before a smaller league/team goes out of business, the networking opportunities gained may lead to sport business positions elsewhere.

For international students studying in North America or for anyone wishing to work internationally, we have included a short listing of world-wide leagues, but not individual country leagues. We could not list every existing league. Our advance apologies if we have left out a league in which you are interested in working. However, Wikipedia has a pretty extensive list of professional sport leagues at en.wikipedia.org/wiki/List_of_professional_sports_leagues (Wikipedia is a free encyclopedia built by contributors posting information that may be incorrect or outdated, but it is a good starting point).

Please explore links on each of their websites to gain access to affiliated teams and leagues.

BASEBALL

Major League Baseball (MLB)
http://mlb.mlb.com/careers/index.jsp
Headquartered in New York, NY

Minor League Baseball (MiLB)
http://www.milb.com/milb/info/jobs.jsp
Headquartered in St Petersburg, FL

American Association of Independent Professional Baseball
http://www.americanassociationbaseball.com/
Headquartered in Durham, NC

Atlantic League of Professional Baseball (ALPB)
http://atlanticleague.com/
Headquartered in Lancaster, PA

Canadian American Association of Professional Baseball
http://www.canamleague.com/
Headquartered in Durham, NC

Empire Professional Baseball League
http://empireproleague.com
Headquartered in Ruskin, FL

Frontier League
http://www.frontierleague.com/
Headquartered in Sauget, IL

Pacific Association of Professional Baseball Clubs (PABBC)
http://pacificsbaseball.com/index.php/team-info/pacific-association
Headquartered in Northern CA

Pecos League
http://pecosleague.com/
Headquartered in Houston, TX

United Shore Professional Baseball League (USPBL)
https://uspbl.com/
Headquartered in Utica, MI

BASKETBALL

National Basketball Association (NBA)
http://www.nba.com/
Headquartered in New York, NY

Women's National Basketball Association (WNBA)
http://www.wnba.com/
Headquartered in New York, NY

NBA Gatorade League (G-League) (originally D-League)
http://dleague.nba.com/
Headquartered in New York, NY

American Basketball Association
http://abaliveaction.com/
Headquartered in Indianapolis, IN
Note. This is a minor league with existing divisions across the United States, not to be confused with the old ABA that merged with the NBA.

FOOTBALL

National Football League (NFL)
http://www.nfl.com/
 Headquartered in New York, NY

Arena Football League (AFL)
http://www.arenafootball.com/
Headquartered in Las Vegas, NV

Canadian Football League (CFL)
http://www.cfl.ca/
Headquartered in Toronto, Canada

Champions Indoor Football League
http://gocif.net/
Headquartered in San Angelo, TX

Arena Development League
http://www.arenadl.com/
Headquartered in Columbus, GA
Note. This league was announced in June 2016 as a developmental league for Arena football with official play beginning in 2017.

Independent Women's Football League (IWFL)
http://www.iwflsports.com
Headquartered in Round Rock, TX

GOLF

Professional Golf Association (PGA)
https://www.pga.org/employment
Headquartered in Palm Beach Gardens, FL

Ladies Professional Golf Association
http://www.lpga.com/careers-home
Headquartered in Daytona Beach, FL

ICE HOCKEY

National Hockey League (NHL)
https://www.nhl.com/
Headquartered in New York, NY

American Hockey League (AHL)
http://theahl.com/
Headquartered in Springfield, MA

USA Hockey, Inc.
http://www.usahockey.com/employment
Headquartered in Colorado Springs, CO

East Coast Hockey League (ECHL)
http://www.echl.com/
Headquartered in Princeton, NJ

National Women's Hockey League (NWHL)
http://www.nwhl.zone/
Headquartered in New York City, NY

Canadian Women's Hockey League (CWHL)
http://www.thecwhl.com
Headquartered in Toronto, Canada

Federal Hockey League (FHL)
http://www.federalhockey.com/
Headquartered in Syracuse, NY

Ligue Nord-Américaine de Hockey (LNAH – Canada's North American Hockey League)
https://lnah.com/
Headquartered in Quebec, Canada

Southern Professional Hockey League
http://www.thesphl.com
Headquartered in Huntersville, NC

Western Hockey League
http://www.whl.ca/
Headquartered in Calgary, Canada

LACROSSE

Major League Lacrosse (MLL—Outdoor)
https://www.majorleaguelacrosse.com/
Headquartered in Boston, MA

National Lacrosse League (NLL—Indoor)
http://www.nll.com/view/nll/home-page-1082
Headquartered in Conshohocken, PA

United Women's Lacrosse League (UWLX)
http://unitedwlax.com/
Headquartered in Boston, MA

RUGBY

Professional Rugby Organization (PRO)
http://www.prorugby.org/
Headquartered in New York, NY

SOCCER

Major League Soccer (MLS)
http://www.mlssoccer.com/
Headquartered in New York, NY

North American Soccer League (NASL)
http://www.nasl.com/
Headquartered in New York, NY

National Women's Soccer League (NWSL)
http://www.nwslsoccer.com
Headquartered in Chicago, IL

United Soccer League
http://www.uslsoccer.com/
Headquartered in Tampa, FL

SOFTBALL

National Pro Fastpitch Softball (NPF)
http://www.profastpitch.com/home/
Headquartered in Hermitage, TN

VOLLEYBALL

Association of Volleyball Professionals (AVP)
(Beach and Indoor)
http://avp.com/
Headquartered in Newport Beach, CA

POPULAR INTERNATIONAL LEAGUES

Fédération Internationale de Football (FIFA)
http://www.fifa.com/
Headquartered in Zurich, Switzerland

International Hockey Federation (Field Hockey)
http://www.fih.ch/inside-fih/our-team
Headquartered in Lausanne, Switzerland

International Basketball Association (FIBA)
http://www.fiba.com
Headquartered in Mies, Switzerland

International Ice Hockey Federation
http://www.iihf.com
Headquartered in Zurich, Switzerland

Fédération Internationale de Volleyball (FIVB)
http://www.fivb.org/EN/FIVB
Headquartered in Lausanne, Switzerland

APPENDIX
C
Sample Résumés

Dorothy T. Brown
808 Larkspur Street – Titusville, FL 32780
dtb@email.com
111-111-1111

SUMMARY OF QUALIFICATIONS	▱ Successful tournament scheduler with advanced skills in set-up and operation ▱ Excellent time management, social media, and web design skills ▱ Experience with a wide variety of sporting events ▱ Effective project manager
EDUCATION	**Ohio State University – Columbus, Ohio – 2008** M.S. – Sport Management 3.78 GPA - Oberteuffer Award Winner **Florida State University – Tallahassee, Florida - 2004** B.S. – Sport Management Minor – Business Law 3.0 GPA
SPORT BUSINESS EXPERIENCE	EVENT AND TOURNAMENT MANAGER – FLORIDA AMERICAN UNIVERSITY – 2009 – PRESENT ▱ Planned, organized, and executed tournaments and meets in eight sports ▱ Designed, sold, and executed tournament sponsorship packages ▱ Assisted with community outreach programs ▱ Competition manager for U.S. Association of Blind Athletes Summer Nationals ▱ Created and maintained day-to-day media relationships ▱ Executed all tournament contractual elements GRADUATE ASSISTANT – OHIO STATE UNIVERSITY – CAMPUS RECREATION 2007 – 2008 ▱ Undergraduate Staff Supervisor – Special Events ▱ Facility management night-time supervisor ▱ Graduate student representative – Recreation Advisory Council SPORTS OFFICIAL – NORTH BREVARD SPORTS ASSOCIATION – SUMMERS, 1998 – 2004 ▱ Softball, volleyball, basketball SPORTS OFFICIAL – DEPT. OF CAMPUS RECREATION – FLORIDA STATE – 2001 – 2004 ▱ Softball, volleyball, basketball, swimming, and track and field VOLUNTEER ▱ LPGA Legends Tour Championship – Player Check-In – Safety Harbor, FL – 2009 ▱ XLIII Super Bowl – Merchandising Stock Manager – Tampa, FL – 2009 ▱ American League Playoffs – Media Security Support – St. Petersburg, FL – 2008 ▱ Little Everglades Steeplechase – Parking Attendant – Dade City, FL – 2007 ▱ Chrysler Championships – Driving Range Concierge – 2004 & 2005

REFERENCES

Name, Title Company Name Address City, State, Zip Approved Phone # Approved e-mail	Name, Title Company Name Address City, State, Zip Approved Phone # Approved e-mail	Name, Title Company Name Address City, State, Zip Approved Phone # Approved e-mail

JOHN E. DAMIAN

5151 NORTHWESTERN ST. BIRMINGHAM, AL 10001
JED@EMAIL.COM 222-222-2222

SPECIALIZED SKILLS

MARKETING & PROMOTIONS
GROUP AND SPONSORSHIP SALES
LEADER AMONG PEERS
CONFIDENT SOCIAL MEDIA COMMUNICATOR

EDUCATION

Bachelor of Science in Sport Management, Minor in Business Administration
Northwestern State University of Louisiana
3.88 – Magna Cum Laude

AWARDS AND HONORS

Dean's List Student
Outstanding Sport Management Major
Track and Field Athlete

REFERENCES

Reference #1 Name, Business title
Company Name
Full mailing address
City, State, Zip
Approved phone number
Approved e-mail

Reference #2 Name, Business title
Company Name
Full mailing address
City, State, Zip
Approved phone number
Approved e-mail

Reference #3 Name, Business title
Company Name
Full mailing address
City, State, Zip
Approved phone number
Approved e-mail

PERSONAL PROFILE

- Proactive, decisive, and result-oriented leader
- Proficient in Microsoft Word, Excel, and PowerPoint
- Effective web and social media designer
- Ethical team player

AREAS OF STRENGTH

SPONSORSHIP SALES
- Proven sponsorship sales record
- Effective communicator with sponsors to maximize year-to-years sales retention
- Detailed sponsorship program designer

GROUP SALES
- Continuous leader in development of group sales packages
- Creative packaging for customer satisfaction and retention
- Developer of innovative services and service delivery
- Effective sales presenter

MARKETING/PROMOTIONS
- Experienced half-time promoter for increasing spectatorship
- Developer of marketing plans for college athletics
- Proven results for increased attendance
- Implemented program social media program for online marketing

VOLUNTEER/COMMUNITY INVOLVEMENT

- PGA Zurich Classic of New Orleans – Media Logistics – April, 2010
- New Orleans Saints NFC Playoff – Game Day Support – 2010
- University of Alabama – Game Day Operations Assistant – 2009
- Northwestern State University – Game Day – Ticketing & Marketing Assistant – All Sports – Four years
- YMCA of Birmingham – Developed Saturday Career Day Program for High School Students – Sport Management and Marketing

PERSONAL PHILOSOPHY

Make each day count, each project your best, each client #1, and keep all promises!

Hazel Lindberg
333-333-3333
hl@email.edu

Permanent Address	**Local Address**
1234 Saragossa Lane	5678 Campus Dr.
St. Augustine, FL 98765	USA University
	Villages, FL 99999

Education

August, 2015 – Present	USA University – Villages, FL
	Major: Sport Business – Donald R. Tapia School of Business
May, 2015	High School Diploma – Titusville High School – Titusville, FL

Sport Business Experience

August, 2015 – Present	USA University Athletic Department – Villages, FL
	Game Management
	- Assisted with development and operation of half-time shows for basketball games
	- Assisted with ticket sales and event set-up/take down
November, 2015	LPGA Legends Championship – Safety Harbor, FL
	- Assisted in media center
	- Standard bearer
May, 2016 –	Orlando Magic – Marketing – Orlando, FL
August, 2016	- Planned, administered, and evaluated research data

Other Employment Experience

January, 2014 -	McDonald's – St. Augustine, FL
	Crew Chief
	- Supervised 10 part-time staff
	- Opened and closed store

Computer Experience

- Microsoft Office – Power Point, Excel, Word, Access
- Archtics Ticketing System
- Statmaster for Basketball

Professional Association Memberships

- Sport Business Association – USA University – Fall, 2015–present
- National Association for Collegiate Marketing Administrators – Current
- National Intramural-Recreational Sports Association – Current
- Florida Student Representative – 2016–2017

Conferences Attended

- Florida State University Sport Management Conference – Tallahassee, FL – 2016
- NIRSA State Workshop - Daytona Beach, FL – Summer, 2016

References

Joseph C. Shimala, Vice President	Dr. John E. Dollar, Professor	Anna Branski
Team Marketing Services	American South University	Head Softball Coach
National Basketball Association	Department of Sport Business	Titus High School
3444 5th St.	1234 Flagler Way	St. Augustine, FL 54321
New York, NY 12345	New Orleans, LA 66666	909-999-8888
123-456-7890	444-444-4444	anna@aol.com
joseph@nba.com	jed@asu.edu	

Sample Functional Résumé

Student Name

Address	Phone Number	Email Address

Education

Saint Leo University, 2005	MBA – Sport Business – Saint Leo University, Saint Leo, FL
Eastern Illinois University, 2000	BA Degree – Business Administration – Eastern Illinois University, Charleston, IL

Experience

Proven leader with 10+ years of various managerial experiences that includes managing people of teams, streamlining organizational procedures, and identifying new processes within that facilitate decreased expenditures. Independent and group-oriented work with exceptional time-management skills. Strong managerial skills with the ability to get the most out of staff members under my direction.

Facility Management (Can substitute sections such as Event Management, Sales, Etc.)
- Recommended, created, and implemented training tools for Aware Manager for the Tampa Bay Lightning
- Prepared, implemented, and evaluated annual educational plans based on individually assessed needs
- Planned, implemented, and evaluated Special Olympic projects and programs for foundation implementation
- Developed successful annual schedules for training of staff for event set-up and take down
- Developed and managed a successful 8-week summer camp for ice skating
- Created and managed an inventory system for facility equipment needs

General Management
- Train, schedule and supervise personnel for events
- Complete and submit compensation reports
- Handle customer service issues in a timely and sensitive manner
- Evaluation of employees on a weekly basis, closely monitoring individual growth
- Plan and execute weekly, monthly and seasonal facility staff schedules
- Participate in organizational strategic planning initiatives and supervise annual department SWOT analysis development

Chronology

July 2012 to Current	Facility Associate Director, Tampa Bay Lightning	Tampa, FL
2011 to 2012	Business Manager, Spectra	Tampa, FL
2008 to 2011	Event Manager, Flagler College	St. Augustine, FL
2005 to 2008	Director of Summer Camps, Parks & Recreation	Land O'Lakes, FL
2001 to 2005	Self Employed, Personal Trainer	Tampa, FL

Personal

Outstanding Staff Member	2014	Tampa Bay Lightning
Community Volunteer Service Award	2008	St. Augustine, Florida
Outstanding Sport Business Student	1999, 2000	Eastern Illinois University

References

Reference 1	Name, Title – Organization – email – phone number
Reference 2	
Reference 3	

APPENDIX
D

Sample Interview Questions

GENERAL QUESTIONS

- What are some of your qualities on which you need to improve?
- What are your strengths? Weaknesses? How would you evaluate yourself?
- Who could I talk with about your work ethic?
- What one college class has most prepared you for this type of work? Why?
- How would you handle a conflict between yourself and your co-workers, supervisors, or customers?
- What makes you different from the other applicants?
- What would you like to learn during your internship and how will you apply it in the job setting?
- What were your responsibilities during your internship?
- What was the most significant contribution you made to the company during your internship?
- This is an unpaid internship. How will you support yourself during the next three months?
- What is your definition of success? Failure?
- Are you willing to relocate?
- What are your short- and long-term goals for your career? How do you plan to achieve them?
- How would you describe yourself?
- What two or three things are most important to you in your career?
- Describe your concept of the ideal career position?
- What classes at school were most useful to you for this position?
- What courses in ethics did you take in college? How have they helped to shape your perspective of sport ethics?
- Tell me the special qualities you possess and how they will help you with this position.
- Tell me about a project you initiated.
- What can we expect from you if you get this job?

- What were your major responsibilities at your previous job?
- What kind of supervisory experience have you had?
- With what kind of people do you dislike working?
- Do you find yourself to be a self-motivated worker?
- What do you want to achieve as an employee here?
- As an intern, how do you feel you can contribute to our organization?
- Is there anything important that you haven't had the chance to tell me?
- How does your educational background pertain to this job?
- Have you ever been disciplined for any performance-related problems?
- Can you explain your working relationships with peers and supervisors?
- Describe yourself as an individual and as an employee.
- What makes you the best candidate?
- In what community activities do you participate?
- What two or three things are most important to you in choosing a position?
- How would you motivate people?
- Tell me a situation where you had to persuade another person of your point of view.
- Give an example of a problem you solved and the process used.
- Describe a project that best demonstrates your analytical skills.
- Why did you choose this career?
- Which is more important to you, the money or the job?
- In what kind of work environment do you think you would excel?
- What personal accomplishments did you have in your previous assignments?

- What do you see yourself doing next year? In 10 years?
- What benefits are important to you in your career?
- What do you want out of a career?
- How do you feel about traveling on the job?
- What sets you apart from everyone else?
- What types of character traits do you possess that will make you unique for this position?
- Are you better working alone or as part of a team?
- How do you handle pressure situations?
- What are your hobbies and interests?
- Why is this internship good for you?
- What is your ideal job?
- What are some of your goals?
- What made you decide to go into this field?
- What are your strongest computer skills?
- What determines a winner?
- What brought you to our organization? Where did you learn of this organization?
- Why do you deserve this position?
- How do you think this organization will benefit by hiring you?
- Would you consider yourself more of a leader, follower, or a person who just gets (stays) out of the way?
- What did you do with your spare time during the four years you were in college?
- On a scale of 1 to 10 (10 highest), how would you rate yourself on dependability and the ability to work with others? Why?
- Describe your best time management skills.
- At any given point in time, did you ever think about giving up on receiving a college diploma? If so, what made you stick with it?
- What would you be doing right now if you were not out on this interview?
- How would you handle being placed in charge of a group of 10-15 employees that were all twice your age?
- If you saw an employee stealing money who had been with the company for a long time and never caused any trouble, would you report the incident? Why or why not?
- My theory is the more people you empower, the more room there is for a mistake. Do you agree or disagree?
- My theory is the more people you empower, the better the organization. Explain what you believe this means.
- Would you prefer to do everything yourself or delegate important tasks to others?

- What do you know about our company? Why do you want a position with us?
- Do you have a role model? Who? Why?
- Do you prefer to work with an individual or a group?
- With what aspects of the industry are you looking to get involved?
- How do you feel about changing your plans with little notice?
- Why did you choose to attend the college(s) you attended?
- What do you look for in a boss or supervisor?
- Give an example of how creative you are.
- Tell me about a time when you had to make a decision but didn't have all the information you needed.
- What is the biggest mistake you've made in your work and how did you recover from it?
- Give me a specific example of something you did that helped build enthusiasm in others?
- Give me an example of a time you had to persuade other people to take action. Were you successful?
- Tell me about a time you had to handle multiple responsibilities. How did you organize these responsibilities?
- As of right now, our organization is running perfectly fine without you. We do not need you as much as you need us. So from our viewpoint, we have nothing to offer you. Tell us what you have to offer us?
- There are larger schools and other schools that can offer you more in internships. So, other than the fact that we are in close proximity to where you live, why do you want to do your internship here?
- Describe your fantasy job, its benefits and salary, where it is, and how long you plan to be on that job.
- We see on your résumé that you interned the same place you worked as an apprentice. Why did you decide to do this instead of learning new ways of doings things by selecting a different organization?
- What two or three things are most important to you in your career?
- If you could pick a position, any position anywhere in the United States, where would you like the position to be?
- Tell me about any group work experience you have that would be relevant to this position.
- Where do you see our organization in five years?
- Have you done any volunteer work in this field?
- What qualifications do you have that makes you more marketable for this position?
- What past experience, person, or information led you into this field?

- What new insights can you bring to our organization?
- How would you rate, from 1 to 10 (10 highest), your public speaking and communication skills?
- What is the most self-fulfilling thing that you have done in your life regarding the sport management field?
- Are you more of a leader or follower?
- What is one new idea you would bring to our organization?
- Will you be able to work weekends and evenings?
- What previous experience do you have that makes you more qualified for this position?
- Is money a strong motivator for you?
- With what type of work environment are you most comfortable?
- How long could we count on you staying with us?
- When can you start if given this position?
- Would you mind working in any geographic location, if we do hire you?
- How long do you think it would be before you could make a contribution to our company?
- Could you handle taking instructions and orders from your supervisor? A female supervisor? A younger supervisor?

- What qualifications do you have to be successful?
- How will you review the performance of your employees?
- You've never supervised anyone. What makes you believe you will be a good supervisor?
- We like to hire interns into full-time positions. At the end of this internship, why will we hire you?
- Explain your technical skill set.
- Do you work well under pressure? Give us an example when you were asked to handle a situation under pressure.
- Would you work holidays and weekends?
- Have you ever had difficulty with a supervisor?
- Who has impacted your career the most?
- Do you have a mentor? How has that mentor assisted you?
- What was your favorite class in college? Why was it your favorite?
- Are you better at math or writing?
- What is your favorite sport to play? Watch?
- Growing up, what influenced you getting involved in sport?
- Are there any questions you would like to ask me?

COLLEGE ATHLETIC ADMINISTRATION/COACHING

- What experiences, good or bad, have you had that you believe will be most helpful to you in accomplishing the responsibilities in this position in our athletic department?
- What do you see as the biggest threat to big-time college athletics?
- When and why did you decide to take an interest in being a _____ for an athletic department?
- If you were in a position at a university where the program was illegally giving money to players, how would you go about handling the situation?
- What is your overall career goal in college athletics?
- For which sports have you fitted equipment? With which do you feel most comfortable?
- If a player came to you complaining that equipment hindered movement, how would you handle this?
- Describe the procedure for fitting a football helmet?
- What is the most important job of the equipment manager?
- Do you know the recommended maintenance/replacement schedule for football equipment, helmets in particular?
- Why do you enjoy coaching?

- What style of coaching do you use?
- At what level would you like to ultimately coach?
- What goal would you like to achieve in coaching?
- What do you consider success in coaching?
- What if your top quarterback was considering transferring to another top university and one of our biggest alums decided to buy him a brand new Porsche? The deal was totally under the table and nobody found out. What would be your feelings on this situation as an assistant coach? What would you do?
- What is your position on Title IX?
- What type of things would you suggest to increase attendance?
- Football is a big revenue sport at this university. However, women's soccer is an important part of the women's program and does not receive as much funding. As an athletic director, if there was extra money in the budget and both programs were requesting money, to which program would you allocate the money? Why?
- What would you do if another university had an away game and didn't show up? How would you handle it?

- Have you taken care of athletic equipment before?
- Do you plan to stay in college promotions?
- How are you going to handle the drug testing policy?
- What penalties would you like to see enforced?
- How would you get students more involved in college athletics?
- Why should we hire you as a graduate assistant for our athletic department?
- How did you get involved in compliance?
- What is your experience with Division ___ compliance rules?
- What do you perceive as the main difference between NAIA and the NCAA?
- At your previous university where you interned, what did you learn about their operations when they moved from NAIA to NCAA? From Division II to Division I?
- Coaches are expected to fulfill other roles in their off season. What can you contribute?

- Do you have any teaching experience? Would you be willing to teach at our university on top of your primary duties?
- What makes a college coach an effective classroom teacher?
- Have you ever failed a compliance test given by your athletic department?
- As a graduate assistant, what were your coaching responsibilities?
- How did your graduate assistantship prepare you for this position?
- What do you know about the position of a senior woman administrator?
- What do you know about eSport as the next college athletic sport?
- What aspect of eSport would make you believe our university should add this as a new sport?
- Where do you think college athletics will be in the next ten years?

COLLEGE PROFESSOR/INSTRUCTOR

- You have not finished your dissertation. How will you handle this with a full-time teaching position, especially when your first year is very time demanding with the development of classes?
- As a new professor, how do you plan progressing toward promotion and tenure?
- What will be your area of research?
- Do you prefer teaching or research?
- What experience do you have in academic advising?
- Describe to us the role of an academic advisor.
- You will be starting a new sport management program. What is your first order of business?
- Have you ever hired faculty?
- How do you feel about committee work?
- Have you ever served on a committee or chaired a committee?
- How good are your time management skills?
- Describe your most creative teaching methodology.
- How do you get a student who is underperforming in your class to improve?
- We get quite a few athletes in our major. What is your attendance policy and how lenient are you with students missing classes?

- How are you a good fit for our institution?
- Our typical class load is four course per semester. How do you feel about that?
- In your graduate assistantship, what duties did you perform for your professors?
- How did your graduate assistantship prepare you for teaching?
- Explain the administrative responsibilities you had in sport management as a graduate assistant.
- What responsibilities did you have as a graduate assistant that would enhance our sport management program?
- How do you feel you will work with graduate students since you just finished your degree?
- How in depth are your research skills? Do you feel you could teach research courses?
- Tell us about your thesis/dissertation. What were your results?
- What do you consider your teaching specialty? If someone already teaches this, what other courses do you feel capable of teaching?
- What different courses do you feel you can teach in sport management?

FITNESS/WELLNESS MANAGEMENT/STRENGTH AND CONDITIONING COACH

- What are your salary expectations as a manager of the fitness club?
- This is a large fitness facility. How will you keep everyone working together cohesively?
- What will you do to increase the number of clients without sacrificing quality of their experience in this facility?
- What will you do to ensure the clients are satisfied?
- How will you review the performance of your certified fitness trainers?
- What is your philosophy of requiring certifications for fitness trainers and what certifications do you prefer?
- What type of experience have you had in working at a health and fitness club?
- A fitness club manager should have a strong background in management and exercise science. Explain how your background fits this position.
- What training have you had working as a wellness director?
- While working as a wellness director, what would be the most important programs you would implement? Which ones would you focus on the most in helping your members?
- What have you already done and what will you do in the future to benefit other people's health through your work as a wellness director?
- What certifications would you require your employees to possess if hired as manager of our club?
- Explain your personal training experience and the type of client with whom you most prefer to work.
- Have you encountered a serious health situation with a member in which you have had to help rehabilitate (e.g., paralysis, heart attack, broken bone)? If you have encountered this or other type of serious situation, how would you go about rehabilitating the patient?
- Have you ever run a cardiac rehabilitation program in concert with physicians?
- What ideas might you have for workouts?
- What kind of safety procedures do you think should be used?
- How might you motivate members to stay with their rehabilitation program?
- What do you think is the best way to keep customers safe?
- How would you deal with someone who is not adhering to fitness club rules?
- How important is it to enforce safety rules?

- What should a fitness center/weight room contain?
- Do you have experience with the elderly?
- How would you motivate a person who is out-of-shape and doesn't like physical activity to begin to enjoy an exercise program?
- With what brands of equipment are you familiar? Weights? Cardiovascular? Stress tests or computer programs dealing with nutrition or fitness?
- Have you ever conducted any classes or workshops on nutrition or fitness?
- In your opinion, what is the ideal fitness club?
- How do you assist your client who has difficulty in communicating with you in a foreign language?
- Let's assume that it is 15 minutes before closing time and your client visits you to have some kind of assistance. What will you tell this client?
- Describe to us what you believe should be included in a wellness program.
- What aspects of your character will enable you to become a successful strength coach?
- A team strength and conditioning coach must be a leader. What type of leader are you?
- What is your position on supplements in the strength and conditioning of young players?
- You have been the strength and conditioning coach of this team for __ years. As a new head coach, why should I retain you on my staff?
- Explain a typical individual workout for a certain position player on the team?
- What is your philosophy on strength and conditioning of baseball players? Track athletes? Swimmers?
- You have a pure strength and conditioning background but no educational background in management. Explain how this makes you an effective coach.
- You have a bachelor's degree and good experience. Would you be against getting an advanced degree to assist you in management philosophy while serving as a strength and conditioning coach full-time?
- Explain your experience in maintaining an injured player's conditioning status.
- Risk management in a strength and conditioning facility is paramount. Explain basic safety rules.
- We would like our new strength and conditioning coach to also assist in the development of programs for the recreational athlete. What experience do you have with this and how would you fit it into your daily schedule?

- Describe your greatest success in conditioning an injured athlete.
- Why should we hire you as a graduate assistant in our fitness center?'
- In your opinion, what is the Cadillac of fitness certifications?
- Our campus is building a new fitness center with student fees where we will have faculty staff memberships. The person we hire will be heavily involved in generating income so this facility will be self-supporting. How will you get faculty and staff members to pay for a membership when, in the past, they could use our small fitness center without a fee?

- The person we hire will be in charge of hiring and training all staff. What staff training programs have you initiated for students in the past?
- Athletes and students will be sharing this new facility. What is your philosophy for these two groups sharing this facility?
- You will be required to hire graduate assistants to assist in running our new facility when you are not working. Graduate students often have night classes. What will you do?

PROFESSIONAL SPORT MANAGEMENT

- What would be a promotional plan that you could come up with while doing your internship?
- Why do you want to be a marketing promoter for this company?
- If you were put in a position where there was a new race track (NASCAR) being built, how would you be able to promote the track to the surrounding area and fans?
- In what area of professional sport are you most interested in building a career?
- What is your career goal in professional sport management?
- If you could make three changes in this league, what would they be?
- How would you handle a coaching change after a popular coach has been fired?
- If your team has had a bad attendance year, what would you do to make sure this improved next year?
- How would you promote your star player in order to raise the popularity of the rest of the team?
- NASCAR has grown in terms of popularity. What would you do to continue this trend?
- NASCAR has an image with some people of being entertainment for old-fashioned country boys. How would you change this perception or do you think a change is necessary?
- How would you promote a motorsport event after a bad accident has occurred and is fresh on the fans' minds?
- What is your outlook on pro-sports and sports equipment industries for the future? Positive or negative?
- Do you have any ideas about new and different activities you might plan for a professional golf/tennis tournament that would raise more money for our community's charities?
- In your own words, what does marketing and promotions mean to you?

- What do you know about the Super Bowl as an event? World Series? World Soccer Cup? Master's?
- Have you had any promotions experience? Concessions/field maintenance?
- Describe your golf background and experience and how it pertains to this job.
- Do you feel pro sports salaries for players are too high?
- Explain your job duties and projects you may have developed with other professional teams.
- What do you think is the main problem in professional sports and what would you do to solve this problem?
- Where do you see yourself 10 years from now if you stay in professional sports?
- What would be your top organizational goal for this professional sport organization?
- How can we overtake the number one team in the NFL in the area of merchandising sales?
- What is your view on teams moving elsewhere to new locations and leaving their fans behind?
- Why did you choose a minor league team opposed to a major league team? Why did you choose baseball?
- If you are hired, give me an example of how you would market our team to boost attendance.
- Why did you choose to apply to our organization for your internship?
- What do you know about baseball?
- What is your goal in professional baseball? Other sport?
- How can your experience relate to minor league baseball?
- Are you willing to put in 60+ hours a week during the season?
- What do you know about our organization?
- Where do you see professional baseball 10–15 years down the road? How do you fit in that scenario?

- What changes would you lobby for in major league baseball? Other sport?
- What experience have you had in the administration of our sport?
- What is your position on the steroid issue?
- When you hear our team name, what is the first thing that comes to your mind?
- What suggestions do you have for getting more people to leave the TV and come to the games?
- At this entry-level position, you will be required to work in several different aspects of the organization such as tickets, concessions, promotions, etc. You will be working long hours and will see very little or none of the games or players. Since you grew up as a fan of this sport, would this present a problem for you?

- One of your players has just been arrested for possession of marijuana. The player has won numerous MVP awards and is one of your position players. How would you handle this?
- Professional lacrosse is beginning to take hold and there are rumblings that our city wants to attract a team. Is the leisure spending of our citizens such that you believe there is still enough to support the existing pro teams?
- What do you feel is the role of community relations in a professional sport organization?
- Our website has a lot of information about our community relations department. What do you know about it?
- Why do you want a career in player development? What scouting experience do you have?

RECREATIONAL SPORT MANAGEMENT

- Why do you want to be an intramural director?
- What experience do you have in working with intramurals? Family or youth programming?
- How would you get more student involvement in intramurals?
- Title IX impacts collegiate recreational sport. Do you feel it is important to have as many opportunities for women as you do for men in the intramural program?
- Since students serve as program supervisors, what type of staff training would you develop to assure the liability is decreased and program quality is enhanced?
- What do you see as some of the most important issues facing the recreation field in the future?
- How do you feel about working in several areas of the recreation field?
- Where do you see yourself in recreation ten years from now?
- How would you start a disc golf league?
- How would you approach the current generation of college students in your attempts to get them to participate?
- How would you deal with underage drinking and drugs on campus, especially when you find an incident occurred resulting from a recreational sport program you sponsored?
- What are your career goals in recreation management?
- If you obtain this job, what do you feel you can contribute to our campus recreation organization?
- What are your major strengths and weaknesses in the area of recreation?
- What type of experience have you had working with campus recreation? Any branch of recreation?

- Why do you choose to work in the recreation field?
- Have you ever had experience in planning recreation programs on your own?
- We run family programs on our campus. Do you enjoy working with children?
- How do you believe children benefit from recreational sport programming?
- How would you promote summer sport camps?
- Let's say one of your programs reached its capacity and a few parents were irate because their child couldn't be enrolled. What would you do?
- What do you know about sport clubs? Instructional programs housed in our department?
- This is a golf community, and our largest enrolled class for children is golf. However, most of our kids hate golf. How would you teach the class to make it fun?
- You have a plan to initiate a new sport for our community. What would it be and how would you sell it?
- What would be your first project as a new assistant director?
- Can you give me any ideas which you think might improve how YMCAs are run?
- What referee experience do you have?
- Do you feel you could revamp our referee training program?
- Do you have experience with starting/sponsoring an official's club to promote professionalism?
- Do you know how to set-up different types of tournaments including single and double elimination, round robin, and ladder tournaments?
- Explain a situation you have observed or have had to manage when you had a large tournament bracket set up and a team did not show up but did not give any notice. What did you do?

- We would like to build a climbing wall. What experience do you have with managing this type of facility?
- We want to improve our programming for the physically challenged student. What ideas do you have?
- Do you believe young children (under age 8) should be exposed to competitive sports?
- Wellness programming should be a big part of any campus recreation facility. How would you go about starting such a program?
- We plan on building a new wellness facility. With your recreation background, what experience do you have in designing such a facility? What would you include?
- Do you believe in hiring students to staff a campus recreation wellness facility? If so, what credentials would you require?
- College students do not have very good diets and sometimes do not make very good choices when it comes to wellness behaviors. Describe a program you could institute that would assist them in making better choices.
- Describe one situation where you feel recreational/wellness programming turned around a young person's life.

- Why should we hire you as a graduate assistant for aquatic programming? Sport club programming?
- Do you have any facility management experience?
- Have you used any software programs applicable to facility management?
- Our university president has asked us to raise money for campus recreation program. What is your best idea for doing this?
- We are in need of a campus recreation facility. Did you have any exposure to feasibility studies in a college facility management class?
- Are you familiar with NIRSA, and have you attended any of their professional conferences?
- Do you have any experience working with a local YMCA or local youth recreation program?
- Do you have any league administration experience?
- What is your favorite accomplishment in recreation?
- What is your favorite thing to do at work in the recreation field?
- How did you get involved in recreation management?

SPECIAL EVENTS/FACILITY MANAGEMENT

- In what type of facility do you wish to work?
- What experience do you have with facility management?
- In your opinion, what is the most important aspect of facility management?
- What types of research do you need to perform to promote a show?
- What types of programs could you use to sell your facility?
- What classes did you take in school which may have helped you the most to enter event/facility management?
- Why did you choose facility management as a career field?
- How do you feel you can help manage this facility?
- If you are having an event in this facility, do you feel it is necessary to have a liability plan?
- How would you train your staff and all employees in risk management?
- Tell us about any risk management experience you have.
- What salary do you expect?
- Are you a people person?
- What do you know about our facility?
- How would you market our facility?

- How would you pack our arena for a basketball game?
- How would you promote a business convention in our arena?
- Why did you choose our facility?
- Are you willing to work in other areas within the organization?
- We have a lot of down time and want to bring in more events to our facility. What types of events do you feel would be good for our community or clientele?
- What do you feel is the most important characteristic an event/facility manager needs to be effective?
- Why do you prefer a pro facility in comparison to a collegiate facility?
- What are your goals in event/facility management?
- If you were put in charge of an event with 50,000 people and there was a person who sustained a major injury, what would be one of the first forms of action you would take beyond medical care?
- How important is advance risk management planning to the operation of an event or facility?
- Have you developed a risk management plan for a facility or event?

- Can you describe the necessary components of a successful risk management plan that would help us prevent injury to our spectators?
- Do you have any experience in designing any type of facility even if it was a class project?
- Have you ever participated in a feasibility study?
- What professional memberships do you hold with any sport related facility management organization?
- Did you purchase a student membership with any facility management organization?
- As an intern, what will be your first contribution to our facility management staff?
- What experience do you possess in attracting major events to a sport facility?
- Did you run any tournaments as part of a class in college? If so, tell us about it.
- We want to improve our recreation facilities. After your tour of our physical plant, do you have any ideas on what would be the first facility you believe we need?
- Have you used any software programs for facility management?
- We have been asked to develop a sales campaign to get students to vote for a student fee that would support new sport and recreation facilities at our institution. As a student, what would make you become a leader in convincing other students this is important for the future of their alma mater?
- Did you have any facility projects in a facility management class required for your degree?
- Colleges are not building eSport facilities. We do not have the money build a new facility. What type of facility might we be able to find on our current campus that could be adapted for this emerging sport?
- Have you ever toured facilities to get new ideas or to learn how others run their facilities?

SPORT BROADCASTING, SPORT INFORMATION, AND SOCIAL MEDIA

- What is your technical skill set?
- Do you have any experience with recording and playback equipment?
- Discuss your current or past involvement with script writing.
- Tell me about your current or past experience with ad campaigns.
- Do you have any mass media experience?
- Describe the most creative work-related project you have created.
- Why do you want a career in this field?
- How do you effectively relay information to listeners?
- How do you conduct live interviews?
- What type of experience do you have in this industry?
- What experience have you had as an announcer for live streaming, radio, or television?
- What do you consider your most significant accomplishment in this field?
- What would be your ideal working environment?
- Explain your experiences working in a control master room.
- What was your greatest accomplishment as an announcer?
- What was your biggest disappointment as an announcer?
- What is your secret to a successful career as an announcer?
- Why are you the best announcer for us?
- As an announcer, what do you believe is your greatest asset?
- If you were hiring a person for this job, what skills would you be looking for?
- Explain any previous positions you have held tied to sports information.
- What sports do you prefer to cover as a writer? As a broadcaster?
- What software programs have you used for print and internet writing?
- What sport statistics programs have you used?
- If you were invited to vote for the Heisman Trophy winner, what do you think are the most important qualifications?
- Have you ever promoted a student athlete for an Academic All-American award? If yes, describe what you did.
- Do you have any experience working in public or media relations?
- Do you have experience using video editing or video recording?
- How proficient are you in utilizing social media?
- What specific area of sports information would you like to work?
- What are your experiences in working with the press and media?
- Have you ever written a press release?
- Have you ever constructed or updated a website?
- Have you ever had to address the media?
- Do you have any experience creating pregame notes for the media?

- Have you ever worked in a press box before?
- How are your communication skills on the phone?
- Have you ever conducted an interview for an athlete?
- Describe your most satisfying interview you have conducted.
- What objectives do you have to help improve the sports information department at our school?
- Have you ever moderated a press conference?
- Do you have any experiences working alongside student athletes and coaches?
- Are you able to manage a sporadic work schedule as well as adapt to the many different sports that our department covers?
- Is there any job in sports information you really do not like?
- Give an example of how you are detail oriented.
- What is something our sports information department can do better if you have visited our website?
- How proficient are you in utilizing social media?
- What ways can you use social media for the organization to reach new audiences?
- What ways can you improve the organization brand with social media?
- What social media platform do you use best?
- How would you handle an organization problem through social media?
- What are your strengths and weaknesses in social media?
- What social media platform do you believe is most effective for our organization?
- Have you been able to build an organization audience through social media?
- What is the next best social media site out there that you have seen but not used?
- How do you measure the effectiveness of social media?
- What is your social media strategy as a whole?
- Have you ever run a social media campaign?
- How would you grade our organization on its social media presence?
- What are the best things to advertise on social media?
- How would you handle criticism of our organization online?
- What company do you think has the best social media presence?
- What is the least effective social media site to reach our customers?
- How would you use social media to increase sales?
- What are the new innovations in social media?
- What are some examples of a successful social media campaign?
- What is an example of a social media campaign that failed?
- How can you improve the company's social media presence?
- How do you attract followers on social media?
- What policies would you create for athletes and their use of social media?

SPORT SALES/MARKETING

- What experience do you have in sales?
- What qualifications do you have that would increase ticket sales for our organization? Group sales?
- How do your communication skills complement this sales position?
- Tell us about some of the sales software programs you have used.
- How will your background aid you in selling sporting goods?
- Do you want to own a sports store or actually be a sales person?
- Do you have any desire to become a sporting goods sales rep for a large corporation?
- About what types of sport merchandise are you most knowledgeable?
- What are your views on company travel with regard to the sales staff budget?
- What salary/commissions do you expect?
- We need to know about your product knowledge. Convince us that you can sell our products.
- How would you advertise our product line?
- Give an example of sales goals you have set in the past for yourself.
- If I were in your pro shop looking for a new wedge or tennis racket, how would you persuade me to buy your new state of the art equipment?
- How have your past sales experiences prepared you for this position?
- With what clientele are you most comfortable?
- Explain a new product and tell us how you would sell it.
- What different sales techniques would you use in selling to the 30–40 age group versus the 15–21 age group?

- In what aspects of marketing are you most interested?
- Are you good with people? In the field of marketing, a lot of one-on-one sales must be done. Describe the first thing you would do when contacting a potential sponsor.
- How do you perceive your career path in sales?
- How would you deal with an interested buyer that is not completely sold on the product?
- What approach would you use on a skeptical buyer?
- How many times would a consumer have to say no before you would give up?
- In what branch of athletic apparel would you like to work?
- In what area of sales would you like to work for our team?
- How will you continue to innovate the product lines in which you are specializing?
- Within our company, which main sporting goods product do you feel is on the rise and will create much revenue, as well as success, for the company? Which product is on the decline and you feel we should drop?
- What new product idea would you like our company to consider bringing to market?
- You are in charge of advertising and want to promote your product the best by allowing a sport celebrity to promote that certain product. How would you go about finding that celebrity, getting him or her to endorse the product, and what will you do to make sure that product sells successfully?
- Shoes are the most poorly fitted item of athletic clothing. For which sports can you fit shoes properly?
- What type of clothing would you recommend for running in cold weather?
- If a customer is 6 feet tall and 245 pounds, how much longer than a standard length club should this individual use?
- What is the significance of the number of dimples on a golf ball?
- What marketing and previous sales experience have you had in an area other than golf? Tennis? Bowling?
- Would you consider yourself a reasonably good golfer? If so, would you use the product you sell even if the product was different than what you are presently using?
- Can you analyze a golf swing and recommend equipment that would help improve that swing?
- What is your perception of the major colleges across the United States that have our logo on their jersey? Do you think it's fair to the smaller schools that we are more interested in making deals with larger schools?

- What is your previous experience in the area of marketing?
- Can you sell yourself to me?
- We are currently involved in marketing a tennis racquet the pro tour has ruled as too big. How would you market this racquet?
- Tell me the qualities of a successful sales person.
- How do you handle your customers who are not satisfied with your product and want their money back, especially if you can tell the product has been used?
- There is an old saying the customer is always right. Is this always true? Why or why not?
- If you are not doing well in sales for a particular month, how would you motivate yourself to do better?
- How do you feel about our company—size, industry, and competitive position?
- What are your views on customer relations?
- Give me an example of a marketing research project in which you have taken part.
- Our team just suffered a terrible season. Obviously, sponsorships are going to be harder to get and season tickets will be harder to sell at the price they were last year. How will you go about getting those sponsorships from the companies that supported the team last year as well as gaining new sponsorships?
- What other majors (if any) did you consider in college and why was sport marketing your final decision? What influenced these decisions?
- Where do you see the professional sports market in 15-20 years? Do you think that fan involvement will continue to increase or do you think fans will get fed up with high salaries?
- Do you think promotions at games take away from the enjoyment of the fans?
- Do you have a portfolio of any marketing projects you've done in college or any other time?
- Describe your hands-on experiences in the field of marketing. What was your role?
- Given the task to come up with a slogan to try and attract fans to our games, what would it be and why?
- How would you compare sponsorship in college with professional teams?
- If given the opportunity to change the team name, what would it be and why would the fans like it?'
- Have you ever written any promotional ads?
- Have you ever helped in the promotional aspect of any event?
- Have you ever conducted or participated in any sport marketing research studies?
- What does sport marketing involve? Define it.

- What effective marketing ideas have you seen persuade the buyer? The spectator?
- How would you market an event that would need contributions from the public to get established?
- What do you believe to be of great importance in the marketing of our organization? Product?
- You are a new sponsorship account executive. An alcoholic beverage company wants to give you a large account, but we have typically shied away from these. However, we might be willing to consider it if it is structured properly and family friendly. It's the largest account you have ever been offered. You work on commission. What would you do?
- You are in charge of the family section of our stadium. Tell us about your sales/marketing ideas?
- Have you ever written a business plan?
- Why did you decide on sport marketing as your sport industry specialization?
- You were a college athlete. How did you juggle classes, projects, and practice?
- We are down to you and one other candidate for our sport marketing internship? What project would you propose to work on for us during an internship?

GENERAL QUESTIONS AN APPLICANT COULD ASK IN/AT END OF AN INTERVIEW

- Is there any chance of advancement in this position?
- What will be the duties for this position?
- What is a typical work schedule for individuals in the off season?
- What is your strategic planning process?
- Does everyone get to participate in strategic planning?
- I could not find a mission or vision on your website. What is your mission and vision?
- Where does management see this organization in five years? 10 years?
- What is your timeline for making the final hiring decision and making an offer to someone?
- I noticed you have a generous benefits package. Could you explain a little more about your dental/vision/medical plan?
- I noticed your sales staff works on commission. What is the typical commission for selling a group plan? Sponsorship signage?
- I am anxious to contribute 100% in this internship. Will I get to participate in the sales of sponsorship signage?
- I am passionate about tournament scheduling. Will I be able to set up any tournament schedules in this internship?
- I noticed there are several vacancies on the sales staff. Is there a particular reason for this?
- How are sales staff members evaluated? How will I be evaluated if hired?
- How does the organization use ticket sales to evaluate their marketing efforts?
- What is the history of returning sponsors with this organization?
- I noticed the organization has several foundations. As an employee, would I get to participate in fundraising for these foundations?
- How involved is the staff in the community?
- With the new facility opening, what is the plan for the selection and hiring of new staff members to staff the facility?
- I noticed an extensive event schedule on your website. Who is responsible for establishing the schedule or selecting events?
- What is your anticipated salary range for this position? Have you decided on an exact starting salary?
- I've noticed that many individuals have been with this organization quite a while based on their bios on your web page. Why do people like working here? Why would I like working here?
- I am passionate about safe activities and facilities. Is there a risk management plan in place? If not, will I be able to develop one that is supported at all levels?
- Is your staff open to me bringing in a new strength and conditioning program for your athletes?
- I believe in a team self-scheduling system for intramural programs where teams self-select a day and time slot for all of their regular season contests. How do you think the students would adjust to this type of system?

Index

About the Authors

Dr. Susan Brown Foster, Professor, possesses academic degrees from Florida State, Eastern Illinois, and a PhD with an emphasis in sport management and higher education from the Ohio State University. Foster has been elected three times to *Who's Who Among America's Teachers,* having been nominated by students in her programs. In 2017, she received Ohio State University's College of Education and Human Ecology Award of Distinction given to alumni for outstanding professional, personal, or community contributions in their field. In 2006, she received the Sport and Recreation Law Association (SRLA) Honor Award for support of undergraduate student legal research, after which three of her previous students won the outstanding undergraduate legal research award. She has also been honored with the prestigious National Intramural-Recreational Sports Association service award and Saint Leo University rewarded her, in 2012, with the Donald R. Tapia School of Business Technology in Teaching Award for the use of different technologies in the classroom.

Dr. Foster was hired in 2003 as Chair to create the Department of Sport Management for Saint Leo University's School of Business. As Chair, she designed and oversaw the development of the concentration in Sport Business for the university's MBA program, enrolling more than 80 students in its first four years. Under her leadership, the Sport Business Advisory Council was established and the undergraduate program grew from 70 to over 160 majors before stepping down to pursue writing and the authorship of the first edition of this text. Since 1985, she has supervised more than 1000 students in their field experiences at both the undergraduate and graduate levels. She considers her teaching specialties to be legal issues, risk management, strategic planning, event and facility management, and recreational sport management. She also has a sincere passion for academic advising and preparing students for entry into the sport business industry through professional development senior seminars and their senior internships.

She has delivered more than 80 presentations and workshops from the state to the international levels. From 2008–2011, she was the lead-off speaker presenting on the topic "So You Want to Work in Baseball" for the more than 500 attendees at the Business of Baseball Seminar held annually at the Baseball Winter Meetings, sponsored by Minor League Baseball. Writing is a passion, and Dr. Foster has been a co-author/co-editor for six books and has authored 10 book chapters in leading sport management texts. Her journal articles have been published in the *Journal of Sport Management, the Journal of the Legal Aspects of Sport, the International Journal of Sport Management, Sport Marketing Quarterly, the Sports Business Journal, the NIRSA Journal,* and the *Journal of Physical Education, Recreation, and Dance.* Throughout her career, she has served on the editorial boards of four different professional journals. In 2009, she received Saint Leo University's Lifetime Publication Award.

At all three institutions where Foster has taught full-time, she was appointed to and has served a combined nine years on President/Chancellor Strategic Planning Committees. While also serving on numerous professional and institutional committees, she has chaired faculty athletic, internal and external affairs, institutional effectiveness, curriculum, and search committees, and was an elected member of the Faculty Senate at Western Carolina University.

Foster was appointed in 2016 to serve on the NIRSA Core Competency project for campus recreational sport managers after serving three years as a national faculty representative to their Registry of Collegiate Recreational Sports Professionals. She has been a site reviewer for the Council on Sport Management Accreditation (COSMA) and served for three years as a member of their Board of Commissioners. Previous to this, she was the elected chair of the Sport Management Program Review Council (SMPRC), where she guided the national approval program for sport management curriculum at the undergraduate, master's, and doctoral levels. This body was the forerunner to COSMA. She has also served as a consultant/external reviewer for institutions reviewing their sport management programs and curricula. In 2007, she created her own business, Sport Business Consulting, LLC.

Dr. John E Dollar is a professor in the sport administration graduate program, and Department Head for Health and Human Performance at Northwestern State University in Natchitoches, Louisiana, where he earned his Master's degree in Secondary Education. In January, 2017, Dr. Dollar was announced as the Director for the Quality Enhancement Plan (QEP) for NSU, the focus of which will be experiential learning as a capstone for all undergraduate students by 2022. He completed his undergraduate degree at the University of Central Arkansas in Conway, Arkansas, where he was a 4-year letterman in track. Prior to his appointment at NSU, Dr. Dollar was a visiting assistant professor, interim program coordinator, and internship coordinator for the sport management program at Texas A&M University, where he also received his doctoral degree.

Dr. Dollar's publications have appeared in *Sport Marketing Quarterly, Athletic Business,* the *International Journal of Sport Management,* and in the online publication *Sociology of Sport.* He has co-authored abstracts that appear in several conference proceedings including the Annual Conference on Girl's and Women's Physical Activity in Sport; the Louisiana Alliance for Health, Physical Education, Recreation and Dance; and the National Association for Girls and Women in Sport. He also has a published abstract of completed research in the *Research Quarterly for Exercise and Sport.* He has presented at state, regional, national, and international workshops and conferences. Included among his publications and presentations are 20 topics involving mentoring, experiential learning, internships and supervision, service learning, career development, and curriculum development in sport management. He has also served on numerous doctoral dissertation and master's theses committees. His personal philosophy is that learning is a lifelong process.

Institutionally, Dr. Dollar has served on numerous committees and councils including Graduate Council Faculty Senate, standards, academic advising, scholarship, distance learning, and faculty guidelines. He received the Advisor of the Year Award in 2007 at NSU, and he has been nominated for the same award on multiple occasions. In 2006, he received the Peacemaker of the Year Award, a domestic violence victim's service award from D.O.V.E.S. in Natchitoches, Louisiana.

Dr. Dollar has taught courses in sport law, ethics and sport governance, human resource management, recreational sport management, research in sport, and of course, has supervised more than 1,300 experiential learning experiences for his students at both the graduate and the undergraduate levels. He also possesses lifetime teaching certificates in Texas and Louisiana.